J. MASS
2
BP
BOSCH
BILSTEIN
TELETRON
DUNLOP

LE MANS

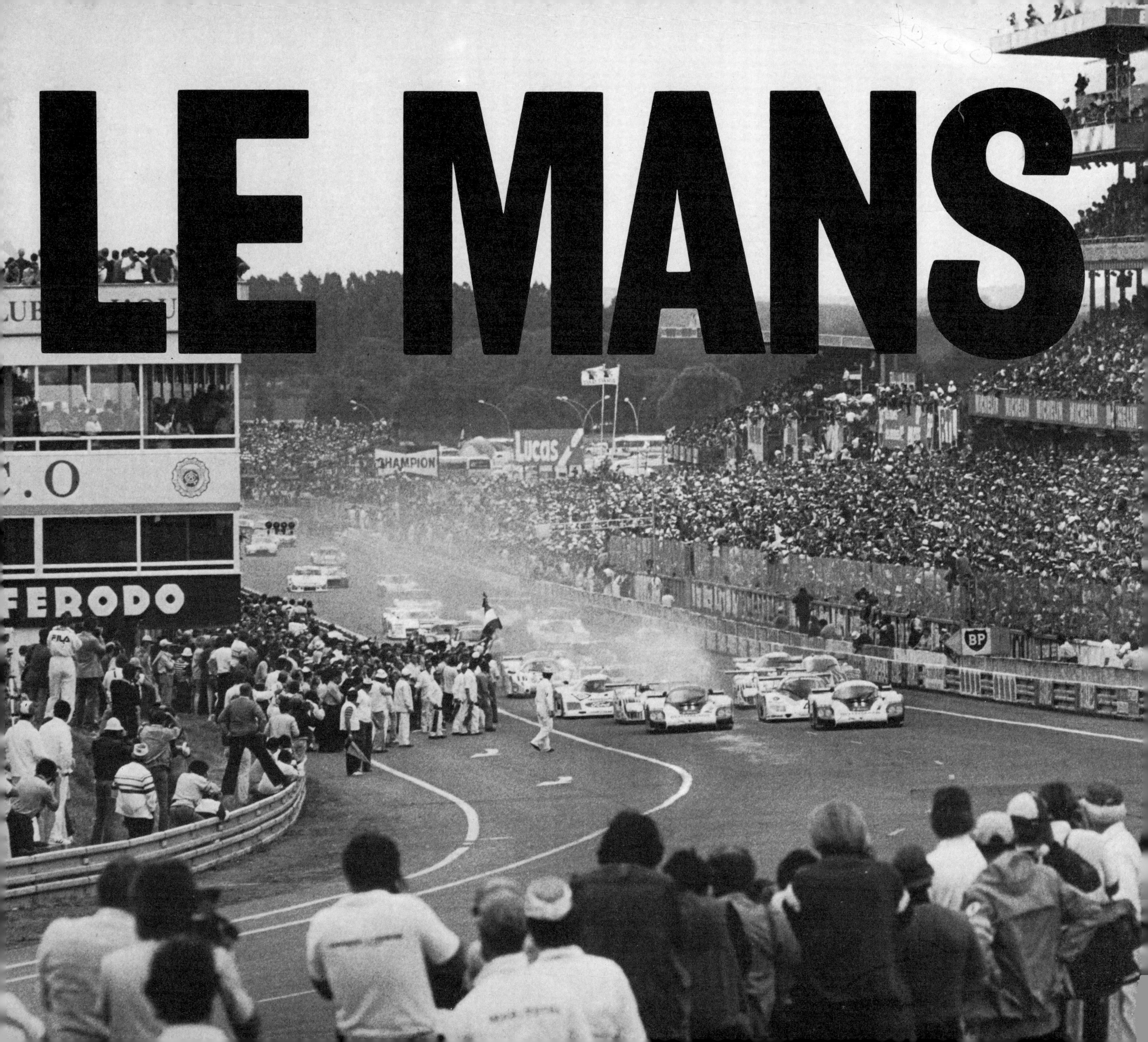

Le Mans 1982
Aston Martin returned to Le Mans with the Nimrod which finished 7th driven by R. Mallock/S. Phillips/M. Salmon. Here it passes the 24 Hours Restaurant on the Mulsanne straight.

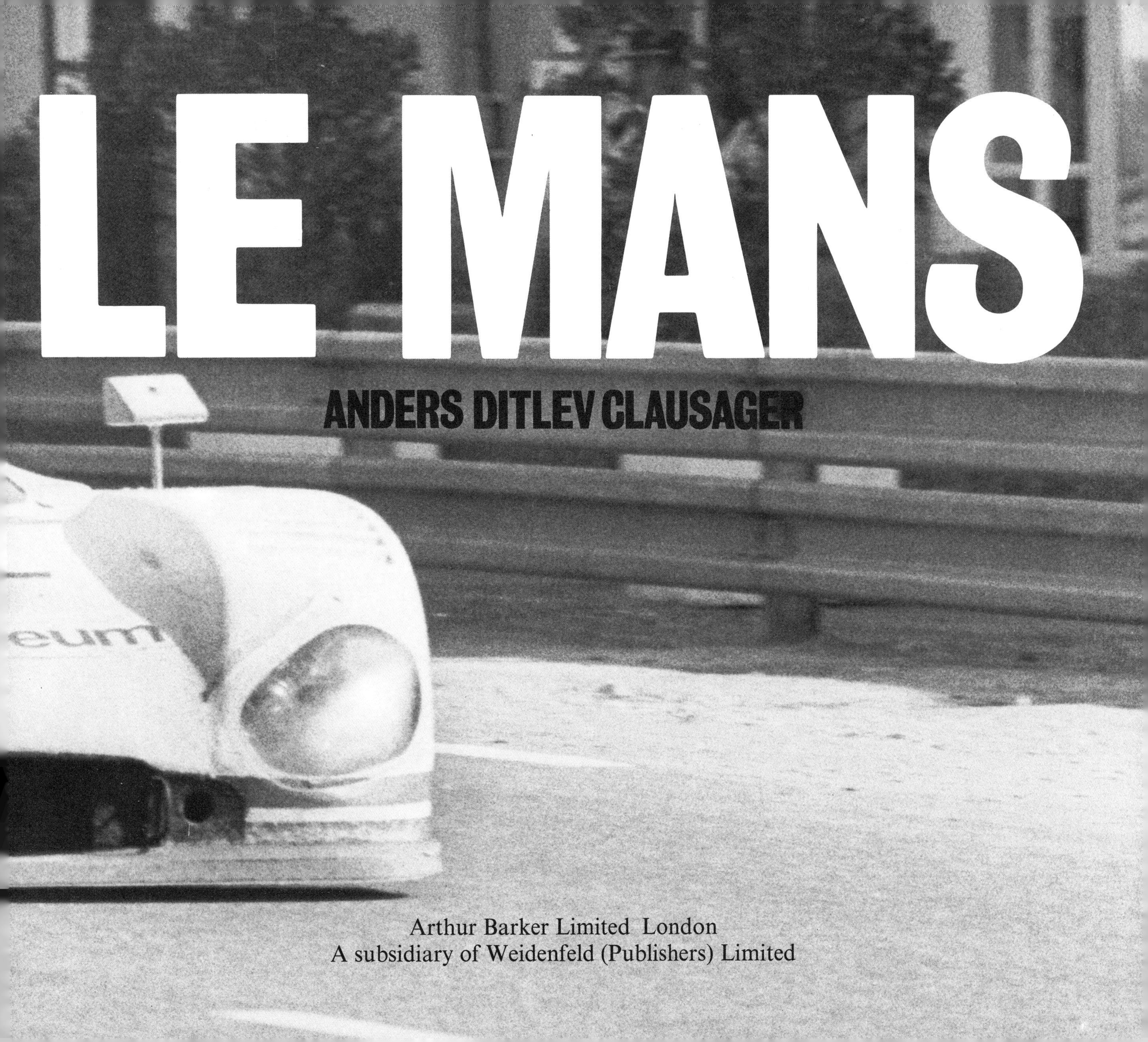

LE MANS

ANDERS DITLEV CLAUSAGER

Arthur Barker Limited London
A subsidiary of Weidenfeld (Publishers) Limited

Published in Great Britain by
Arthur Barker Limited,
91 Clapham High Street,
LONDON, SW4 7TA

Produced by Winchmore Publishing
Services Limited,
48 Lancaster Avenue,
Hadley Wood, Herts

Edited by Sue Butterworth
Designed by Roy Williams
Picture Research Sports Agency
Magazines – Paris

ISBN 0 213 16846 4

Printed in Holland

FOREWORD 6
1. A TOWN THAT BECAME A RACE 8
2. LE MANS TRADITION 16
3. 1923-1939 THE VINTAGE YEARS 26
4. 1949-1965 THE CLASSIC YEARS 76
5. 1966-1981 FROM RECORDS TO RECESSION 138
6. 1982 THE YEAR OF REVIVAL 188
RESULTS 196
INDEX 206

FOREWORD

To take an interest in the '24 HOURS OF LE MANS' is to be interested in the monument of automobile sport and almost the entire story of motor sports.

The Automobile Club de l'Ouest who have set this trial, as it were, annually from 1923, has had in my estimation the ability to instantly perceive in the new form of Motor Races devised by the brilliant young Charles Ferroux a lasting future. And also the ability to confidently and decisively adopt the idea of the Editor of 'l'Auto' for a contest of endurance which should provide motor sport with a true test of its technical progress.

What amazes me even more is that 'l'A.C.O.', as we commonly refer to it, has shown such great determination in the undertaking of this venture, and by their staying power have ensured that we are privileged to experience, annually, the '24 Hours'.

It is absolutely remarkable that despite so many obstacles and difficulties the creators of Le Mans, admittedly assisted by good engineers, have managed to promote their contest through the upheaval of the inevitable and necessary evolution of the car and the sport. Together we pay tribute, actors on the track and actors in the grandstand, to those who create and dominate each year such a momentous event.

Together with you, dear reader, I am about to look back with some emotion, and with thanks to Anders Ditlev Clausager, to the great beginnings of 'Le Mans' and the story of its continued progress.

I know personally what an excellent place for experimentation and progress 'Le Mans' promises to remain and it is one of the main reasons for my love of the competition.

Jacky Ickx

June '82

PORSCHE
Jules
11
Jules
Shell
Shell
BP

All the fun of the fair: Main entrance to the grandstands in 1952.

1. A TOWN THAT BECAME A RACE

Le Mans – the words inevitably conjure up thoughts of the motor race. 'Le Mans' is the colloquial way of referring to the race which is officially known as 'Le Grand Prix d'Endurance de Vingt-Quatre Heures du Mans'. But Le Mans the city is the capital of the department of Sarthe in north-western France, the French equivalent of an English county town such as Norwich – they are of approximately the same size, and both are cathedral cities. Le Mans is set on the sandy plains of western France; the surroundings are pleasant, the flat countryside is partly covered by forest, deciduous as well as coniferous. As is so often the case in France, the 'department' derives its name from a river; the Sarthe is a tributory of the Loir which runs some miles to the south.

Le Mans has a respectable history of a thousand years or so. Its cathedral dates back to the twelfth century; at that time Le Mans was the capital of the province of Maine, a countship which together with Anjou was ruled by England until 1203 as part of the original possessions of Eleanor of Aquitaine. It was regained for France by Philippe II, and formerlly annexed by the French crown after the Hundred Years' War. One wonders whether the fact that Le Mans was once under English rule is an inspiration for present-day British competitors in the 24-hour race, or whether the city's history is known by the thousands of British enthusiasts who make the pilgrimage to the Sarthe circuit for that week-end in June every year.

With the dawn of the era of mechanised road transport towards the end of the nineteenth century, Le Mans became the birthplace of some of the most remarkable of the early horseless carriages, thanks to the efforts of the Bollée family who were originally bell-founders. Amédée Bollée, *père*, built a steam carriage called *L'Obéissante* in 1873 – obedient she certainly was, completing a successful run from Le Mans to Paris and back via Orleans in 1875. Further experimental steamers followed, and in 1885 Amédée Bollée, *fils*, entered the picture when the two Amédées, father and son, built a vast steam coach to an order placed by the Marquis de Broc – by all accounts the first vehicle in history built for sale. Eventually the younger Amédée forsook the steam engine in favour of internal combustion, his first production car with a petrol engine was ready in 1896 and two years later he built a remarkable racing model with the world's first streamlined bodywork.

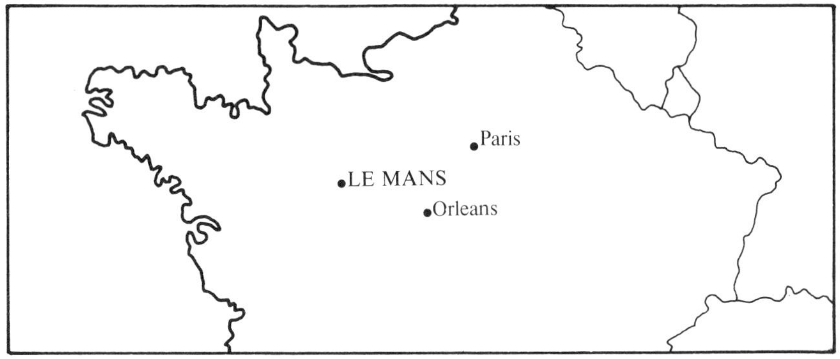

The Amédée Bollée company continued to make cars in limited production until the outbreak of the First World War, mostly largish touring models with big four-cylinder engines and chain drive, typical of the Edwardian period. A few cars were built after 1918 but an attempt at re-starting production with a new model in 1922 came to nothing. Meanwhile Amédée's brother Léon had entered motoring history. As a young man in the 1890s Léon was a keen cyclist but was advised by his doctor to give up this exercise as too strenuous for his health. Loath to give up his trips into the countryside, Léon decided to put a petrol engine on his tricycle. The result was the Léon Bollée Voiturette; by the standards of the 1890s as revolutionary a concept as the Mini 60-odd years later on.

The Léon Bollée Voiturette was the first small, lightweight and therefore fast petrol engined vehicle. It had three wheels, with the air-cooled horizontal single cylinder engine slung next to the single driven rear wheel. The rider sat more or less in the geometrical centre of the vehicle and a brave passenger could be accommodated in a front seat or 'fore-carriage'. The Léon Bollée caused considerable furore when it was first introduced in December 1895; the notorious H. J. Lawson bought the British patent rights for the fantastic sum of £20,000 and produced a version under license as the Coventry-Motette, while Herbert Austin's first Wolseley car of 1896 was surely inspired by the Léon Bollée as it was shelved because it would have infringed the patent rights. The Léon Bollée was perhaps the fastest thing on wheels which was on general sale in 1896 and not surprisingly became the preferred vehicle of many sportsmen, including C. S. Rolls. It was however somewhat temperamental; the most famous of latter-day Bollée owners, S. C. H. 'Sammy' Davis (one-time Le Mans winner) often had a struggle to finish the Brighton veteran car run in his aptly-named *Beelzebub*.

After the turn of the century, the Léon Bollée name was found on a range of largely conventional cars, and production continued into the 1920s. By this time Léon had died, and his widow sold the company to William Morris in 1924. Keen on establishing a French company in order to circumvent French import tariff barriers, Morris was intent on repeating his outstanding British success but was foiled by a number of factors – he would later blame this failure on the company's French staff and workforce whom he considered intransigent and un-cooperative in their chauvinistic attitude to the British. The truth was that the products of Morris-Léon Bollée were not suitable for the French mass market – the first model, a 2½ litre four, was of a type turned out by dozens of small French manufacturers in the 1920s and while sound enough was hardly an outstanding machine, nor was it cheap enough to compete outright with the wares of M. Citroën. While their 12 CV was good for perhaps 2–3,000 sales per year, Morris-Léon Bollée courted folly with their next effort, a Wolseley-inspired three-litre straight-eight in 1928, followed by a six-cylinder model a year later. In 1931, Morris gave up and sold his French company to a syndicate which attempted to continue car production but only lasted two years, and after that the Bollée name was used only for piston rings. The Morris-Léon Bollée production period coincided with the early years of the 24-hour race but the make never participated in the great race held on its home ground – the only tenuous connection was that British teams were occasionally given workshop facilities in the Morris-Léon Bollée factory.

While Le Mans never became a centre of the French motor industry, the city was not without its motoring traditions, nor without a sporting tradition. The Automobile Club de la Sarthe – the forerunner of the Automobile Club de l'Ouest – was formed in 1905, and in the following year it was a circuit proposed by the Sarthe club which was adopted by the Automobile Club de France for a new motor race, the Grand Prix de l'A.C.F. – popularly referred to as the French Grand Prix.

The first French Grand Prix was held on 26 and 27 June 1906 over a 64-mile course consisting of a triangle of main roads to the east of Le Mans, its nearest point – the Fourche hairpin – about five miles from the centre of the city. The winner was Ferenc Szisz on a 90 hp Renault who averaged 62.88 mph over two days' racing, six laps of the circuit per day. His historic win was aided by the first use of detachable wheel-rims as an aid to tyre changing.

Another important historic event near Le Mans in the early years of the century was Wilbur Wright's first flight in Europe in a powered heavier-than-air flying machine which took place over the Hunaudières horse-racing course on 8 August 1908, and over the next few years Wright continued his flying activities around Le Mans which thus also became an early centre for aviation. The spot where Wilbur Wright made his first flight is a few hundred yards from the Mulsanne straight of to-day's Le Mans racing circuit, and a monument to Wright is on the site. There was an aerodrome here for many years after Wright's experiments and this became of special relevance to the history of Le Mans in the years of the Second World War.

Motor racing returned to Le Mans in 1911 when the first Grand Prix de France – not the same thing as the Grand Prix de l'A.C.F. and by all accounts a rather second-rate event – was held over a triangular 33½ mile circuit to the south of Le Mans. This was significant as the circuit later used for the 24-hour race incorporated parts of the 1911 Grand Prix circuit and indeed continues to do so. The 1911 Grand Prix circuit entered the suburbs of Le Mans at the Pontlieue hairpin, from there it ran for a long stretch down the Route Nationale no. 158 towards Tours, before turning west and later north to return to Pontlieue. The 1911 race has become famous not so much for Hemery's win on a 10.5 litre Fiat but because Ernest

A picnic scene in the Sarthe Forest during the 1934 race.

Friderich came second on a tiny 1.5 litre Bugatti Type 13. Similar races were held over this circuit in 1912 and 1913, won by a Lion-Peugeot and a Delage respectively, and there were also motor-cycle and cycle-car races held during these years.

In 1919, the new Circuit Permanent de la Sarthe was marked out by the Automobile Club de l'Ouest. This was a circuit of 10.726 miles in length over public roads to the immediate south of Le Mans, incorporating parts of the 1911–13 circuit, including the northern-most point which was the Pontlieue hairpin. Going round the circuit clockwise, it followed the R.N. 158 Tours road through the Tertre Rouge curve onto the Mulsanne straight which was almost $3\frac{1}{2}$ miles long, stretching past the race course and Les Hunaudières to the outskirts of Mulsanne village. Here a 90-degree right-hand bend led onto the next part of the circuit, the Arnage section, about $1\frac{1}{2}$ miles of almost straight road, ending in an S-bend or to be more precise, the 'Indianapolis' left-hand bend followed almost immediately after by the Arnage right-hand bend. Here the circuit joined the Laigne road and turned north back towards Le Mans; $1\frac{1}{2}$ miles on came the Maison Blanc – White House – double curve, fast but treacherous owing to the view being blocked by the farmhouse from which this bend took its name. After White House, the finishing straight where the starting line, the pits and the grandstand have been situated for all but one of the 24-hour races (the exception was 1925 when the starting point was at Les Raineries, on the opposite side of the circuit near Hunaudières). From the starting line, the road went back to the Pontlieue hairpin, also in an almost straight line.

The first race over the new circuit was the Coupe Internationale des Voiturettes in 1920, won by Friderich on a Bugatti. This event

Tertre Rouge to-day: looking south from the Cafe towards Mulsanne.

1931: Lorraine and Aston Martin at Tertre Rouge.

The start of the 1929 French Grand Prix run over the Sarthe Circuit.

was repeated for the next three years while there were also Cycle-car Grand Prix and motor-cycle races over the Sarthe circuit in the early years. But by far the most important event prior to the beginning of the 24-hour race was the Grand Prix de l'A.C.F. of 1921. The first French Grand Prix to be run after the First World War, this was run to a three-litre formula with a stipulated minimum weight of 800 kg. The race was over 30 laps of the circuit and the winner was Jimmie Murphy on a Duesenberg, at an average speed of 78.1 mph, with a standing lap record of 82 mph. This was the first win for an American car and driver in an important European motor race but a victory which America was unable to repeat for 40-odd years. The French Grand Prix was also run at Le Mans in 1929, to a fuel consumption formula, and there were the Bugatti-only Grand Prix races on the circuit in 1928–30. In 1922 the Sarthe circuit was the stage for an early economy run named after its inventor Doctor Collières; the idea was to drive as far as possible on five litres of fuel, the winning Peugeot Quadrillette covered nearly 200 km which was the equivalent of around 110 mpg.

But the lasting fame of Le Mans sprang from the decision in 1922 of the Automobile Club de l'Ouest to organise a 24-hour race for touring cars as a demonstration of the reliability and efficiency then achieved by modern production motor cars. The idea of a 24-hour race where cars would have to run all night was then, as now, unusual, if not particularly novel. The first 24-hour race appears to have taken place almost 20 years before the first such race at Le Mans; it was held over a dirt track near Indianapolis in the U.S.A. in 1904, and there were several 24-hour races over various American tracks prior to 1916, especially on the board tracks which were then at the height of their popularity. Annual 24-hour races were held at Brighton Beach on Coney Island near New York in the years from 1907 to 1910.

The first 24-hour record – as opposed to a race – was also established in America, where Merz and Clemens covered 1,096 miles at an average of 45.6 mph in November 1905. This record was the inspiration for the British driver S. F. Edge to attempt to do the same – but single-handed. His machine was a stripped six-cylinder Napier of the marque with which Edge was connected commercially, and his attempt took place on the brand-new motor racing track at Brooklands on 28 and 29 June 1907. Together with his riding mechanic Blackburn, and accompanied by two other Napier cars for part of the run, Edge duly accomplished a record at the remarkable average speed of 65.91 mph (total distance 1,582 miles) which makes an interesting comparison with the speeds and distances at the early Le Mans races. His record stood for an extraordinary long time and was in the end beaten by Edge himself in July 1922 when he drove a Spuker 30/40 hp at Brooklands for two 12-hour sessions (as racing at night was no longer permitted following complaints from neighbouring Surrey landowners) at an average of 74.27 mph. Three years later, Thomas Gillett drove a two-litre A.C. Six for 24 hours at the French Montlhery track at an average of 82.58 mph. After that, speeds increased quickly, and by 1936 Captain Eyston held the absolute world's 24-hour record at 149.19 mph, an average that has yet to be reached during a Le Mans race but which demonstrates the difference between setting a record in a lone car on a purpose-built track, and running in a race with 50 other cars over a road circuit.

The first 24-hour race in Europe was the Bol d'Or which was first held at the St Germain circuit near Paris in 1922. The Bol d'Or was always a slightly peculiar race. It was originally open only to cars of less than 1,100 cc, together with three-wheelers and motor-cycle combinations. In consequence it attracted some weird and wonderful machinery among the cycle-cars of the period. Only one driver was permitted but a passenger or riding mechanic had to be carried throughout the race. Although the racing did continue for 24 hours, each driver was permitted a rest period of four hours. A minimum average speed of 30 kph (19 mph) was necessary to qualify and a vehicle was automatically disqualified if this speed had not been maintained at the end of the first three hours; a similar rule was often applied to the Le Mans 24-hour race.

The Bol d'Or race was held annually until the Second World War, a single race (in 1927) was held at Fontainebleau but otherwise the event took place at St Germain until the race moved to Montlhery in 1937. In the following year the capacity limit was upped to 1.5 litres, and the last pre-war race in 1939 was won by an Aston Martin Ulster. The race was revived at St Germain in 1947, and the 1948 and 1951 races were also held there but the other post-war races took place at Montlhery. In 1954 two drivers were finally permitted, and the last Bol d'Or was held in 1955; the capacity limit had then gone up to two litres and Porsches came first and second in the 1955 race. However, the Bol d'Or never attracted the same interest as Le Mans, although there is no doubt that it was the first Bol d'Or which inspired the A.C.O. to organise their first 24-hour race at Le Mans.

A straight-forward copy of the Le Mans race was instituted in 1924, a year after the first 24-hour race at Le Mans. This was a 24-hour touring car Grand Prix organised over a triangular road circuit at the Francorchamps village near Spa in the Ardennes in Belgium. It was won by a Bignan at 48.7 mph. This touring car GP was run until the war and revived in the 1948–53 period but there was then a break until 1966 before there was another 24-hour race at Spa. Then the present series was begun, and the 1966 race was won by Hahne and Jacky Ickx in a BMW. The Spa 24-hour race is still an annual fixture and normally takes place in the late summer, some weeks after Le Mans. While it is part of the drivers' endurance championship, it does not count towards the manufacturers' championship. It is therefore perhaps a less prestigious race than Le Mans and is contested by many more touring cars than those running at Le Mans – in 1981, it was won by a Mazda RX-7 at an average of little more than 80 mph.

The other contemporary 24-hour race is the Daytona, held on a speedway in Florida which was opened in 1959 primarily for stock-car racing. The first sports car event was the Continental race in 1962, a 3-hour race run over a combination of a road circuit and part of the speedway oval. By 1966 this race had developed into the 24-hour race which has been held regularly ever since each year in January or February. On a par with the Le Mans race, Daytona is a drivers' and manufacturers' championship race and is well supported by the same sort of cars that race at Le Mans; Ferrari, Ford and Porsche have all been winners in turn, and the 1981 race brought victory for the Porsche 935 of Redman/Rahal/Garretson at an average speed of 115 mph. Bearing in mind that this race was sponsored by a well-known American soft drinks manufacturer one might be forgiven for concluding that this was a race-winnin' combination!

Before turning to the history of the Le Mans 24-hour race, it is worth remembering the closest equivalent held on a British track, the Double-Twelve Hour race organised by the Junior Car Club at Brooklands for three years, in 1929, 1930 and 1931. The title of the race was owing to the fact that as mentioned earlier, night racing was not allowed at Brooklands, so the cars ran for twelve hours on the first day, were then locked away in a *parc fermée* and brought out for the second round of twelve hours' racing the following day. It was a sports car race with the cars running on handicap in traditional Brooklands style. The 1929 race was won by Ramponi in an Alfa Romeo at 76 mph, and in 1930 Barnato and Clement won in a Bentley at an average of 86.88 mph. The final race was the 1931 event, won by the MG Midget of the Earl of March and C. S. Staniland, at 65.62 mph. Afterwards, the event was changed completely to become a 1,000-mile race held in one day. Today, the premier British sports car event is the BRDC 6-hour race at Silverstone.

In the 1932 race, Minoia made the fastest lap on this 2.3 Alfa Romeo.

2. LE MANS TRADITION

Nuvolari (on the right) watches the Alfa being re-fuelled in the 1933 race. Co-driver Sommer on the pit counter is ready to take over.

THE NICE THING ABOUT the Le Mans 24-hour race is that it is such a traditional event. Anyone who had witnessed the first race in 1923 and then had been transported magically forward in time to 1982 would probably feel quite at home, once the initial shock of seeing such outlandish cars had worn off. Basically, the circuit is the same as in 1923 though with many improvements and somewhat shortened; and the format of the race is equally unchanged. The starting time of 4 pm on a Saturday afternoon has occasionally been moved one or two hours forward but has always returned to where it was in 1923. Of 50 races, only three have not taken place in June; these were the first race which took place in May, the 1956 race in July and the 1968 race in September. Of the famous traditional motor races Le Mans has survived for longer than most in the same format and on the same circuit. Only the Indianapolis 500-mile race and the Monte Carlo Rally which both started in 1911 have remained as unchanged for longer, while the French Grand Prix, the Targa Florio and the Tourist Trophy which all go back to 1906 have all been changed drastically at least once if not several times.

We owe the birth of the 24-hour race to the ideas, initiative and foresight of three men. Georges Durand, secretary of the Automobile Club de l'Ouest, wanted to organise a unique and outstanding race at Le Mans and had the idea of promoting a race to demonstrate the reliability of ordinary touring cars. He took his ideas to Paris and discussed them with Charles Faroux, editor of *La Vie Automobile*, during the Paris motor show in October 1922. Faroux thought of Emile Coquille, the French agent for the Rudge-Whitworth detachable wire wheel, who had once suggested a night race to encourage improvements in lighting and electrical systems. Faroux initially suggested an eight-hour race – to be run half during daytime and half during the hours of darkness – but he and Durand soon decided to make it a 24-hour race. Coquille promised to put up a trophy – the Rudge-Whitworth Cup – and made a donation of 100,000 Francs.

Durand went back to Le Mans and set about obtaining all the necessary permissions to close the roads of the circuit to the public during the race, and also undertook the organisation of the race and all the attendant facilities – not the least of the problems involved would be to arrange artificial lighting over part of the circuit. Charles Faroux set about drafting a suitable set of regulations. It was decided that Coquille's Rudge-Whitworth Cup should not go to an outright winner of the race – instead the 1923 race should be considered as the first qualifying round for a Triennial Cup which would only finally be awarded after the 1925 race. Of the three originators of the race Faroux functioned as clerk of the course until 1956 when he was over 80, while both Durand and Coquille had died during the Second World War.

The first regulations intended to make sure that the cars taking part were standard touring models. Initially it was required that exact duplicates of the cars in the race should be present at the circuit, but this was soon discontinued in favour of a solemn declaration signed by the entrant to the effect that at least 30 similar cars had been manufactured. The cars had to conform with the manufacturer's catalogue specification and had to run fully equipped with wings, running-boards and hoods in addition to lamps, horn, mirror etc. 1,100 cc cars got away with just two seats but larger cars had to have four seats, and in addition to the driver 60 kg of ballast had to be carried for every passenger seat.

During the race itself cars had to cover a minimum distance depending on their capacity – originally ranging from 570 miles for 1,100 cc models and going up to 990 miles for six-litre cars – and there were systematical eliminations every six hours of those cars which dropped behind their required averages by a certain percentage. All tools and spares to be used during the race had to be carried on the car – initially this included even jacks, pumps and cleaning materials – and only the driver was permitted to work on the car during the race. All re-fuelling had to take place at the pits, using fuel supplied by the A.C.O.

These regulations were soon amended and for 1924 it became a requirement that oil, water and fuel could only be replenished after the first 20 laps, and then at 20-lap intervals. During the years 1924 to 1927 it was stipulated that hoods had to be raised during part of the race but it is interesting that the A.C.O. has right from the start been completely neutral on the question of open versus closed cars, and closed cars appeared at Le Mans very early on; ever since the popularity of either type has changed almost as fashion dictated. Before 1939, some of the bodywork requirements were relaxed a little, for instance rear seats became optional on all cars and doors were no longer required on open cars. The co-driver, and later a mechanic, were permitted to work on the car during the race. Above all the minimum distances required were steadily increased over the years and by 1939 had virtually doubled.

The original Triennial Cup was only awarded once, over the 1923–4–5 races, and in 1924 a Biennial Cup – still known as the Rudge-Whitworth Trophy – was instituted complementing and then replacing the Triennial award. The Biennial Cup continued for many years after the war. It was awarded on the basis of an Index of Performance which took a car's actual race distance compared to the set minimum distance into account. From 1928 an annual winner was recognised, the Annual Distance Cup simply going to the car which had covered the greatest distance in the race, but for reasons of convenience and continuity it has long since been the custom to refer to 'winners' – meaning those cars which covered the greatest distances – of the 1923–27 races. An annual winner of the Index of Performance was also recognised but often the same car won the Index and the Biennial Cup – 1930 was the first year in which this did not happen.

The 10.726-mile circuit which had been marked out in 1919 was only used for the first six 24-hour races. The Pontlieue hairpin was a narrow street lined with houses, and it had become a favourite vantage point for spectators; it was soon realised that this was a dangerous spot so for the 1929 race, the A.C.O. built a road – the

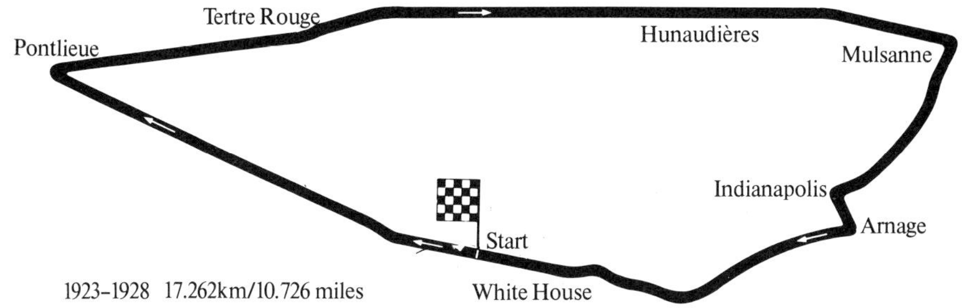

1923–1928 17.262km/10.726 miles

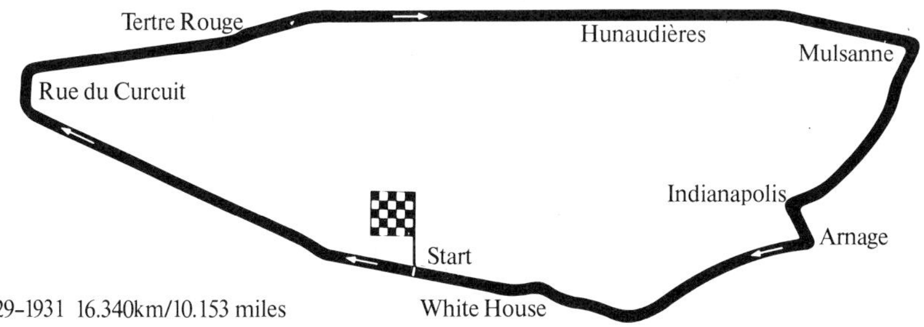

1929–1931 16.340km/10.153 miles

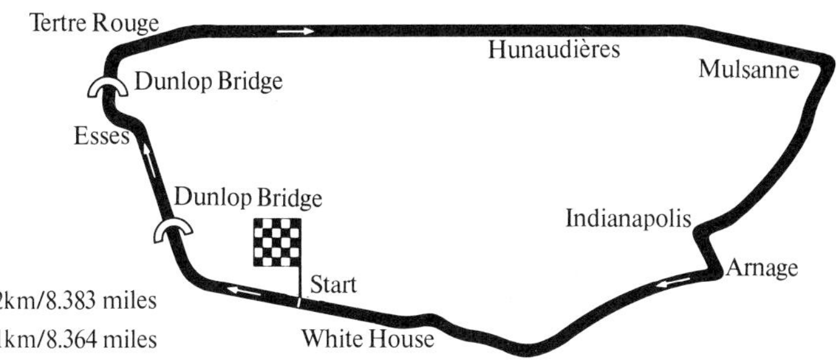

1932–1955 13.492km/8.383 miles
1956–1967 13.461km/8.364 miles

Rue du Circuit – which cut across the Pontlieue hairpin approximately a quarter of a mile from the apex. The Rue du Circuit was not more than a few hundred yards long and began and ended with two sharp right-hand bends. The length of the circuit was shortened to 10.153 miles by this amputation, but in this form the circuit only lasted for three years before the A.C.O. decided to perform major surgery. For 1932 a new road connecting the two sides of the circuit was built on land acquired by the A.C.O. well clear of the built-up area of Le Mans. Soon after the starting line a fast right-hand curve

The Dunlop Bridge to-day.

swept on to the new section – named Tertre Rouge, or 'Red Hillock' – which was about a mile long, taking in the Esses and re-joining the original circuit via the sharp right-hand Tertre Rouge corner. The circuit was reduced to 8.383 miles in length and in this form lasted until 1955. Two pedestrian bridges, which have since assumed the shape of Dunlop tyres, spanned the circuit in the Tertre Rouge section where on both sides of the track the fairground-like 'Village' began to grow up.

The 1939 start – Delahayes and Talbots dominate the picture.

For the first race in 1923, the facilities were on the primitive side, with tents acting as pits and only a small grandstand. Then in 1925, the pits had to be moved from their original position midway between White House and Pontlieue, across the circuit to a point near Les Hunaudières – the A.C.O. was having trouble with the original land-owner but soon managed to purchase the site so for 1926 the pits and the grandstand were back in their original place, where they still are. A permanent wooden structure was built and in 1934 a second storey was added; this was also the year in which the first high-pressure fuel systems were installed. The amenities gradually improved, with grandstands, a club house, press-box, time-keepers' boxes etc.

Everything had to be rebuilt after German attention during the war but the circuit and its facilities largely followed the pre-war pattern up to 1955. Then the great disaster brought with it the realisation that some drastic alterations were necessary to cope with the much-increased speeds of which modern sports-racing cars were capable. Between Arnage and the Esses the track was re-modelled, widened and re-surfaced, while impressive new three-storey pits were constructed in concrete, with viewing balconies topping entertainment suites above the pits themselves. A deceleration zone and pit lane were provided, and a sunken road was put between the circuit itself and the barrier opposite the pits for the protection of spectators in the grandstand area. A permanent signalling station was built at the exit from the Mulsanne corner, at a spot where 20 years before the Bentley team had been the first to establish a signalling post linked by telephone to the pits. The 1955–6 alterations shortened the circuit very slightly from 8.383 to 8.364 miles.

For the first post-war race in 1949, prototypes had been given admission for the first time – 'as an exceptional measure' – provided the prototypes were accepted by the French Ministry of Mines, or the corresponding licensing authorities abroad. It may be argued that this was only to some extent regularising the tendencies that had prevailed towards the end of the 1930s when many cars taking part, while ostensibly catalogued touring models, were in fact virtually specially built for Le Mans and other races and any member of the public would have found it difficult to purchase some of the cars –

Porsche came to the fore in the 1960s – the Mitter/Davis 904/8 in 1965.

such as the Adler Renn-Limousinen. The A.C.O. naturally hoped that manufacturers would enter bona fide prototypes which might form the basis of next year's production model but mostly such hopes were thwarted as 'prototypes' became more and more special and were often entered by companies which did not have the slightest intention of ever offering a catalogued touring sports model. However, at least on one occasion has a Le Mans win – that of Mercedes-Benz in 1952 – led directly to a production version of the winning prototype, while outstanding post-war winners from the ranks of production sports cars have included the Jaguar D-type, the Ford GT 40 and the Porsche 935. These reflect the A.C.O.'s intermittent concern over the prototype issue and their occasional efforts to make Le Mans a more attractive race for proper sports cars again, as opposed to what has aptly been called two-seater racing cars.

But the return of real touring cars does not seem likely under current F.I.S.A. regulations, while the A.C.O. is well aware that the prestige and popularity of Le Mans is to some extent dependant on having the fastest category of sports car at any time in the race – whether they are called prototypes, Group 6 or Group C cars. Naturally, there are those who regret that modern series production touring sports cars are virtually without a chance of even qualifying for the race and over the years there has been no shortage of suggestions of what could be done to turn the clock back and have Le Mans races as they used to be. My favourite suggestion on the lunatic-nostalgic fringe was a proposal made in the 1960s at the time when seven-litre Fords were bombing down the Mulsanne straight at record speeds – the idea was quite simply that cars should be capable of carrying the same number of passengers (with, of course, luggage) as the engines' capacities in litres. Ford might have made the first seven-seater limousine to win at Le Mans!

Changes in the post-war regulations have more or less reflected the increasing speeds in the race. The set minimum distances were increased regularly until they were abolished in 1972 in favour of a rule that in order to classify a car must cover a certain proportion (originally 70 per cent) of the distance of the overall or the class winner The stipulated minimum number of laps to be covered between fuel stops, some times allied to maximum tank capacity thereby effectively dictating minimum fuel consumption, lasted until 1959; similar rules were revived in 1975, and are incorporated in the Group C regulations which applied from the 1982 race. In post-war years the specification of cars has been dictated in various ways in the rule book which includes a number of stipulated measurements, of for instance windscreens, internal width, ground clearance and turning circles. Safety has become a pre-occupation of the organisers, particularly after the 1955 race – safety harnesses became compulsory in 1970, and their introduction meant that the Le Mans start which had been used since 1925 had to be sacrificed: instead of running across the road to start their cars, drivers had to be strapped in when the signal to start was given. Now there are numerous clauses in the rule book governing the design of fuel tanks and fuel lines, roll-over bars, seat belts, impact absorbing structures and many other items, which are carefully checked by the scrutineers before the race.

The A.C.O. scrutineers have always had an important fall-back clause – that cars must confirm to 'the spirit of the race'. This has been used to exclude cars at scrutineering as happened in 1962 when two Lotus 23s were excluded for this reason – and Colin Chapman swore never to return to Le Mans again! – but the same clause was not invoked when the extraordinary twin-boom Nardi was entered in the 1955 race. Another famous example was the Morgan which was excluded as being 'old-fashioned' in 1961 but which was admitted in the following year and duly won the two-litre class. All of these cars brought criticism of the scrutineers but there can be little doubt that on the whole, the A.C.O.'s staff perform a difficult job in a competent and very fair-minded way.

As far as the race itself is concerned, an important change to the regulations in 1953 forbade solo drives – in the year after Levegh's 23½-hour solo drive had almost brought him victory. Although some winners had driven almost solo – such as Sommer in 1932 and Chinetti in 1949 – by all accounts the only time when a car has actually finished at Le Mans without the driver being relieved at all at the wheel was when E. R. Hall took his Bentley through to an eighth place in the 1950 race, leaving a frustrated would-be co-driver in the pit. But from 1953 onwards there have been rules governing the length of time each driver is permitted to spend at the wheel, both in terms of the number of consecutive laps and overall time. In later years, three drivers per car became accepted and now a driver may even change cars within the same team during the race, provided he or she has qualified in both cars during the practice session. A rule used to good effect by Jacky Ickx in recent memory. The present-day running start after one lap behind a pace car came in in 1971, and 1981 saw pace cars being used for the first time during the race, at such times when the road was being cleared after accidents.

One of the original ideas was that the 24-hour race should be a demonstration of reliability and efficiency. The rule dictating that only two persons (the two drivers, or a driver and a mechanic, or two mechanics) might work on the car during the race persisted into the 1960s, but by then the parts and tools carried in the car were for use during stops on the circuit while all equipment – often of a very sophisticated nature – in the pit, could be used during pit stops but at no other times. Replacement of major units and ancillaries was then still forbidden but this rule was abolished and in the 1970s it was not uncommon to see engines replaced during the race, or complete rebuilds being performed in record time by teams of mechanics. It is encouraging that in 1980, the rule prohibiting changes of major components was re-introduced, and extended to cover the practice period as well. But during an involuntary stop away from the pit, the driver still has to rely on his own wit and resources and is limited to

The Reed/Arents Ferrari 250 GTO was an early retirement in the 1961 race.

using tools and spares already in the car, while acceptance of outside assistance leads to automatic disqualification – if discovered.

The fuel consumption rules as such were abandoned after 1959, but a new Index of Thermal Efficiency was introduced as a subsidiary competition in the same year, using a complex formula to determine the index figure – taking into account the weight of the car, its average speed and fuel consumption. While the old Index of Performance disappeared together with the minimum set distances in each class after 1971, the Index of Thermal Efficiency continued but became of less importance as it no longer applied to all cars in the race, only to certain categories. But a similar notion was re-introduced in 1981 when the Le Mans Chamber of Commerce put up a special award for efficiency based on fuel consumption, with sponsorship from the Esso petroleum company.

The circuit was lengthened slightly to 8.369 miles in 1968 when a new artificial chicane – the Virage Ford – was built just at the approach to the pits, as a means of slowing cars as they come up to

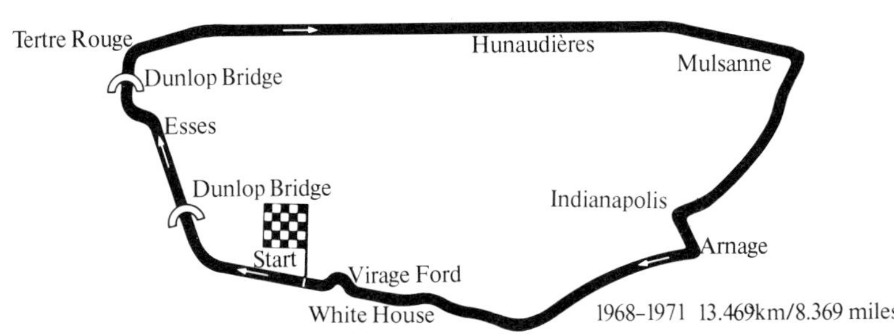

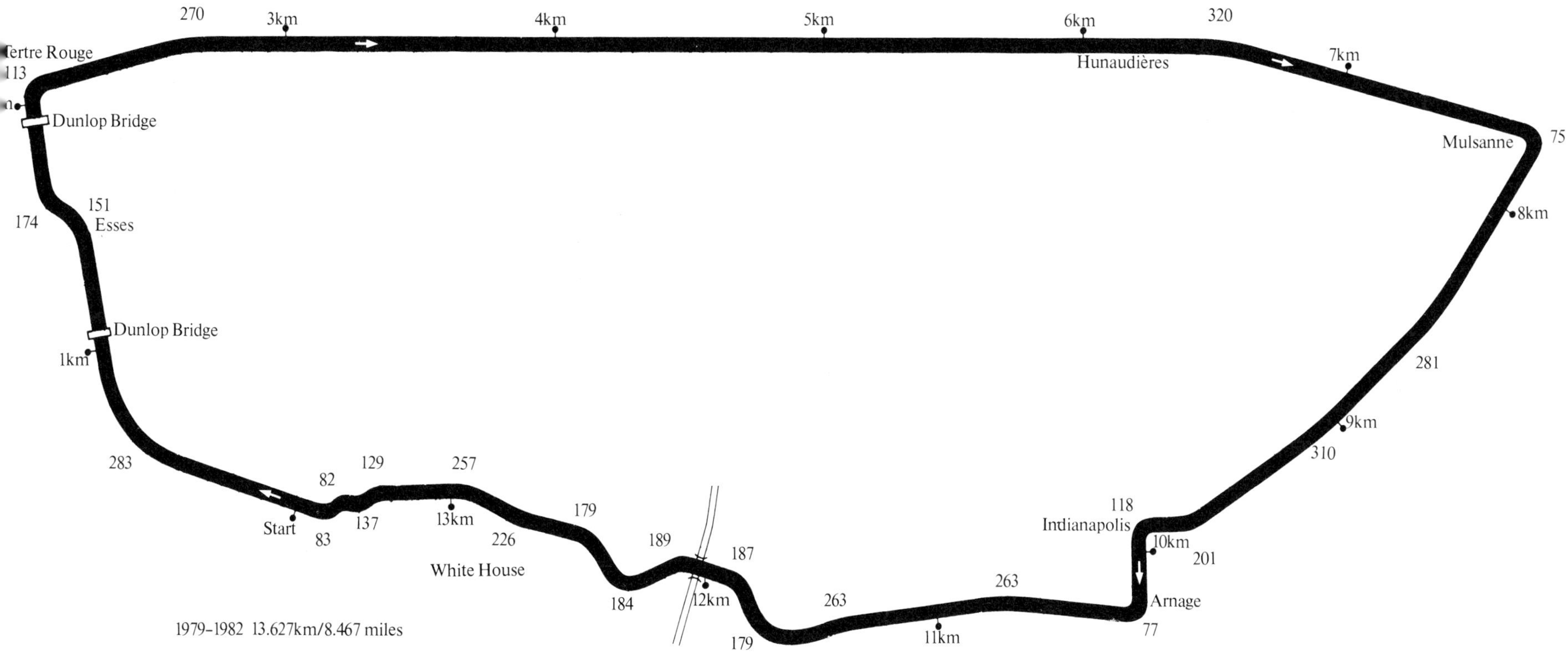

Note: All speeds are approximate and in kilometres per hour.

the pit area. A major re-modelling of the circuit took place in 1971–72 when the entire section from Arnage to the pits was reconstructed. For the first mile from Arnage the route of the circuit was unchanged but the standard of the road was improved while a completely new section was added from then on, by-passing the old White House curve with a series of new curves and bends beginning with the Virage Porsche, leading up to a re-designed Virage Ford and then on to the pit section. The new part of the circuit was called the 'Technical' section and was designed to increase the interest for the drivers as well as for the spectators, besides slowing down the cars as they go past the pits and the grandstand. Also during this period the entire circuit was lined with Armco steel safety barriers. With the 1972 alterations the circuit was lengthened to 8.475 miles.

Small retouches since – notably to the Tertre Rouge corner in 1979 – have shortened the circuit to 8.467 miles. An ambitious re-construction programme was scheduled to have been carried out in the 1975–76 period – this would have included the building of a completely new Mulsanne straight, a new Mulsanne corner short of the existing corner and a new section leading on to the old circuit between Mulsanne and Arnage so the circuit would have been shortened somewhat – but the A.C.O. has had to shelve these plans for the time being. A new circuit had been constructed at Le Mans some years previously – the so-called Bugatti circuit of 2.7 miles which takes in

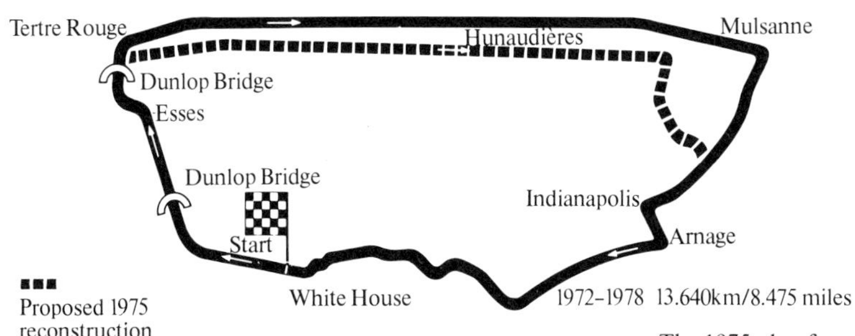

The 1975 plan for a new Mulsanne straight was not executed.

Everyday traffic at Mulsanne – note the permanent Armco barriers.

the pit straight and part of the Tertre Rouge section of the 24-hour circuit, but then veers away before the Esses and loops back in complicated bends through the car parks to re-join the main circuit at the Virage Ford. The Bugatti circuit was used for the French Grand Prix in 1967 but is now considered too short and unsuitable for major races.

So Le Mans to-day – despite all changes made over the years – still retains its basic concept in a recognisable form, 50 races on. As a race it has had its good and bad periods; but it is more firmly lodged in the public mind in France and internationally than any other motoring event in the calendar. It is possible to distinguish between different eras at Le Mans quite clearly. The 16 pre-war races must stand on their own – they may be considered as the touring car races. The first few races, largely dominated by the multitude of French cars, were perhaps the least typical of all Le Mans races as the race had still not found its final form. The Le Mans stone age perhaps – followed by what we can only call the iron age, the period when the heavy metal from Bentley dominated the scene with four wins in a row from 1927 to 1930 – wins which helped to put both Le Mans and Bentley on the map and fostered the enormous interest in Le Mans in the Anglo-Saxon world. No less outstanding were the four Alfa Romeo wins from 1931 to 1934 while British cars continued to play an important part in the race with several wins on Index. After Lagonda's one-off win in 1935 the last few pre-war races were marked by a return of the originally strong French interest and all three races from 1937 to 1939 brought victory, overall and on Index, for French makes – Bugatti, Delahaye, Simca.

The next era in Le Mans history is for many enthusiasts still the golden age. The 1950s and early 1960s brought us some of the greatest classic sports cars from Ferrari, Jaguar, Mercedes-Benz and Aston Martin which all took turns to win at Le Mans – Ferrari established a unique record with nine wins, 1949, 1954, 1958 and no less than six wins in a row from 1960 to 1965. Jaguar's record was no less impressive – winning five times was a remarkable performance in its own right while Jaguar's and Dunlop's efforts at Le Mans gave us the disc brake, perhaps the greatest legacy of motor sport in modern times. Mercedes and Aston scored one victory each while

Grandstands dozing in the sunshine.

The pits – as built in 1955–56 – with the race control box.

during this period the only win for France was that of Talbot in 1950. After that the French had to content themselves with winning the Index of Performance which was won no less than ten times by Panhard-engined cars between 1950 and 1962. Above all the sheer variety of cars encountered at Le Mans – a very high proportion of them British – made the early post-war races of outstanding interest. And from modest beginnings, American and German entries gradually grew in stature to challenge for overall victory at Le Mans.

It is a question of definition when the modern era began for the 24-hour race. Perhaps in 1963 when for the first time a rear-engined car won and the Rover-B.R.M. turbine car made its convincing demonstration; perhaps in 1972 or 1976 which saw major changes in regulations and categories. But by choosing to begin a new era in 1966 the post-war races are neatly divided into two equally-sized groups while it was also the year of the first Ford win and the year in which British participation declined so drastically. After Ford's splendid and well-earned victories – four in a row – Porsche's long-standing dedication to Le Mans finally bore fruit with their two wins in 1970 and 1971. The impressive performance of the 917s at Le Mans is a legend and the records for speed and distance set in 1971 had yet to be beaten ten years later. Porsche became the leading marque at Le Mans succeeding to the throne that had once been Ferrari's, and for the rest of the decade victory went either to Porsche or to one of the new French cars that emerged after the long hiatus of French competitors. From 1972 to 1980 Matra-Simca and Porsche won three times each, Renault-Alpine and Rondeau once each. The only victory that did not go to either France or Germany was in the subdued 'economy' Le Mans in 1975 when a British car with an Anglo-American engine and American sponsorship took the winner's place – the Gulf-Mirage-DFV, the first win for the Formula One-dominating Ford-Cosworth engine at Le Mans. The 1980s began well for the race, first Jean-Pierre Rondeau became the first man to win Le Mans in a car bearing his own name, then Jacky Ickx made history by scoring his fifth win in 1981 – the first man to reach this number. He had previously won in 1969 in a Ford GT 40, in 1975 in the Gulf, while his 1976, 1977 and 1981 wins were all in Porsches.

The prospects for the fiftieth race in 1982 were good; a new set of regulations had been proposed by F.I.S.A. (Federation Internationale Sportive d'Automobile, the governing body of international motor sport whose president is the controversial Frenchman Jean-Marie Balestre). The new rules were adopted for the Manufacturers' and Drivers' World Endurance Championship consisting of 11 races from March to October, of which the five most prestigious counted towards the Makes' Championship. Le Mans was the premier race among these while the other races were at Monza in Italy, Silverstone in England, Nürburgring in Germany and Spa-Francorchamps in Belgium. Le Mans was the only 24-hour race in the endurance championship as Daytona was relegated to non-championship status and the Spa 24-hours counted in the Touring Car Championship.

Modern-day pit stop: the Porsche 956 of Mass/Schuppan in the 1982 race.

The 1982 rules aimed to improve the general standard of sports car racing by defining a new category of two-seater racing sports car, the Group C cars. Apart from the re-introduction of fuel consumption restrictions and specifying that the cars must be two-seaters of a minimum dry weight of 800 kg, the most interesting idea was that engines must be 'recognised' by a manufacturer who has homologated production cars in Group A or B. This was hoped to attract greater interest from manufacturers' own teams and entries were expected from Porsche, Lancia and Ford in addition to the well-established sports car specialists such as Rondeau, Lola and March with Ford-Cosworth engines, the WM with its Peugeot PRV co-op engine and the British Nimrod with an Aston Martin engine. With unlimited capacity engines and the new rules permitting some measure of ground-effect it was obvious that Le Mans was going to be very fast indeed. The top speed of some cars was claimed to be around 250 mph – would the 1971 records be broken at last? But as history tells us – speed itself has never been enough at Le Mans.

49

3. 1923-1939 THE VINTAGE YEARS

The Chenard et Walcker of Senechal/Loqueheux in the 1925 race – with hood up as regulations demanded. Winner of the Tri-ennial Cup.

LE MANS 1923

All beginnings are difficult and the first 24-hour race at Le Mans was no exception. For a start, the dates chosen – 26 and 27 May – turned out to be too early in the season and the weather was terrible – a hailstorm, heavy rain and high winds combining to make life unpleasant for the drivers. The pits were in tents and the road surface none too good. A total of 33 cars were brought to the start at 4 pm on the Saturday afternoon; the starting time unaltered to this day.

Two entries from Voisin did not materialise but of the 33 starters only three were not French – these were a team of two Belgian Excelsiors with ohc 5.3 litre six-cylinder engines, the biggest cars and therefore given numbers 1 and 2; and a single three-litre Bentley, entered by the maker's London agent John Duff who was partnered by Bentley's works driver Clement. Among the other entries were La Lorraine and Chenard et Walcker in the two- to three-litre class, while at the other end of the scale were five cars in the 1,100 cc class – two air-cooled S.A.R.A.s, two Salmsons and an Amilcar. There were two Bugattis and a Delage; while car number 19, entered as a Montier-Special, was largely Ford Model T; its entrant-driver Charles Montier was Ford's French agent.

Three of the cars had closed bodywork and as yet there were no regulations governing the use of hoods during the race; but most other rules were intended to make sure that the entries were true touring cars. Cars had to be fully equipped with hood, wings, running-boards and electrical equipment; apart from 1,100 cc cars which had only to be two seaters, all entries had to have four seats and ballast had to be carried in lieu of passengers. Repairs could only be carried out by the driver; and while fuel consumption was unrestricted, re-fuelling could only be carried out at the pits.

At first the idea of a 24-hour race had been greeted with derision in some quarters – for instance by W. O. Bentley himself; nevertheless he agreed to act as Duff's pit manager and soon realised that Le Mans was exactly the kind of race that would demonstrate the capabilities of his cars. That year's event was, while undoubtedly spectacular, perhaps the least dramatic Le Mans race ever. Very soon after the start, the two Chenard et Walckers went into the lead, followed by a two-litre Bignan; they were to retain this order throughout the race and eventually finished 1–2–3. The pre-race predictions that no car would stand the pounding for the twenty-four hours were soon shamed, in fact the first retirement (a S.A.R.A.) was caused when the car crashed after the lighting system failed in early evening, and there were only two other cars which had to retire.

Much excitement was provided by the Bentley; this was an early three-litre without front wheel brakes, and the two-wheel brakes were wholly inadequate. An additional problem was created by a headlamp which was inoperative after being hit by a flying stone; another stone holed the petrol tank and the car was delayed for two and a half hours while repairs were made. At the end, Duff and Clement shared a fifth place with one of the Excelsiors; Clement had meanwhile set up a lap record (for sports cars) of 66.69 mph. The race was won by Lagache and Leonard in a Chenard et Walcker covering 1,372.94 miles at an average speed of 57.21 mph; although as yet the A.C.O. did not recognise an outright winner of the individual race, instead all finishing cars had qualified for the Triennial Cup.

1923: Relaxed atmosphere at the pits before the first race.

The Duff/Clement Bentley speeding past the pits in 1923.

Early Bugatti entry – the Mari/Pichard $1\frac{1}{2}$ litre model in 1923.

LE MANS 1924

For 1924 the event was put back three weeks, to 14 and 15 June, as the organisers hoped for improved weather; their expectations were fulfilled, indeed the heat was described as tropical. The number of entries had increased to 40 but the only non-French car was the Bentley of Duff and Clement; this year equipped with four-wheel brakes and proper stone guards to protect lamps and fuel tank. The entry of a three-litre Sunbeam was scratched; the other main contenders were as in 1923, the La Lorraine, the Chenard et Walcker, the Bignan and one of the newcomers, the 3.2 litre Aries.

Apart from the 1924 race being the second round in the Triennial Cup, a new Biennial award was also instituted – the Rudge-Whitworth Cup – which remained a feature of the Le Mans until 1960.

Rare Italian – the three-litre Diatto of Lecot/Renaud in the 1925 race.

The regulations now stipulated that after the first five laps, hoods had to be erected and remain up for 20 laps; and a minimum of 20 laps had to be covered before fuel, water and oil could be replenished.

This was a much more gruelling race than the previous year; 19 cars had retired after 12 hours, and at the finish, only 15 cars were in the running of which one did not classify as it failed to cover the minimum distance required. At the end of the first lap, an Alba and a Corre la Licorne had already retired. The opening stages of the race were dominated by the four-litre straight-eight Chenard et Walcker, the Bignans and the La Lorraines. Lagache in the Chenard pushed the lap record up to 69.076 mph before the car caught fire and burned out, while the pace proved too much also for most of the other big French cars – both the three-litre Bignans, the Aries and the three-litre Chenard were all out by midnight. This left the team of three La Lorraines, all with ohv 3.4 litre six-cylinder engines, as the main competitors for the Bentley, while some of the smaller cars, the two-litre Chenards and Bignans moved up the score board.

At half time Duff in the Bentley was lying second to the Lorraine of Stalter and Bloch; and during Sunday morning Duff eventually overtook the French car which ultimately retired at 1 pm leaving the Englishman in a secure lead, followed by the two remaining Lorraines. Despite losing much time towards the end of the race due to a lengthy pit stop for a precautionary change of both rear wheels, Duff and Clement were the winners; although they had covered 1,380 miles, their qualifying distance was 1,290 miles due to a misunderstanding as Duff had not realised that the long pit stop had pulled his average for the final five laps down below the statutory minimum. The lead over the Lorraine in second place was therefore only 10 miles, and Duff's distance less than that of the 1923 winners. The average speed was 53.783 mph.

LE MANS 1925

The race on 20 and 21 June 1925 brought several innovations, chief among which was the first Le Mans start which was to be a feature of the race until 1969. The cars were lined up at an angle on one side of

Under the marshal's watchful eye: filling up Chenard et Walcker 'tank' in 1925.

The three-litre Sunbeam of Chassagne/Davis which finished second.

Still in 1925, a pre-race photo of the successful O.M. team.

the road, the drivers stood opposite and when the flag fell the driver had to run across, put up the hood and start the car. 1925 was also the one year when the pits and grandstand were moved from their traditional position at Les Raineries across the circuit to the hippodrome at Hunaudières, due to difficulties with a land owner.

Of a total of 68 entries, 49 were brought to the start; but only 16 were to classify, and five cars which were running at the finish failed to cover the minimum distance. Perhaps because of Bentley's win the previous year, there was more international interest in the race; British entries included a team of two three-litre Bentleys, Duff and Clement now supplemented by a works entered car driven by Kensington Moir and Dr Benjafield. Two of the sophisticated and fast three-litre Sunbeams with twin ohc six-cylinder engines were driven by Segrave/Duller and Chassagne/'Sammy' Davis, and while an entry from AC was scratched, an Austin Seven driven by Gordon England and Sir Francis Samuelson was, with its 747 cc engine, much the smallest car in the race. From Italy there were four Diattos – two with three-litre engines, and two two-litres, together with three O.M.s with their remarkably powerful side valve engines; and perhaps the most portentous newcomer was a lone American Chrysler 70, though ignominiously, this first American entry at Le Mans failed to qualify on distance. Among the French contingent most of the interest attached to the Chenard et Walckers – two of the big eights were entered together with two 1,100 cc models, the latter with the fully enclosed streamlined 'tank' bodywork which became a hallmark of this make – and also the team of three La Lorraines. The largest car was a 4.5 litre Sizaire-Berwick; not the British mock-Austin species but the old-fashioned French model which had a side valve four-cylinder engine with fixed 'T' cylinder head complete with valve caps. There were also two three-litre Aries in the large car class. Among the smaller cars, a famous name made its first appearance: two 1.5 litre Talbots, of the French variety, though both retired.

Initially, a fierce duel was fought out between the Bentleys and the Sunbeams from which neither team emerged victorious. Having driven flat out with the hood up, Moir ran out of fuel before the officially permitted re-fuelling stop. The other Bentley and both Sunbeams suffered from various mechanical mishaps, and the Segrave/Duller Sunbeam retired before midnight with clutch

The Chrysler Six of Staffel/Desvaux failed to qualify in the 1925 race. Here seen negotiating the Pontlieue hairpin.

trouble. Duff and Clement in the other Bentley were put out of the race when the float chamber of one SU carburettor broke off and there was an under-bonnet fire.

Of the big French cars, the La Lorraines again proved to have the stamina necessary; one of the cars crashed while lying in third place but the other two finished first and third, sandwiching the only surviving British entry, the Chassagne/Davis Sunbeam, which completed the course with a fractured chassis. But perhaps the most impressive performance was of two of the two-litre O.M.s which finished in a shared fourth place. The 1,100 cc Chenard et Walcker 'tanks' took the honours in the Rudge-Whitworth Cup, one winning the Triennial award (which was not repeated) and the other taking the first Biennial Cup. Before retiring, Lagache in the eight-cylinder Chenard et Walcker had improved his lap record from the previous year to 70.206 mph, while the average speed of the winning La Lorraine was 57.838 mph for a total distance of 1,388.127 miles.

On a serious note, Le Mans claimed its first two deaths this year; Andre Guilbert was killed in a Ravel when practising on Saturday morning prior to the race, and Marius Mestivier lost control of his Amilcar which went off the road on the Mulsanne straight; he was killed instantly.

LE MANS 1926

After one year's absence the race headquarters were back at Raineries in 1926, the un-cooperative land owner having in the meantime decided to sell the area to the A.C.O. at a reasonable price. Chenard et Walcker were conspicuous by their absence this year (and indeed, would only once more return to the Sarthe circuit) so French hopes centred – again – on the La Lorraines, together with the three-litre Aries and for the first time Peugeot, making one of their rare appearances at Le Mans with a team of two 3.8 litre sleeve valve cars. O.M. was back in force but there was no other Italian entry; similarly the three Bentleys were the only British cars. A rather surprising entry came all the way from Toledo, Ohio; the Willys-Overland company (which at the time was among America's leading mass-producers) entered a Willys-Knight with a sleeve valve engine, and two of their Overland Sixes (of which one crashed in practice).

There was still no overall winner officially but the second Biennial Cup was coupled with an Index of Performance, based on actual distance travelled by a car in relation to the required minimum distance set for its class. The Triennial Cup was abandoned. The hoods still had to be raised at the start which gave an immediate but slight advantage to the single closed car in the race, a French Jousset. There were several French entries in the 1,100 cc category – including S.A.R.A., Salmson and Aries – but nothing smaller; while the Willys-Knight was the biggest-engined car at 3.9 litres.

New pits and grandstands had been erected; also a restaurant, bars, much-increased car parks which would accommodate 3,000 vehicles, and a large scoreboard on which spectators could follow the changing positions throughout the race. The press-box was at the top of the new grandstand.

The promised battle between La Lorraine, Peugeot, Aries and Bentley duly unfolded. The dark horse, the American Willys-Knight, was, despite its advantage on engine size, never a serious threat and soon retired; its smaller stable-mate, the Overland, proved to possess more stamina in the long run and was lying sixth when it retired with less than an hour to go. The 1926 race was an unmitigated disaster for two of the favourite teams; of the Peugeots, the Wagner/Dauvergne car suffered from long drawn out electrical troubles and finally had to retire when the electrical starter refused to work after a pit stop – hand cranking was interestingly enough disallowed. Their Boillot/Rigal team mates were disqualified while lying second at half time – the windscreen had broken earlier and the jury-rigged remains had now given way. The disqualification was unpopular with the crowd of spectators and the luckless officials had to make themselves scarce until the hubbub had died down.

The Bentley team fared even worse. 'W. O.' attributed his cars' failure to lack of preparation as Bentleys were preoccupied with record-breaking at Montlhery; but there was no real reason why all of the three green cars should fail and indeed they did so for different reasons. First to go, at about half-distance, was the Duller/Clement car which suffered a broken valve, and by mid-morning the Gallop/Thistlethwayte car was out of the race with a broken rocker arm. This was particularly disappointing as this was one of the new short-chassis super sports three-litre models and it had been lying as high as second. Final hopes were pinned on the Davis/Benjafield car which had moved up to third but was wearing out its brakes rapidly; it had covered 1,480 miles and had less than half an hour to go when Sammy Davis slid into a sandbank at Mulsanne. The Aries had both retired earlier in the race, and the result was therefore a remarkable 1–2–3 for La Lorraine; all three setting average speeds over 100 kilometres per hour, the first time this barrier was broken. Winners were Bloch/Roissignol at 66.083 mph, total distance 1,585.99 miles. In fourth and fifth places followed two O.M.s, and Minoia and Foresti in the leading O.M. were also the winners of the Biennial Cup and the Index. Fastest lap speed was pushed up to 71.112 mph by Courcelles in the second La Lorraine.

Pontlieue was a favourite spot for photographers. Corre La Licorne in 1926.

LE MANS 1927

Was this the classic 24-hour race? It may certainly have done more than any other single Le Mans to bring the event to the notice of the British public, containing as it did all those ingredients that would have been necessary for a 'Boy's Own Paper' version of the great race: near disaster, followed by heroic effort resulting in a British victory.

The beginnings were inauspicious; a mere 22 cars came to the start on 18 June, and most peoples' money would have been on the team of three Bentleys, two three-litre cars and one of $4\frac{1}{2}$ litres. All the big French cars had disappeared with the exception of a single Aries three-litre. Otherwise there was a gaggle of French cars in the smaller capacity classes up to two-litres; notably the air-cooled S.A.R.A.s, the beautifully made twin ohc Salmsons in the 1,100 cc class, and one of Gregoire's front-wheel drive Tractas co-driven by the designer himself.

Frank Clement and Callingham drove the $4\frac{1}{2}$ litre Bentley which went into the lead right from the flag. Hoods had been raised at the start but despite this handicap Clement broke the lap record on the second lap of the race. This was the last year that regulations demanded that hoods be raised for the first three hours of the race. The two three-litre Bentleys followed, driven by Baron d'Erlanger/Duller and Sammy Davis/J. D. Benjafield; the latter car was 'Old Number 7' which had crashed so close to the finish of the 1926 race. The Bentleys led the Aries driven by Chassagne/Laly, and this in turn was followed by the three Salmsons. The Aries sported somewhat ungainly bodywork, the front half was of traditional aspect but the long slab-sided tail was reminiscent of the 'tank' bodies already seen on the Chenard et Walcker.

Then at 9.30 in the evening, just as the summer night was closing in, all calculations were upset. A two-litre Th.Schneider (driven by Tabourin/Poirier) skidded at White House corner, less than a mile before the pits and came to a halt blocking the road. Callingham was just behind in the $4\frac{1}{2}$ litre Bentley; taking to the ditch, he managed to avoid the French car but his car rolled over behind the stationary Th.Schneider. The mêlée was soon joined by a second Th.Schneider and Duller's three-litre Bentley; then an 1,100 cc Aries added itself to this monumental pile-up, and finally came Sammy Davis in the third Bentley. Apparently he had some notion that the road ahead was not clear so he approached White House rather more slowly than he would otherwise have done; he was able to brake, bringing the heavy Bentley into a skid so that it hit the assembled wreckage sideways on.

The most remarkable thing about the White House disaster was that nobody was actually killed. Of the six cars involved, five were totally wrecked, but Davis was able to extricate his Bentley and drive it back to the pits for closer examination. The frame was bent, and so was the front axle; the offside front wing and running-board were in tatters, and the headlamp was smashed. But it was a runner; Davis frantically set about rectifying some of the worst damage as best he could – the rules stipulated that only the driver could effect repairs, and he was only allowed the use of tools carried on the car. After half an hour, the Bentley re-joined the race; and when co-driver Benjafield later took over, he reported a slight tendency to pull to the right when braking, otherwise the massive solidity of the Bentley appeared to have withstood the effects of the crash remarkably well.

By now the big Aries was leading the race, and throughout the rainy night the chase went on. During Sunday morning the French car's lead was eroded from four laps to one, as it had a lengthy pit stop with starter trouble. But with Chassagne at the wheel, the Aries was still faster than Benjafield in the Bentley; then in the final stages of the race it was apparent that the French car was in trouble. It stopped at the circuit with an hour and a half to go, and the Bentley took the lead. It was the only big car left in the race, and was followed home by a pair of 1,100 cc Salmsons; only seven cars finished, last home was the Tracta. It makes an interesting speculation that if Davis had not got the Bentley going again, outright victory could have gone to one of the Salmsons which would have been the smallest-engined car ever to succeed at Le Mans. As it was, Casse and Rousseau won the Index of Performance and the Biennial Cup in addition to their third place overall.

The average speed of the Davis/Benjafield car had been 61.354 mph for a total distance of 1,472.52 miles; well below the figures

Reproduced from a 1927 French picture magazine, not all these photos are from Le Mans but they give an impression of the period:
1: The winning three-litre Bentley of Benjafield/Davis passes the pits.
2: A typical pit-stop scene. Le Mans pits were still only semi-permanent.
3: Mistinguett and Charles Carpentier in the artists' motoring gymkhana.
4: Morane monoplanes at the Orly air display.
5: A pair of Salmsons at Pontlieue.

achieved by any of the first three Lorraines in the previous year, but it should be remembered that the car was stopped for a long time after the crash, and its average speed was probably rather lower afterwards. Frank Clement, in the $4\frac{1}{2}$ litre Bentley, set a new lap record of 73.4 mph before being put out of the race.

This then was the start of Bentley's fame – if not fortunes; but as W. O. Bentley himself said, '. . . from this time we had no need to worry about publicity'. If the Le Mans victories did not help towards putting the Bentley company on a sound commercial footing, at least they created the legend of the green cars at Le Mans, and a heritage that lives on in the name of the current Bentley 'Mulsanne' model; even if no Bentley has raced at Sarthe since 1951. As a fitting finale to the 1927 victory, the winning car was the star guest at a party given by *The Autocar* in the honour of the Bentley team at the Savoy Hotel soon after the race, when 'Old Number 7' still bore its honourable battle scars.

LE MANS 1928

Undoubtedly all the publicity generated by Bentley's dramatic win in the previous year had helped to increase British interest in Le Mans and apart from three $4\frac{1}{2}$ litre Bentleys, there were teams of two-litre Lagondas and $1\frac{1}{2}$ litre cars from Aston Martin and Alvis; the last-mentioned entries were two of Alvis' front-wheel drive cars. Aston Martin also had two cars, neither of which finished, so it was an inauspicious start for what, over the years, became the most consistently-entered British marque – 25 races to 1964, two private entries since and Aston Martin engined cars in 1967 and 1982.

1928 was also the year in which the American challenge had to be taken seriously. The biggest-engined car was a 4.9 litre straight eight Stutz, and this was backed up by four Model 72 Chryslers with 4.1 litre engines. Two two-litre Italas were the sole representatives of Italy – this marque's only appearance at Le Mans. The only French contender for victory was the Aries which had challenged Bentley in 1927; otherwise the French entries were all in the classes below two-litres, including, among others, two Salmsons and three Tractas. The total field numbered 33 cars.

For the first time, an annual distance award was officially recognised in addition to the Biennial Cup and the Index of Performance. First car to lead was the Brisson/Bloch Stutz, and the lap record was broken in rapid succession by Woolf Barnato in a Bentley, then the Stutz, then Clement in another Bentley, all in the first hour of the race. The big Aries had the dubious distinction of being the first car to retire, after only two laps. From then on the battle became Anglo-American; Bentley v. Stutz and Chrysler. Birkin in the third Bentley driving on a punctured tyre (he carried no jack) suffered a collapsed wheel and his car went off the road; his co-driver Chassagne struggled for three hours before being able to re-join the race. During most of the night the Stutz led followed by the Barnato/Rubin Bentley, one of the Chryslers and the Clement/Benjafield Bentley; but the latter had to retire with a cracked chassis frame, caused by metal fatigue induced by vibration, and this in turn pulled the radiator hose away.

Bentley's three-car team was therefore effectively reduced to one, and as the cars were all similar the Bentley team fully expected the Barnato/Rubin car to succumb to the same problems as the Benjafield/Clement car. Meanwhile, one of the Lagondas had got stuck in the sandbank at Mulsanne corner; it was rammed by the second Lagonda driven by the Baron d'Erlanger who was, however, able to continue and finished the race in eleventh place. One of the Chryslers dropped down the field and finally retired; another had only lasted ten laps but the two surviving cars kept well up with the race leaders.

Meanwhile Birkin and Chassagne were working their way up through a depleted field of smaller cars; in his efforts Birkin ultimately set a new lap record of 79.29 mph and finished fifth. The Bentley–Stutz duel for the lead was intensified when, on Sunday afternoon, the Stutz lost its two lower gears; but it was apparent that Barnato too was in trouble. He had passed the American car while it was being re-fuelled, but now had to slow down and from the Bentley pits it could be seen that the $4\frac{1}{2}$ litre was beginning to distort its shape – the sign of a cracked chassis. As his radiator began to leak water Barnato lowered his speed, nursing the car through the last few laps to win at a margin of less than eight miles from the Stutz. The winning car's average speed was 69.108 mph and the total distance

1,658.6 miles, handsomely beating the 1926 record. Two Chryslers followed in third and fourth places and the first of the Alvises was a very creditable sixth, its team mate ninth. All three Tractas also finished, and for the second year in succession, Casse and Rousseau (who finished tenth overall) took the Index and the Biennial Cup with their 1,100 cc Salmson.

If lacking the spectacular drama of the 1927 race, 1928's race provided more excitement as the outcome was in doubt right up to the end; although there is no doubt that the excitement and the worry were more pronounced in the Bentley pit than on the grandstand. Bentley's third victory, and the second in succession, did nothing to harm the already excellent reputation of the make; but the 4½ litre's hitherto undiscovered tendency to fracture its chassis under strain was a warning to the company.

LE MANS 1929

The entry of 25 cars was composed largely as in previous years – French cars in the minority, and of these the biggest were 1.8 litre S.A.R.A.s. The Bentley team consisting of five cars were the favourites; there were four 4½ litre cars of which three had run in the previous year's race – their chassis now suitably strengthened – but Woolf Barnato and Sir Henry 'Tim' Birkin were entrusted one of the new Speed Six models: Bentley's first six-cylinder car, a 6½ litre developed to challenge the Rolls-Royce Phantom but in short chassis sports form a formidable weapon in their Le Mans armoury.

Ranged against the Bentleys were the American cars: a straight

The twin ohc Stutz of Brisson-Stoffel at the new Pontlieue corner in 1929.

eight 5.3 litre Du Pont, three Stutzes, now of the twin ohc DV.32 model with four valves to each of the eight cylinders, and two Chryslers. A potential British challenge might come from a lone $4\frac{1}{2}$ litre Invicta, and there were also single entries from Lagonda, Alvis and Lea-Francis. There were no Italian cars entered, and in the absence of Salmson, the most important French entry was that of four Tractas. A 749 cc d'Yrsan provided an almost comic contrast to the enormous Bentley Speed Six.

The circuit was shortened fractionally as the Pontlieue hairpin – virtually in Le Mans itself – was cut off by a new road, the Rue du Circuit, in the interest of safety; the distance was now 10.153 instead of the original 10.726 miles. This arrangement was, however, of a

The $4\frac{1}{2}$ litre Bentley of Benjafield/D'Erlanger was third in the 1929 race.

The Bentley team with the spoils of victory in 1929. Barnato and Birkin on the Speed Six, car no. 1, were the winners.

Artist impression of Barnato and Kidston's Bentley Speed Six.

makeshift nature and only lasted three years before the much more radically altered Tertre Rouge stretch was opened.

As expected, the Bentleys took the lead from the start, only two of the Stutzes keeping up with them. Lord Howe, who was driving a 4½ litre Bentley together with Bernard Rubin had trouble first with plugs, then with the magneto, and was obliged to retire at the end of the afternoon; but nothing could impede the progress of the other Bentleys. At 8 pm the Bentleys, and one of the Stutzes driven by the British record breaker Captain George Eyston, had lapped the rest of the field.

And so the race went on. Little short of a multiple disaster, as in 1927, or wholesale mechanical breakdown, could have destroyed the Bentleys' lead which was gradually extended. Their opponents did not fare so well. One of the Stutz drivers was badly burned when petrol was spilled on the red-hot exhaust pipe during a pit stop; his co-driver bravely continued in the face of a possible 18 hour solo drive but was eventually put out of the running with a leaking petrol tank. A similar fate overtook Eyston's Stutz, leaving only the Bouriat/Philippe care in the race. The Du Pont had retired early when the ballast it carried fell through the floor and damaged the prop shaft! And the Invicta ran a big end early on Sunday morning.

In the end, it was a rather predictable Bentley walk-over; with Bentleys in the first four places, the most magnificent victory so far at Le Mans, and not equalled before 1957. It was also the most impressive demonstration of the qualities of the Bentley, speed coupled with stamina and reliability. The green cars were followed home by the surviving Stutz in fifth place, and two Chryslers were sixth and seventh after an undramatic race. Only three more cars finished; the Lea-Francis, and two of the Tractas. The winning Bentley was the Speed Six; Birkin set the lap record for the new circuit at 82.984 mph, and he and Barnato also won the Biennial Cup and the Index of Performance – the biggest-engined car ever to win this Index which has tended to favour cars of smaller capacity, but a good measure of the margin of performance enjoyed by the big Bentley. For the first time all three major awards therefore went to the same car, a feat only repeated twice in Le Mans history. The winner's average speed was 73.627 mph and the distance covered was 1,767.07 miles.

LE MANS 1930

The result of the 1929 race led to violent criticism of the passivity of the French motor industry in not entering Le Mans with cars which had a chance of winning on distance; but there was no sign that such criticism had been heeded for the 1930 race, indeed, if anything, the French interest was even less – of the 17 starters (the smallest-ever field) only three cars were French, two Tractas and a 1.5 litre Bugatti; the first time the Molsheim factory had been represented at Le Mans since 1923, and the first time a female crew – Mesdames Mereuse and Siko – had been permitted to start in the race.

The 1930 winner: Barnato and Kidston in the Bentley Speed Six.

1930 newcomers: Earl Howe's 1750 Alfa Romeo in the Rue du Circuit. Followed by a British Talbot.

However, it is likely that the economic depression had affected manufacturers in general; the American entries were down to two Stutzes, but two important newcomers to the Sarthe circuit were Mercedes-Benz and Alfa Romeo, with one entry each. The race was still somewhat of a British, not to say Bentley, benefit: there were ten British cars entered, of which five were Bentleys. This year the Bentley entry came from two different stables, the factory team ran a trio of Speed Sixes led by Barnato and Kidston in 'Old Number One' which had won the 1929 race; they were supplemented by two supercharged $4\frac{1}{2}$ litre 'Blower' Bentleys, from the team of the Hon. Dorothy Paget. Two Talbots – from the British company – were entered: 2.3 litre machines, their tall bonnets hiding Roesch's compact six-cylinder engines and they could easily be identified from their three closely-set headlamps. A Lea-Francis was the sole contestant in the $1\frac{1}{2}$ litre class apart from a Bugatti, and finally there were two MG M-type Midgets, of the 'Double-Twelve' type which had won the team prize in the British equivalent of Le Mans, the Brooklands Double-Twelve hour race.

The race that unfolded proved to be a Mercedes-Bentley duel; the Stutzes were never really in the running, one car set itself on fire and the other broke its rear axle. Caracciola (whose co-driver was Werner) took the lead from the start in the Mercedes, but was passed on the fourth lap by Birkin in one of the blown Bentleys. In doing so Birkin shed a tyre tread and although he continued at first, the tyre ultimately burst forcing him to stop to change it. The other Bentleys continued the chase, after the first pit stop the Barnato/Kidston Speed Six was less than two minutes behind the Mercedes, and the two cars passed and re-passed each other several times as the evening wore on. Then, in the middle of the night, the Mercedes failed to re-start after a pit stop; it seems the dynamo had stopped charging and the battery was flat, and of course Le Mans regulations forbade push-starting as well as the use of a starting handle.

The start of the 1930 race, with Bentley, Stutz and Talbot to the fore.

This left the Bentleys firmly in control of the race, if anything the two teams could indulge in some private sport but as it turned out, the 'Blower' Bentleys lived up to their reputation for mechanical unreliability and both had retired by midday Sunday. Lower down the scale, the Alfa Romeo driven by Lord Howe and Callingham challenged the pair of Talbots but was unable to pass either of them. Both the MG Midgets had retired, and in the end only nine cars finished, led home by the Barnato/Kidston Bentley which also took the Biennial Cup, its average speed was 75.876 mph and distance 1,821.02 miles. The Clement/Watney Bentley followed, then came the two Talbots and the Alfa Romeo; the Lea-Francis beat the Bugatti in the $1\frac{1}{2}$ litre class, and the two Tractas rounded off the list, despite Gregoire in one of the Tractas getting stuck in the ditch on the last lap, getting free only just in time with a little unofficial help from the spectators standing by. The Index of Performance went to Talbot, and Birkin – before retiring – pushed up the lap record to a remarkable 89.696 mph.

After this, their fifth victory, the Bentley works team retired from racing; indeed, the original Bentley company lasted only just another year, as the receiver was appointed in July 1931 and eventually control passed to Rolls-Royce. For three years a single Bentley was entered privately at Le Mans but without any success, and although a Rolls-Royce type Bentley put up an impressive performance in 1949 and 1950, it was not really competitive. The Bentley days were over on that June Sunday in 1930, but what a splendid final chapter in their saga.

ENTRE L'OBSTACLE ET VOUS, PLACEZ...
LES FREINS
BENDIX
ETABLISSEMENTS
Castrol
BOUGIE K L G
L'ATOMISOR

LE MANS 1931

There was a marked contrast between the line-up of cars for the 1931 race and those that had gone before. There were fewer works teams, and more private entries and even if there were remembrances of the past in the form of single entries of Bentley, La Lorraine and Stutz, more importance attached to the presence of works teams from Bugatti (three 4.9 litre Type 50s, managed by Jean Bugatti) and Alfa Romeo (three 8C-2300s, a brand new model that had made its first appearance in the Mille Miglia two months previously; although

The Chryslers getting away quickly at the 1931 start, bracketing Mercedes and Stutz.

only two came to the start). Most important among the bigger cars was an SSK-type Mercedes similar to the one that had been entered in 1930; it was the only German car, while two Chryslers represented America. Apart from the privately entered Bentley, British hopes centred on two three-litre Talbots, and among the smaller cars were three 1½ litre Aston Martins and a brace of supercharged C-type MG Midgets. A perhaps unlikely entry was a lone 2.6 litre Arrol-Aster complete with sleeve valves, the only time a Scottish-built car has contested the race, but its performance hardly compared with that of the Ecurie Ecosse cars 25 years later. But it was encouraging that a total of 26 cars started, and for the French more encouraging still that the Bugatti works team held out the prospect of victory.

With such hopes riding on the three black Bugattis, it is difficult to understand the reason for the events that followed. If, as has been claimed, the Bugatti's tyres had already proved unreliable, and further misadventures had occurred in practice with treads being lost

The 1931 winner: the Alfa Romeo 8 C 2300 of Earl Howe and Birkin.

– and their team mates, Zehender and Marinoni with a similar Alfa.

at high speed, it is surprising that the tyres were not changed altogether – one wonders whether national pride played a role, as the Bugattis rode on Michelin and to change to a non-French make of tyre would undoubtedly entail a loss of face. In any case, as Dumont has argued, the road holding and the stability of the Type 50 were hardly sufficient for its top speed of 112 mph. But whatever the real reasons, ostensibly it was the tyre problem which caused Bugatti's difficulties at Le Mans: first the Chiron/Varzi car threw a tread; then, at 6.30 pm, the tread of the left rear tyre wound itself round the brake drum of the car being driven by Maurice Rost. He went off the road, hitting several spectators of whom one was killed and several injured. Rost was thrown clear and badly injured; he never raced again. The car was a complete wreck. Chiron's car lost another tread, and Jean Bugatti decided to withdraw the remaining two team cars. This was not Bugatti's year: two privately entered cars retired and the women's team, Mesdames Mereuse and Siko, were disqualified for re-fuelling too early.

This left the race between the Alfa Romeos, the Mercedes-Benz and the Talbots. One of the Alfa Romeos crashed, and one of the Talbots retired with a cracked chassis. But the remaining Alfa Romeo, driven by Lord Howe and Sir Henry Birkin, was the first car home, at an average of 78.13 mph and a total distance of 1,875.1 miles – a fraction over the 3,000 km barrier which was broken for the first time in the history of Le Mans. Howe and Birkin took the 'triple crown' by also winning the Index, and the Biennial Cup. They were followed by the big Mercedes-Benz driven by Iwanowski and Stoffel; Iwanowski put up the fastest lap but failed to break Birkin's 1930 record. The surviving Talbot was third, and this was amazingly enough followed by the ancient La Lorraine. Only two more cars finished, an Aston Martin and a 1.1 litre Caban; this was the smallest number of cars ever to have finished at Le Mans. One of the MGs finished but was not classified; it had broken a piston but managed to keep going, but took more than the permitted 30 minutes to complete the final lap.

The first victory for Italy, and for Alfa Romeo, brought congratulations from Mussolini; yet both drivers were British and experienced veterans from the Bentley team; indeed, it was Sir Henry Birkin's second win.

1931: Ill-fated Bugatti, the type 50 of Varzi/Chiron while still in the running.

LE MANS 1932

This was the first year of the 'new' circuit; a new road had been built specially to the A.C.O.'s requirements across the circuit just after the pits and grandstand, rejoining the original circuit at Tertre Rouge. This new stretch included the 'Esses'. The new circuit cut out the Pontlieue section completely and kept well clear of the suburbs of Le Mans. The Tertre Rouge section soon became a favourite vantage point for spectators, and the centre of the gradually growing 'Village' with all its side-shows and fun fair atmosphere. The circuit was somewhat shortened and the lap distance was now 8.383 miles; in this form, the Circuit Permanente de la Sarthe survived largely unchanged until 1967.

Another small field of 26 cars, numerically dominated by seven Alfa Romeos: six 2.3 litre cars, two works entries with some assistance also given to last year's winners, Howe and Birkin, and one 1,750 six-cylinder model. Ranged against these were only three big-engined cars, all privately entered by French drivers: a Mercedes-Benz, a Stutz and Sir Henry Birkin's old Blower Bentley. There was a single British Talbot, and two 2.3 Bugattis – the Type 55s. Aston Martin brought three works cars and there were single entries of Alta and MG but no other British cars. Among the smaller French cars a 1½ litre Citroën made a unique appearance for a make renowned for endurance in long-distance record attempts, but hardly

1932: The old Bentley of Trevoux/'Mary' before the White House debacle.

capable of the speeds required to be competitive at Le Mans. It soon retired . . .

From the start it seemed to be mainly a question of which Alfa Romeo would take the lead, individual drivers jockeying for position. But on the first lap, the French driver Trevoux overturned the old Bentley at White House, setting in motion a train of events that seemed to be almost a repetition of the 1927 drama, and would probably have been far more serious, had it happened after dark. As it was, the Bentley merely proved an irritating artificial chicane, defeating all efforts to shift it, until just after 6 pm when Minoia in one of the works Alfas came down towards White House too fast and, trying to avoid the wreck, skidded into a field. Here it was soon joined by the Stutz and, eventually, Marinoni's Alfa Romeo also

Madame Siko in conference at the Alfa pit during the 1932 race.

Pierre-Louis Dreyfus and Schumann raced this 2.3 litre Alfa under the pseudonyms 'Ano' and 'Nime'.

fetched up against the immovable bulk of the Bentley.

Of the remaining Alfa Romeos, the Schumann/Dreyfus car rolled at Arnage, and at 3 am Birkin's head gasket blew and with it his and Lord Howe's chances of a repeat win. The Mercedes-Benz and the Bugatti Type 55 driven by Chiron/Bouriat had both retired, so the main contestants were now the two Alfas of Sommer/Chinetti and Cortese/Guidotti (the remaining works car); the other Bugatti driven by Czaikowski and veteran driver Ernest Friderich (his only drive in the 24-hour race, but as the winner of the 1920 Voiturette G.P. he was no stranger to the Sarthe circuit); and the Talbot. This would in fact have been the finishing order had it not been for the retirement of the Bugatti at noon on Sunday.

The Cortese-Guidotti Alfa was constantly plagued by parts working loose and falling off, and its mudguards gradually took on a distinct non-regulation shape; meanwhile Raymond Sommer in the leading Alfa had to drive solo, as Chinetti was taken ill after only three hours at the wheel. The Talbot in third place also had its

Inset: 1932's winner – almost solo: Raymond Sommer on the Alfa Romeo.

The Bugatti 2.3 litre model of Bouriat and Chiron.

troubles to contend with; it was running on only five cylinders, and was harrassed by the little 1,750 cc Alfa Romeo which eventually finished fourth. In the end the race was Raymond Sommer's; his winning average was 76.48 mph and the distance 1,835.55 miles; even if the figures were lower than 1931's record, it was a remarkable performance by this French driver whose second Le Mans this was – in the previous year he had driven a Chrysler which had retired. Sommer also won the Index. The Biennial Cup was taken by one of the two finishing Aston Martins, just snatching it away from a faltering Caban which had finished ninth and last.

LE MANS 1933

Although surely a well-meant gesture, undertaken in all innocence by the pious burghers of Le Mans, the building of a small chapel at the track might have had somewhat cynical overtones – the French are primarily a practical race. Mass was said here on Sunday morning during the race. For those in peril on the track . . .?

A total of 29 cars were brought to the start on 17 June after a

Two of the Aston Martins entered in the 1932 race in the pits.

The Alfa of Nuvolari/Sommer during a 1933 pit stop. Nuvolari looks agitated. Inset: Sommer doing his bit for victory in the 1933 race.

When Madame Siko's Alfa crashed near Arnage early Sunday morning during the 1933 race, she was fortunate in being thrown clear.

Chinetti and Varent were the runners-up with this Alfa in 1933.

record 13 entries had been scratched. Again, there were seven Alfa Romeos; five 2.3 litre eight-cylinder models, of which two were short chassis Mille Miglia replicas, and two 1.75 sixes, of which the Rousseau/Paco car was a coupé. Among the Alfa drivers, the partnership of last year's winner Sommer with the Italian master Tazio Nuvolari (his only Le Mans appearance) attracted attention. The Frenchman Louis Chiron had been tempted away from the native Bugatti into another Alfa, together with Cortese; another change of allegiance was the British duo of Lewis and Rose-Richards who had taken the Talbot into third place in 1932 but were now to be found in an Alfa.

Among the more unusual entries was Prince Nicholas of Roumania, in a giant 6.9 litre Model J Duesenberg; Trevoux persisted with the old Bentley, and Labric-Daniel with an equally venerable La Lorraine. The last big car was a single five-litre Bugatti. Apart from the Bentley, all the British cars were small fry, comprising three Aston Martins in the $1\frac{1}{2}$ litre class (in one of these Sammy Davis had his last Le Mans drive), two 1,100 cc Rileys (these were the Nine Brooklands models; one had won the 1932 TT, and it was Riley's first entry in the 24-hour race) and finally a Singer Nine, two MG Midgets and an Austin Seven. All the remaining entries were various small French cars, including a farewell appearance of that Le Mans stalwart, the air-cooled S.A.R.A.

Right from the start a most punishing pace was set up, the Alfa Romeo driven by Sommer eventually set up a new lap record of 90.96 mph, at last beating Birkin's record from 1930. The five 2.3 Alfa Romeos led, and were followed by the Bentley and the Duesenberg; but the final Le Mans appearance of a classic Bentley soon ended in the sandpit at Mulsanne, while the Roumanian prince was disqualified for re-fuelling too soon. The only car left to threaten the Alfas was the big Bugatti, driven by Mesdames Desprez and Tarante. Before 2 am the first of the 2.3 litre Alfas, that of Moll/Cloitre, retired with lighting trouble. Otherwise the lead still changed between Sommer/Nuvolari, Chinetti/Varent and Chiron/Cortese, with Lewis and Rose-Richards never far behind.

Early Sunday morning, Nuvolari stopped for 16 minutes while a leaking fuel tank was plugged, and shock absorbers were also a cause of trouble. Then Cortese had a dramatic accident, turning a somersault at the Esses, while the Bugatti had given up with mechanical trouble. Nuvolari had managed to regain the lead after some brilliant and furious driving but was still challenged by the Chinetti/Varent car; particularly as his fuel leak grew steadily worse, despite much dedicated gum-chewing by Nuvolari, Sommer and even the entire pit crew of Lewis and Rose-Richards. The last hour of the race was of a drama unparalleled in Le Mans history; Nuvolari led by two minutes at 3 pm; fifteen minutes later Varent was in the lead, but Nuvolari passed yet again. At 3.52 pm Chinetti (who had taken over from Varent and who was spurred on by a promised 60,000 francs bonus should he win) passed a stationary Nuvolari at the pits; Nuvolari got going again, and on the last lap the lead changed three times. Finally, Chinetti missed a gear change at Arnage, he went off the road and Nuvolari got by; when Chinetti resumed the chase, he found the road blocked by a smaller car – and Nuvolari won by a margin of a quarter of a mile, or about ten seconds.

Tazio Nuvolari, the flying Mantuan – winner of the 1933 Le Mans.

The winner's average was 81.4 mph and the distance 1,953.61 miles, handsomely beating the previous records set up in 1931. Sommer and Nuvolari also won the Biennial Cup. They were followed home by Chinetti (who got his 60,000 francs bonus all the same) and Varent, and in third place was the Alfa of Lewis and Rose-Richards. Fourth was the little Riley of von der Becke and Peacock and this team won the Index of Performance; they were followed by an Aston Martin, the supercharged MG J4 Midget and the other Aston Martin driven by Bertelli and Sammy Davis. The closed Alfa was eighth, and the next four places were occupied by small French cars; thirteenth and last to finish was the Singer Nine.

Thus ended a most memorable race; Nuvolari's only Le Mans drive, resulting in a dramatic victory at one of the narrowest margins ever in the history of the 24-hour race. But Alfa Romeo's 1–2–3 victory was tinged with regret; after having run into financial problems, the company had been taken over by the state-owned I.R.I. organisation which had announced the withdrawal from racing of the Alfa works team at the end of the 1933 season.

LE MANS 1934

Although there were no further changes to the circuit, the aspect of Le Mans was changed drastically for the 1934 race as impressive new two-storey pits had been erected, and new high-speed fuel pumps had been installed courtesy of the petrol companies. The new pits would cater for a maximum of 60 cars – a figure which was occasionally reached in the 1950s although since then the number of entrants has normally been limited to 55.

Perhaps because of the much improved amenities, perhaps because of Nuvolari's dramatic victory the year before, the 1934 race attracted 44 starters, of which Britain provided the biggest number, but none with the chance of an outright win as the biggest British cars were the Aston Martins, Rileys and Singers in the 1½ litre class; Britain also dominated the 1,100 cc class with MG Magnettes, a Lagonda Rapier and Riley Nines, and in the small car class there were Singer Nines, MG Midgets and a single Austin Seven. The total number of British cars was 23; but the favourites were yet again the 2.3 litre Alfa Romeos, of which four were entered privately, making up for the absence of the Milanese works team. France fielded 17 cars, including five Bugattis ranging from 1½ to five-litres; the old La Lorraine; assorted small cars, including the last appearance at Le Mans of Rally, Tracta and Salmson, although the last mentioned would make a brief re-appearance in 1955–6; and two of the new front-wheel drive Derbys with two-litre V-8 engines, one driven by Englishwoman Mrs Gwenda Stewart.

1934 and the last win for Alfa Romeo, by Philippe ('Phi-Phi') Etancelin (seen here) and Luigi Chinetti.

Raymond Sommer in one of the Alfa Romeos led from the start, closely followed by the other three cars of this make; but after less than two hour's racing, the Sommer car caught fire and had to retire, putting the British entered Alfa of Lord Howe and Rose-Richards into the lead. Sommer's early retirement was a bad omen for the Alfa camp; another British crew in an Alfa, Saunders-Davis and Clifford, had to retire during Saturday evening, and after having dropped down the field due to lighting problems, Lord Howe and Rose-Richards were finally defeated with clutch trouble.

As Sunday dawned it therefore appeared that the remaining Alfa Romeo – driven by Louis Chinetti and Philippe Etancelin – would have the race in the bag, if it would last; but there seems to have been a repeat of the leaking fuel tank problem which all but defeated Sommer and Nuvolari in the previous year. Of their rivals, the five-litre Bugatti had already retired the previous evening; so had one of the 2.3 litre Bugattis while the other was disqualified. The three-litre Bugatti and the venerable La Lorraine still kept going but they were well down the scoreboard, behind many of the smaller cars; indeed, the leading Alfa was hunted by a pack of assorted Aston Martins, Rileys and MGs. But when the Aston Martin which was running second retired, Chinetti had a comfortable lead over the following Riley which enabled him to relax a little. He finished the race as winner but without breaking any records – the average speed of the Chinetti/Etancelin Alfa Romeo was 74.74 mph and the distance covered 1,793.85 miles, lower figures than at any time since 1929, nor was the lap record broken.

Apart from the victorious Alfa Romeo, the honours of the race went to British cars; of 23 finishers, 16 were British, and the achievement of Riley was particularly noteworthy: of six cars entered, six finished, taking second, third, fifth and sixth places, while the Riley of von der Becke/Peacock, which finished fifth, also won the Index of Performance and the Biennial Cup. One of the MG Magnettes was fourth, MG's best ever Le Mans placing, and Singers filled seventh and eigth places.

With four consecutive victories to their credit, the Alfa Romeos were obvious rivals to the Bentleys for the best overall performance at Le Mans, but the Italian cars still needed a fifth victory to equal the achievement of the British cars. This is exactly what Alfa Romeo entrants intended to do in 1935 . . .

LE MANS 1935

The biggest number of cars so far came to the start this year: 58 cars were lined up on Saturday afternoon 15 June. British cars again dominated, with a total of 37 cars, most of them in the $1\frac{1}{2}$ litre or smaller classes – Singer fielded the largest entry of nine cars, followed by Aston Martin and MG with seven cars each, six Rileys, four Austin Sevens (three works entries). Two Frazer-Nashes were the first representatives of this marque to race at Le Mans. But this year Britain also fielded a contestant in the big car class: two $4\frac{1}{2}$ litre Lagonda Rapides, entered by Fox and Nichol. Among the drivers of

The Aston Martin of Elwes/Morris-Goodall sweeps onto the new Tertre Rouge section in 1935.

the smaller British cars were Mr and Mrs Wisdom – Tommy and 'Bill' – but in separate cars, a Singer and a Riley respectively. Both retired without completing the race.

Among the French cars the La Lorraine made its final appearance – appropriately enough on the tenth anniversary of the win of this make. It was also the last year for entries from BNC and Derby. Bugatti was the only French make with more than a single entry; no less than seven cars of the Molsheim make took part, in assorted sizes from $1\frac{1}{2}$ to five-litres. Talbot – now under the control of Anthony Lago – made a welcome re-appearance with a three-litre coupé; this operation was probably in the nature of testing the water, as was the first entry of a Delahaye. These two marques would be more prominent in the future. Undeterred by previous bad luck – he was disqualified in 1933, and his engine seized in practice for the 1934 race – Prince Nicholas of Roumania once again brought his gigantic out-moded Duesenberg to the starting line. But popular imagination seized on the Alfa Romeos yet again; four of the 2.3 litre supercharged eight-cylinder cars which now had four wins to their credit, backed up by a 1,750 cc six-cylinder car. This year, however, there were two other Italian cars entered: a pair of Fiat Ballilla Sports with 995 cc engines, although their entry was due to Frenchman Amedee Gordini who had his first Le Mans drive in one of these cars.

As could be expected, the Alfa Romeos took the lead initially. Among their drivers this year were Sommer/de Sauge; but as the latter was taken ill, Sommer would have to drive solo. Lord Howe was partnered by Brian Lewis, Chinetti by Gastaud, and Stoffel by Pierre Louis-Dreyfus. Each of these cars took turns to lead the race, and were meanwhile challenged by the Lagondas of Hindmarsh/Fontes and Benjafield/Gunter, and also by the big Bugatti of Labric/Veyron. The Duesenberg retired before midnight; Sommer was in the lead at the time but a lengthy pit stop delayed him, and he ultimately abandoned the race before dawn on Sunday. He was followed by the Bugatti and the Alfa Romeo of Chinetti/Gastaud which twice had been in the ditch and the second time was too badly damaged to continue. Next to go was Lord Howe – his Alfa holed a piston – so in almost a repeat of the sequence of events in 1934, there was now only one big Alfa left, the car of Stoffel and Louis-Dreyfus. The main challenger was now the Hindmarsh/Fontes Lagonda – the other

1935: The $4\frac{1}{2}$ litre Lagonda of Hindmarsh and Fontes . . .

Lagonda eventually dropped down the field with gearbox problems, although it did finish the race.

The Hindmarsh/Fontes car overtook the Alfa on Sunday morning; then in the final hours of the race its oil pressure failed and Dreyfus gained on the Lagonda as it made several pit stops with its speed dropping. When Dreyfus passed the British car, his pit manager was confused and signalled that he was now in the lead when in fact he still had one lap to make up; but when the mistake was realised it was too late. Hindmarsh and Fontes nursed their sickly Lagonda home to the first British victory since 1930, their distance was 1,868.33 miles and the average speed 77.847 mph – they were just five miles ahead of the Alfa Romeo. But the 1933 record still stood.

In all 28 cars finished, third place went to Martin/Brackenbury in an Aston Martin and they also won the Index as well as the Biennial Cup. A Riley was fourth and the French newcomer, the Delahaye, placed fifth. Among the MGs, three PA-type Midgets driven by all-female crews, managed by George Eyston, finished in twenty-fourth, twenty-fifth and twenty-sixth positions; they were followed home by two Austin Sevens. So ended a memorable race with a surprise finish – the Alfa Romeo robbed of its ultimate triumph by a British dark horse, and Britain confirming its supremacy in the smaller capacity classes.

. . . and after their victory.

LE MANS 1936

A unique year in the history of the Le Mans 24-hour race – the year it was cancelled. If not quite on the brink of a civil war such as the one which broke out in Spain in June 1936, France was plagued by civil unrest, her industries paralysed by strikes – not least of course the motor industry: this was the year when Ettore Bugatti was denied access to his factory at Molsheim; when 25,000 workers occupied the Renault factory at Billancourt for almost a month; when the strikes and occupations spread all over France until 5 million workers were involved. But with the Matignon agreements most of the demands of the workforce were met – a 40 hour week, paid holidays, and the recognition of collective agreements – and before the end of the year the socialist Leon Blum had formed his Popular Front government. The Third Republic was saved – for the time being . . .

But one casualty had been the Le Mans race which was cancelled only a week before it was scheduled to take place, at considerable cost to the A.C.O., not to mention the 60 entrants. There had been much increased support from the French manufacturers this year, including works teams from Talbot, Delahaye and Delage (the two latter companies were now merged), and Amedee Gordini for Simca-Fiat. Aston Martin, Austin, Frazer-Nash and Riley continued to support the race, and there were numerous private entries from both France and Britain. Two Alfa Romeos were scheduled to defend the Italian colours, and an intriguing newcomer was the German Adler; after Mercedes-Benz, only the second German make to enter Le Mans.

LE MANS 1937

However, the entry list for 1937 promised a more interesting race still, particularly with the official return of a Bugatti works team – two of the stunning Type 57 G 'Tank' models with all-enveloping bodywork which had already proved their merit by winning the French Grand Prix at Montlhery in 1936 (run that year to a sports car formula when the French decided they could not compete with the new German Grand Prix cars). One car was entrusted to Le Mans veterans Veyron and Labric, the other to Benoist and Wimille – for the latter it was his first experience of the Sarthe circuit. Against the Bugattis were ranged no less than seven 3.6 litre Delahayes – part works, part private entries – a single Delage and two Talbots. There were also two privately entered Bugattis. Two other French makes made a return to Le Mans – Chenard et Walcker had two cars, appearing little different from their 1925 entries with the same streamlined bodywork; and Peugeot was seen at Le Mans for the second time, with a trio of the 402-based 'Darl' Mat' Specials.

The Delahaye of Paul and Mongin which was second in 1937.

Recalling past glories were single entries from Alfa Romeo – a 2.9 litre model driven by Sommer and Guidotti – and a Lagonda $4\frac{1}{2}$ litre, but both these cars retired early on, leaving the big car class an all-French preserve. Britain was well represented otherwise, by Aston Martin, Frazer-Nash – even if their entries were BMW's in all but name – Riley, Singer, MG and the Austin Seven 'Grasshoppers' which this year were joined by a 1,500 cc HRG and a somewhat unlikely contender in the shape of a stripped-down Ford Ten, with the 1,172 cc side valve engine. From Germany, the Adler entry promised for 1936 materialised – three outstanding cars, combining lowly-stressed 1.7 litre side valve engines with front-wheel drive and

1937: Bugatti has won for the first time – Benoist and Wimille, after their victory . . .

streamlined coupé bodywork in the manner of Jaray; on the track they looked like whales surrounded by sharks. Under the skin they were in fact remarkably standard Trumph models. They were joined by a single BMW 328. Finally, the main French entries in the smaller classes were three 1,100 cc Simca-Fiats and two Simca Cinqs – with the diminutive 569 cc Fiat 500 engine, much the smallest type of car ever to compete at Le Mans. Of the total field of 48 cars, 24 were French, 18 British, five German and one Italian.

As the race unfolded, the opening battle was between Sommer in the Alfa Romeo and Wimille in the Bugatti; but within the first hour of the race a multiple crash happened between the White House – scene of similar accidents in the past – and the pits. Six cars were involved; first Kippeurt rolled his Bugatti – he was thrown clear but had been killed instantly – then the single BMW ran into the wreckage, followed by Pat Farifield's Frazer-Nash-BMW and a Delahaye. Finally, one of the Talbots and a Riley added themselves to the pile-up; only Forestier in the Riley was unharmed, and Pat Fairfield died from his injuries. The dual tragedy cast its shadow over Le Mans but the race continued. Kippeurt and Fairfield were the first two drivers to be killed while racing at Le Mans since 1925.

. . . and during the race itself.

Soon after came Sommer's retirement, leaving the works Bugattis firmly in charge of the situation. Wimille and Benoist both set new lap records in turn; at midnight they had a three lap lead over the Delahaye which was running second, while the Veyron/Labric Bugatti was third. When this car retired on Sunday morning, another Delahaye automatically moved into third spot, and this was eventually the finishing order – the Wimille/Benoist Bugatti, followed by two Delahayes and the Delage. The first non-French car was an Aston Martin in fifth place; two of the Adlers were placed sixth and ninth, and the Peugeots were seventh, eighth and tenth. Wimille's performance in his first Le Mans was outstanding; he was credited with a new lap record of 96.423 mph, and he and Benoist comfortably broke the 1933 records – their distance was 2,043.02 miles and the average speed 85.126 mph; furthermore they won the Index. The Biennial Cup went to the Aston Martin of Morris-Goodall and Hitchens. The Ford Ten actually finished, in fourteenth place.

France had her first Le Mans victory since 1926, and with French cars in the first four places, demonstrated her newly found supremacy in sports car racing in no uncertain way. For Bugatti, a most satisfactory outcome – their first Le Mans win at record speed helped to obliterate memories of the 1931 debacle; and for Wimille an outstanding personal triumph, winning at his first appearance at Le Mans, an achievement shared only by a few outstanding drivers, such as Barnato and Nuvolari.

LE MANS 1938

In view of their victory in 1937 the absence of Bugattis – either works entries or privately owned cars – from the 1938 line-up was remarkable. One supercharged 4.5 litre Bugatti 'Tank', the Type 57 S 45, had taken part in the Le Mans practice run but was withdrawn, apparently because the factory did not consider that the car was ready to race. By contrast, Delahaye and Talbot were out in force; the former fielded two of their Type 145 4.5 litre V 12s – little more than camouflaged Grand Prix racing cars – in addition to five 3.6 litre sixes of the better known Type 135. There were six Talbots, one a $4\frac{1}{2}$ litre, and the rest of four-litres; these were the favourite teams, together with two Alfa Romeos – one a supercharged 2.9 litre coupé driven by Sommer and Biondetti.

Other French entries were a single Delage, two women in an unusual 2.3 litre four-cylinder Amilcar based on the Pegase model but with an ohv engine – the last Le Mans entry for this make – and the three Darl'Mat Peugeots. The one make fielding most entries was Simca, with eight 1,100 cc cars and two Simca Cinqs. There was a total of 28 French entries out of 42 cars altogether; other than the two Alfa Romeos and the two Adlers, there were ten British entries made up from two MGs, two Rileys (French owned), two Singers and single representatives of Aston Martin, HRG and two newcomers: Morgan and Atlanta. Morgan had an example of their first four-wheeler, the Coventry-Climax engined 4/4, and Atlanta a 1.5 litre engined car with fully independent suspension to smoothe out the bumps of the Sarthe circuit.

Raymond Sommer was the favourite, as so often before, and soon took the lead from the big Delahayes; he was briefly threatened by the $4\frac{1}{2}$ litre Talbot driven by Etancelin and Chinetti, but all the three biggest French cars were soon out of the race with mechanical trouble, and Sommer/Biondetti could extend their lead over the following Talbots and Delahayes almost at their leisure. Among the smaller cars, Gordini and Scaron put up a magnificent drive in the 1,100 cc Simca-Fiat, and led not only their own class but all the $1\frac{1}{2}$ litre cars as well. Two of the Peugeots had retired but the third was leading the two-litre class; the Adlers were circulating steadily and unobtrusively, like clockwork; and in a repeat of the 1935 race, a private husband and wife battle was being fought out between Tommy Wisdom in a Singer Nine, and Mrs Wisdom who this time shared a PB-Type MG – neither finished the race. Indeed, for most of the race the British cars were not doing very well.

But this was a Le Mans race with a sting in the tail, fully proving that to win, above all the car must stand the distance. While safely in the lead – despite having burst a tyre – the Sommer/Biondetti Alfa Romeo broke a valve on Sunday afternoon. Suddenly, the Delahaye of Chaboud and Tremoulet, which ran for most of the race with only top gear, was promoted to race leader from having been 12 laps behind, and it was followed by another Delahaye in the hands of

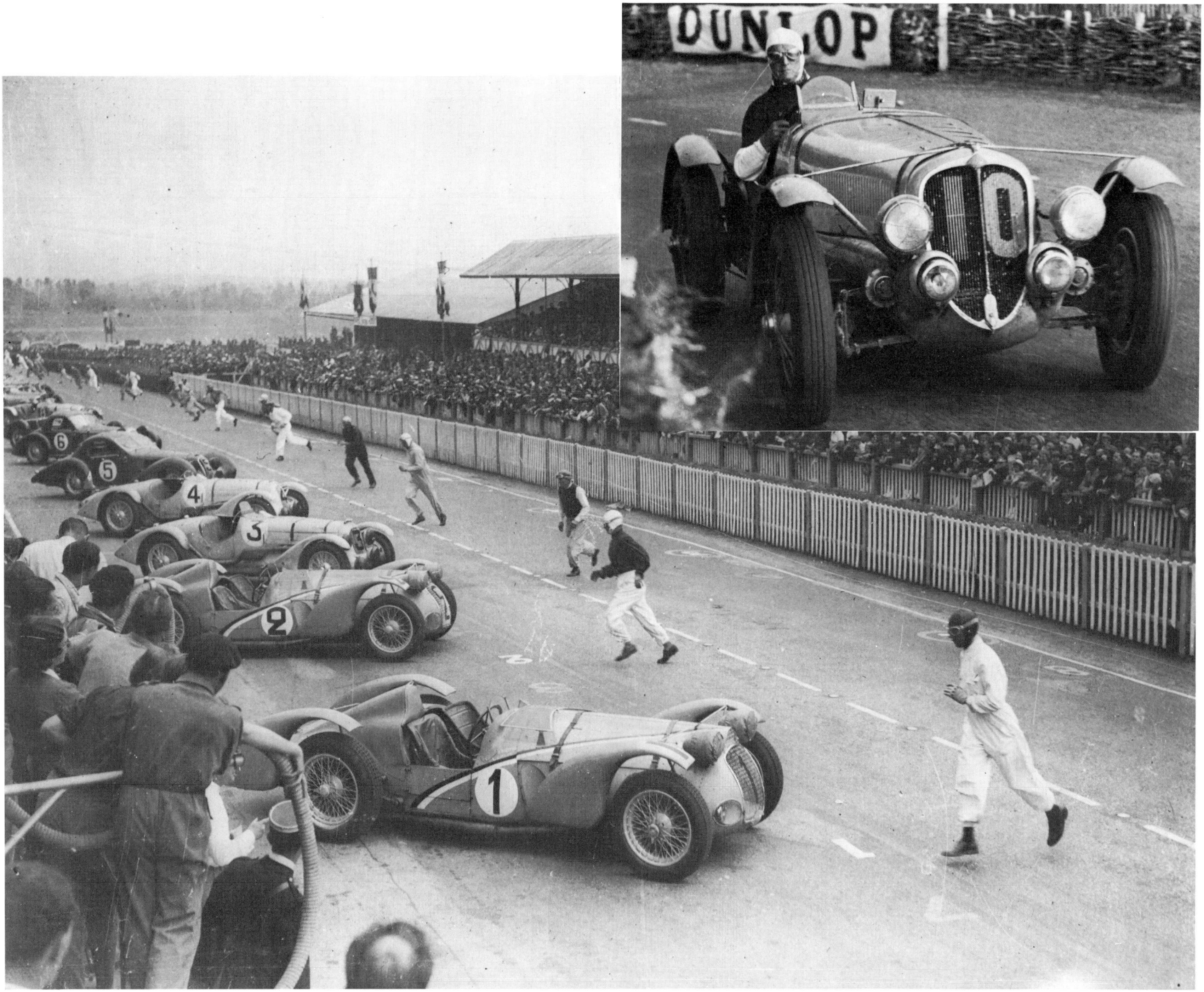

Start of the 1938 race – two Delahayes in front of four Talbots. Inset: This Delahaye of Villeneuve/Biolay was fourth in 1938.

1938 was Delahaye's year. The winning car on the right, number two on left.

Serrauld and Giraud-Cabantous. There was little time left for any other competitor to come from behind and challenge the two leaders, and at 4 pm Sunday afternoon Delahaye could celebrate a 1–2 win, with the third surviving car of this make being placed fourth. A Talbot was third, and the Peugeot fifth – complete French dominance for the second year running, in marked contrast to previous years. But as the winner's distance was only 1,976.54 miles, at an average Speed of 82.36 mph, no new records were set, nor was there a new lap record as Sommer's fastest lap was 96.177 mph, fractionally less than Wimille's 1937 record. Among the smaller cars, there had been another surprising change of fortune when Scaron crashed the leading Simca; this permitted the two Adlers to take sixth and seventh places, and Graf Orssich-Sauerwein in the leading Adler also won the Biennial Cup; but they were just beaten on Index by one of the tiny Simca Cinqs. Highest placed British car was a French-owned Singer Nine which finished eighth; altogether four Simcas finished, as did the HRG, a French-owned MG and the Morgan – there were no more than 15 finishers in 1938.

LE MANS 1939

Again there were only 42 cars in the race; the mixture was more or less as in the two previous years. Bugatti was back with a works entry, another Type 57 'Tank' with a supercharged 3.3 litre engine; the sole example of this make, it was entrusted to the 1937 winner, Wimille, partnered by Veyron who had driven in four previous races but never finished. By contrast, the French opposition was almost

guilty of over-kill; the Delahaye-Delage combine had eight 3.6 litre cars of the former make and two three-litre Delages, and the Lagonda-Talbots were also present in force – six cars of which three were four-litre models, the other three 4½ litre cars with a close relationship with the company's Grand Prix racers. The home contingent was rounded off by eight Simcas taking the total number of French cars to 25.

Adler brought only one of their 'Rennlimousinen' to start this year; they had entertained hopes of repeating their success in a bigger class, and had brought an equally efficiently streamlined 2.5 litre six

The 1939 start: contrast in closed cars – Adler and Simca-Fiat. Inset: The Delage came second in 1939 – here chasing through the Esses.

The BMW team of three 328 models for the 1939 race . . .

along, but this had to scratch after the engine blew up during practice. But German reinforcements came from BMW with three of the two-litre 328 models – one with coupé bodywork. Sommer brought a brand-new 2.6 litre Alfa Romeo coupé, forming an unusual Franco-Italian-Thai alliance as his co-driver was Prince Birabongse of Thailand, better known under his racing pseudonym of B. Bira.

The 12 British cars were mostly as before, small capacity models from Aston Martin, HRG, MG, Morgan, Riley and Singer, but with one very important addition – two Lagondas, of the Bentley-designed $4\frac{1}{2}$ litre V12 model. One was driven by Lord Selsdon and Lord Waleran, the other by Charles Brackenbury and Arthur Dobson. W. O. Bentley had joined Lagonda some years after Rolls-Royce took over the original Bentley company, and while it must have given him some satisfaction to see one of his cars back at Le Mans, he was worried that the cars were not sufficiently prepared

. . . and the streamlined saloon which finished a remarkable fifth.

Night-time pit stop for the Dobson/Brackenbury Lagonda V-12. Inset: The Lagonda at the Esses.

for the race – Lagonda chairman Alan Good had only allowed a few months in which to get the cars ready. In the circumstances, Bentley decided to run the cars at a set speed of 83 mph – slightly faster than the 1938 winner – and see what happened; this was intended mainly as a trial run for later Le Mans races.

Most of the initial excitement therefore centred round the dog-fight of the big French cars – Chinetti's Talbot, Gerard's Delage, Mazoud's Delahaye and Wimille in the Bugatti. Sommer's performance must have disappointed his many supporters – the new Alfa misbehaved, and ultimately had to retire. Among the smaller cars, the Adler was an early retirement – a piston broke – while the BMW led the two-litre class, and Gordini and Scaron once again put up an excellent performance among the 1,100 cc cars.

The pace soon began to tell and several of the big cars retired; the Tremoulet/Forestier Delahaye spilled oil on the track, causing two accidents to other competitors, but fortunately without injury to the drivers. For most of the night the Delage of Gerard/Monneret was in the lead, gaining the lion's share of the newly instituted 1,000 franc bonus which the A.C.O. awarded to the leading car each hour. On Sunday morning they were still in the lead, followed by the Bugatti – but the ranks of the French cars had thinned dramatically and the two Lagondas were third and fourth. Then the Delage ran into

Smallest car ever to finish at Le Mans – the 570 cc Simca Cinq which was twentieth and last home in 1939.

Below: The work of 'Le Sorcier': Gordini and Scaron with the Index-winning Simca-based Gordini.

Inset: Trave-stained winner, the Bugatti of Wimille and Veyron. Above: . . . and how it got stained. Bugatti on its way to victory.

trouble; the engine ran rough, a plug change effected no improvement and the drivers suspected that a valve spring had broken – they carried no spare and were therefore unable to do anything about it. In the course of the Delage's pit stop, it was overtaken by the Bugatti which became the ultimate winner. The Delage still finished second, and the Lagondas – which appeared completely unperturbed by 24 hours of racing and had not needed even a tyre change – followed in third and fourth places. Wimille just beat his own 1937 records, with a distance of 2,084.54 miles at an average of 86.86 mph, while the honour of setting a new lap record fell to Mazoud in the Delahaye at 96.70 mph.

The three BMWs all finished in great style, in fifth, seventh and ninth places – the coupé was first home at a remarkable average speed of 82.55 mph. The surviving Delahayes were placed sixth, eighth and eleventh; and Gordini's Simca came home in tenth place, winning both the Index and the Biennial Cup at the same time, while none of the Talbots made it to the finish. The unanimous opinion was that for the 1940 race the Lagondas and the BMWs would have to be watched.

Bugatti and Delage, first and second in 1939.

INTERLUDE

There was of course no Le Mans race in 1940. The possibility of an Anglo-German encounter had in the meantime taken on an entirely different dimension . . . And even if the initially triumphant powers of the Axis staged a demonstrative Mille Miglia on Italian soil in 1940, the possibility of an Anglo-French Le Mans was denied the Allied powers when German forces crossed the French border on 13 May. At around the time when the Le Mans race would have taken place, the French had other matters to occupy their attention: on 14 June the Germans entered Paris, and a week later the French had been forced to sign a humiliating surrender at Compiègne.

Before the fall of France, the RAF had made use of the small air strip adjacent to the circuit; the Luftwaffe soon took this over and enlarged it into a considerable base for their fighters. Even the Mulsanne straight was used as a runway. In consequence, the circuit did not escape the attention of the Allied bombers; when France was liberated the circuit and buildings were in a sad state – what had not been destroyed in the bombing had been deliberately burned down by the retreating Germans. It was a curious coincidence that with the first British troops to arrive at Le Mans came Sammy Davis – the 1927 winner.

In view of the devastation wrought at the circuit it naturally took considerable time before the Automobile Club de l'Ouest could contemplate holding the 24-hour race again; but in 1948 it was decided to hold the event in the following year and reconstruction work was put in hand, which finished a few weeks before the week-end scheduled for the race – 25 and 26 June 1949. The overall layout of the circuit and buildings was largely unchanged compared to the pre-war plan, but grandstand and pits were thoroughly improved in detail, and the opportunity was taken to re-surface the entire circuit.

There was one highly important innovation in the regulations for the first post-war Le Mans – as 'an exceptional measure . . . the entry of a prototype will be accepted'. More than 30 years on, the prototype entries dominate the Le Mans scene almost totally, and the race is now very far from being what Faroux and Durand originally intended in 1923: a race to demonstrate the reliability of ordinary catalogued touring cars. And, despite the lapse of ten years and the intervening war, 12 cars appeared at the 1949 race to contest the fifteenth Biennial Cup.

Casual spectators at Mulsanne in pre-Armco days. Delage leads Aston Martin in 1939 race.

1958: The Ferrari 250 TR of Rodriguez/Behra no. 25 battles with Sigrand's Stonguillini in the dryving rain.

4. 1949-1965 THE CLASSIC YEARS

LE MANS 1949

The 1949 entries were, as could be expected, a wonderful mixture of ancient and modern. French cars dominated the line-up – there were no less than 29 native cars, including three Talbots, seven Delahayes and four Delages among the big cars; while nine assorted Simcas and Simca-Gordinis contested the smaller classes, together with two DBs, two Monopoles and a single Renault 4 CV, privately entered without the approval of the factory. The odd man out was a 4.4 litre diesel-engined Delettrez, driven by its constructors, the brothers Delettrez.

The biggest British entry came from Aston Martin, with six cars including a venerable antique, a 1936 two-litre model, but more interestingly, also one of the new DB.2 models, with the 2.6 litre dohc six-cylinder Lagonda engine designed by W. O. Bentley. The Bentley make made a re-appearance – a single car driven by Hay and Wisdom, a 1939 4½ litre with streamlined coupé bodywork by Paulin, originally built for Embiricos. There were also single cars of the following makes: Healey – a 2.4 litre Riley engined saloon; Frazer-Nash – a two-litre Bristol engined 'High Speed' model of the type that was subsequently renamed 'Le Mans Replica'; Alvis – entered by two Belgian drivers; Riley – a French entered pre-war model; MG – George Philips' special bodied TC; and a Singer Nine – also French entered. Finally, there were three 1½ litre HRGs. The only other entries were of two makes which were both newcomers to Le Mans: from Italy, a pair of two-litre V12 Ferraris; and from Czechoslovakia, two 745 cc two-cylinder two-stroke Aero-Minors with front-wheel drive.

The big French cars initially set the pace but right from the start it was apparent that the new Italian make was a worthy challenger and both the Ferraris stayed with the leaders of the race; and when the leading Delahaye retired after having caught fire, the Ferraris moved into the lead, although one of them crashed soon after 9 pm. The other Ferrari – driven by Chinetti (who had shared the winning cars in 1932 and 1934) and Lord Selsdon (who had been placed fourth in one of the Lagondas in 1939) – disputed the lead with Talbots and Delages, but when, in the middle of the night, the leading Talbot retired with engine trouble, the Ferrari was able to move up and take the lead.

Among the smaller cars, the Simca-Gordini leading on Index fell victim to clutch trouble, while the little Renault had broken a valve and the MG was disqualified. But there were numerous other retirements due to mechanical failure, and only 19 cars finished the race. While the Chinetti/Selsdon Ferrari held its lead and became the ultimate winner, it was suffering from a slipping clutch which allowed the Delage of Louveau and Jover to gain on it. There was, however, not enough time for the French car to catch up; at 4 pm on Sunday afternoon it was still a lap behind. Third place went to a British car, the Frazer-Nash driven by H. J. Aldington and the motor-cycle racer Norbert Culpan, who was the owner and entrant. These were followed by a second Delage, a Delahaye and the big Bentley. Not only did Ferrari score a notable victory on the first appearance of the marque – although its average speed of 82.281 mph and total distance of 1,974.899 miles were less than those achieved by the two-litre BMW which came fifth in 1939 – but the same car also won the Biennial Cup, and the Index. It should be added that Chinetti drove more than 22 hours, thus completely reversing the result of his and Sommer's 1932 win when Chinetti had been taken ill and was unable to drive for more than three hours.

The fastest lap was put in by Simon in a Delahaye at 96.577 mph but this was no new record either, although it was within 0.4 seconds of Mazoud's 1939 record. One of the small Simca Cinqs with the 569 cc engine finished in eighteenth place, and both of the Czech Aero-Minors finished as well, in fifteenth and nineteenth places – the former winning the 750 cc class as well as setting a new record in its class. The other unusual entry, the Delettrez diesel, had retired when it ran out of fuel.

There had been one fatal accident, claiming the life of Pierre Marechal in an Aston Martin.

The victory of an Italian car must have been a disappointment for the French, not least for the President of the Republic, M. Auriol, who was present at the finish; but they could console themselves with the thought that 1949 was merely the first post-war race and as such could be considered to be transitional.

LE MANS 1950

The revival of interest in Le Mans which had begun in the late 1930s and had continued in 1949 was reinforced this year with 112 applications from which the maximum number of starters – 60 – was selected. Furthermore, these were of 26 different makes, from France, Britain, Italy, the USA and Czechoslovakia. The French contingent was again the biggest numerically, totalling 33 cars, but it was evident that with three Talbots, two Delahayes, and a single Delage, the big French cars were in retreat; on the other hand there were no less than 25 French contenders with engines between 600 and 1,500 cc, from DB (Deutsch et Bonnet), Ferry-Renault, Gordini, Monopole, Panhard, Renault and Simca. The unsuccessful Delettrez of 1949 was brought to Le Mans again, accompanied by another

Like father, like son. Louis Rosier senior is getting somewhere with the Talbot in the 1950 race.

French diesel engined car, the MAP which featured a centrally mounted supercharged engine.

Britain was also well represented; the streamlined Bentley coupé was joined by another pre-war survivor of the make, Hall's 1934 TT car. The three Aston Martins were all of the DB2 type, with the dohc six-cylinder engine; and this year marked the first appearance at Le Mans of another famous British engine of this configuration, Jaguar's XK – three XK120 models were entered. Other British newcomers were Allard – a single J2 model with Cadillac V8 engine, driven by Sidney Allard himself – and Jowett, with one of their recently launched Jupiter sports models, fitted with the unusual $1\frac{1}{2}$ litre flat four engine. There were two Frazer-Nashes, and two Healeys, one of which had a Nash engine; George Philips was there again with his MG, and another famous Le Mans name also made an appearance – sadly, its last – this was the $2\frac{1}{2}$ litre Riley roadster.

The little Aero-Minors were this year accompanied by a compatriot in the shape of a Skoda; while from Italy there were five Ferraris, of two- and 2.3 litres capacity. Obviously the Modenese were becoming keen after their perhaps unexpected victory the previous year; their drivers included both Chinetti and Selsdon, and also the French veteran Raymond Sommer who postponed his retirement for a farewell appearance at Le Mans. Another Italian entry was – unusually – a Fiat 1500. Finally, perhaps the two most remarkable cars on the Sarthe circuit in 1950: the two American Cadillacs, a very standard looking sedan model entered by the Collier brothers (who had done a lot of racing in MGs in the USA) and a very ugly special bodied car entered by Briggs Cunningham – it was soon named 'Le Monstre'. These were given start numbers 2 and 3; number 1 was the MAP with a theoretical engine capacity of almost 10 litres, because of its supercharger doubled from the actual five-litres, under the then current equalisation formula.

From the start, a battle between the favourites Talbot and Ferrari unfolded, but they were ably challenged by the two British newcomers, Allard and Jaguar. Sommer led the opening stages, followed by a Talbot driven by the two Rosiers – father and son – and the Allard. Sommer broke the lap record several times but eventually dropped out with a broken dynamo bracket. Rosier had already moved into the lead in the third hour and apart from a brief period in the early morning when the Meyrat/Mairesse Talbot took over, Rosier led the race throughout and to ultimate victory, with the Meyrat/Mairesse Talbot second.

It was not a good race for Ferrari; all the five entries retired, the Lucas/Selsdon car had an accident and Chinetti's back axle gave up. By contrast, the British cars had a splendid race: 14 out of 16 British entries finished, British cars took third, fourth, fifth and sixth places, four class wins and shared the Index win. The Allard was third after the two Talbots, the Nash-Healey fourth and this was followed by two Aston Martins. One of the Jaguar XK120s driven by Leslie Johnson and Bert Hadley had challenged the leaders strongly, rising as high as third place, but with less than three hours to go had to retire with clutch trouble. The two other Jaguars finished twelfth and fifteenth. The Allard won the five- to eight-litre class; the Aston Martin of Abecassis and Macklin the three-litre class, and also shared the Index honours with a Monopole-Panhard. A Frazer-Nash took the two-litre class, and the Jowett Jupiter the $1\frac{1}{2}$ litre class.

The winning Talbot set new records for average speed – 89.713 mph – and distance – 2,153.121 miles; Louis Rosier also set a new lap record of 102.83 mph, the first time this had risen above 100 mph.

Mesdames Simon, Haig and friends; with their Coupe des Dames-winning Ferrari coupé in 1951.

1950: The winner – Louis Rosier and Talbot no. 5. Co-driver Rosier junior scowls on the right.

Among the other finishers were both the Bentleys – the 16 year old TT car was eighth, which must surely constitute some kind of record – and the 1939 model was fourteenth. Also both the Cadillacs – the Collier sedan was tenth, just beating the Cunningham monster into eleventh place. Rosier's win for France was naturally popular; but it was to be another 22 years before a native car would score an overall win at Sarthe. On the other hand, the many British successes were an indication of events to come at Le Mans over the next few years.

LE MANS 1951

The sensation of 1951 was the new Jaguar XK120 C – the competition model specially evolved by the Coventry company to win Le Mans. With a tuned XK engine in a lightweight tubular chassis and streamlined bodywork, the three C-types were obviously among the favourites of the 60-strong field, despite not being by any means the biggest engined cars at Le Mans. They were beaten on capacity by 19 other entries, headed by two Allard J2s. Also among the big bangers were three Cunninghams, with Chrysler V8 engines of 5.4 litres – the first serious American bid for victory at Le Mans since the Stutzes and Chryslers of 20 years previously.

France was still in the running with a strong entry of six Talbots; however there was only a single Delahaye to keep them company, the last time Delahaye entered at Le Mans, while Delage had bowed out with their 1950 entry. The biggest entry of one make was nine Ferraris, headed by four of the new 4.1 litre America models. There was a single Nash-Healey and the remaining big cars were the Bentley streamliner and the Delettrez diesel, both making their third and final appearances at Le Mans. A standard XK120 kept the three C-type Jaguars company, while their British rivals, the Aston Martin DB.2s numbered five. The rest of the 19 British entries were made up of two Frazer-Nashes, three Jowett Jupiters – two standard models and one of the R.1 type prototypes – and George Philip's MG, now a TD with Syd Enever designed streamlined bodywork, the UMG 400 which was famous for what it inspired – the MGA – rather than for what it achieved: in the race it was soon eliminated with engine trouble.

France dominated the small capacity classes with variations on the Dyna Panhard flat twin theme – from DB, Callista, Monopole and Panhard themselves – together with no less than six Renault 4 CVs and five Simcas and Simca-Gordinis. There were 25 French cars in all. Czechoslovakia sent a single Aero-Minor (for the last time) but this year there was an American challenge not only among the big cars but also in the 750 cc class: a Crosley of 726 cc. Backing up the Ferrari entry was a single Lancia Aurelia GT – the car fresh from a second place in the Mille Miglia. This was Lancia's first Le Mans entry, perhaps a belated arrival of so famous a make but nevertheless typical of Lancia's almost traditional lack of interest in motor sport before the 1950s. Finally, making a very unobtrusive entry at Le Mans, a single 1,100 cc Porsche 356 coupé, privately entered by two French drivers; the first German car to compete at Le Mans in post-war years and the modest beginning of a very distinguished career.

A young Stirling Moss was driving at Le Mans for the first time, together with Jack Fairman in one of the C-types; and it seemed that the Jaguar strategy was to let the Moss/Fairman car play hare to the assorted hounds of Talbot, Ferrari and Cunningham. Moss soon went into the lead, but was in fact driving to a pre-arranged speed, with power in hand; demonstrating the new Jaguar's superiority. All the three C-types were among the leading cars in the initial stages of the race, setting an uncomfortable pace for the Talbots. Within the first hour, the French driver Lariviere was killed when his Ferrari went off the road.

As the evening wore on, the C-type of Leslie Johnson and Biondetti lost its oil pressure and went out; eventually Moss suffered the same fate, and the third Jaguar driven by the two Peters, Walker and Whitehead, took the lead. Three Talbots had retired, leaving only two with a chance of a placing, and both were well down the scoreboard at half time; but a Cunningham was lying second, and one of the big Ferraris third. However, Walters and Fitch in the surviving Cunningham gradually slipped down the field while Hall and Navone in the Ferrari also retired. At their expense, the Talbots of Meyrat/Mairesse and 'Levegh'/Marchand made a partial comeback, challenging the Aston Martin DB.2s which were themselves following the Jaguar.

As it was nothing could erode the lead of the Walker–Whitehead C-type; this was the winner at an average speed of 93.495 mph, a distance of 2,243.886 miles and with a handsome nine lap lead over number two, the Meyrat/Mairesse Talbot. The other Talbot was fourth, and the two Aston Martins third and fifth; this was not the end of Aston Martin's success as the other three entries of this make also finished, in seventh, tenth and thirteenth places. The Nash-Healey was sixth and the first Ferrari eighth – the only surviving America model driven by Chinetti/Lucas. Neither of the Allards finished, and the Walters/Fitch Cunningham had dropped back to eighteenth. The Lancia Aurelia had a trouble free run to twelfth, and won the two-litre class; only one Jowett finished but repeated the $1\frac{1}{2}$ litre class win though be it said at a lower speed than the Porsche which emerged victorious in the 1,100 cc class. The Biennial Cup and Index both went to the Monopole-Panhard of De Montremy and Hemard – for the second year running; and Stirling Moss set a new lap record of 105.232 mph. Not bad for a young driver on his first appearance at Le Mans, in a brand new and untried car. Among the 30 finishers were 12 British cars; but the Bentley failed to complete the minimum distance required for its class and was therefore not classified.

LE MANS 1952

Jaguar had come, seen and conquered at Le Mans the previous year, but they were completely out of luck in 1952; this was a year which was remarkable for three reasons: the appearance of the new gull wing Mercedes-Benz 300 SL coupés; the complete failure of the Jaguar team; and the epic solo drive of Pierre 'Levegh' which almost brought him victory.

Of the *vieux garde*, Talbot was now the only representative, with four cars entered; after repeated fiascos in previous years, Gordini had had his contract with Simca cancelled and now entered two cars in his own right, one a 2.3 litre dohc six; but the remaining French entries were all *petite cylindree*, from Panhard, Renault and Simca,

1951 winners – Walker and Whitehead in their C-type Jaguar.

The first German win came in 1952. The Mercedes-Benz 300 SL of Lang/Riess hurries through the Esses.

The Mercedes-Benz drivers at the start of the 1952 race.

together with a Peugeot based supercharged Constantin special. There were 20 French cars among the 57 starters; the next biggest group were 18 British cars, led by the three rebodied C-type Jaguars and five Aston Martin DB.2s. There were two each from Allard, Nash-Healey and Frazer-Nash; Jowett fielded three cars and, making their first comeback at Le Mans after the war, a single representative from Morgan – a Plus 4 model with the Standard Vanguard engine of the unsuitable capacity of 2,088 cc.

From Italy, the Ferraris were supplemented by two Lancias and a single 1.3 litre Osca – the make built by the Maserati brothers after they sold the company bearing their own name. Briggs Cunningham was naturally back, with three entries one of which was a coupé – incidentally, just over half the starting cars were coupés, including three Porsches and the three new Mercedes-Benz 300 SLs.

The Jaguars had given trouble already in practice; the new bodies had very restricted radiator air intakes and the cars suffered from overheating. Initially, however, all the three Jaguars were among the leaders, together with the other favourite team, the Ferraris; while the Cunningham coupé, the 2.3 litre Gordini and Levegh's Talbot were also among the first ten cars. The Mercedes-Benz team seemed initially content to play a waiting game, keeping quietly in the background and travelling at less punishing speeds. They did not have long to wait; the Jaguars' troubles soon manifested themselves, and within the first four hours all the three C-types had retired with problems brought on by overheating. The Gordini then went into the lead, followed by Levegh while the Mercedes began to move up the scoreboard. The Ferraris suffered mixed fortunes; at half time there were only two Ferraris still in the race of seven starters of this make. Then Chinetti was disqualified for re-fuelling too soon – and then there was one. At about the same time the Gordini had to retire when the brake linings had worn out, but its compatriot, Levegh's Talbot, moved into the number one spot.

He was followed by two Mercedes – the Lang/Riess car and that driven by Helfrich/Niedermayer; Kling and Klenk had retired earlier. Of the other front runners, both the Macklin/Collins Aston Martin and the Chaboud/Pozzi Talbot retired after accidents with less than three hours to go, permitting the Johnson/Wisdom Nash-Healey and the sole remaining Cunningham, driven by Briggs Cunningham himself together with Spear, to move gradually forward. This would have been the eventual order of finishing except for Levegh's retirement in the last hour of the race. He had insisted on driving single-handedly throughout, whether as a point of honour or because he was worried about the Talbot's engine and did not want his co-driver Marchand to suffer the ignominy of mechanical breakdown, is not quite clear; but Levegh drove without a working rev counter and it is possible that, in a state of complete exhaustion, he over-revved accidentally.

So France was cheated of victory; instead Germany won for the first time at Le Mans with the two Mercedes taking first and second place. Lang and Riess had covered 2,320.071 miles at an average speed of 96.696 mph. A new lap record of 107.595 mph had been set by Ascari in a Ferrari before his retirement in the third hour. The Index win went to Hemard and Dussous in the Monopole-Panhard, and they also took the Biennial Cup. Among the class winners was the Jowett Jupiter in the $1\frac{1}{2}$ litre class, for the third year running, while the 1,100 cc Porsche and the two-litre Lancia also repeated their 1951 class wins. The only survivor of the Ferrari team could manage no better than fifth, followed by the class winning Lancia, an Aston Martin DB.2 and another Lancia. The total number of finishing cars was 17, but only four were British, A rather disappointing result after the successes of 1950 and 1951.

LE MANS 1953

This year saw the launch of a revised manufacturer's championship for sports cars which – in a not dissimilar way to the new Group C rules of 1982 – stimulated interest in sports car racing, and therefore Le Mans, enormously. Suddenly, Le Mans became a Mecca for the works teams.

Jaguar, as usual considering Le Mans important enough in its own right without bothering overmuch about the championship, came to the Sarthe circuit intent on erasing the memories of the 1952 fiasco. To this end they brought three lightened C-types, with bodywork similar to the 1951 cars, while the engines were fitted with Weber carburettors and for the first time, Dunlop disc brakes were used. There was also a privately entered C-type of more conservative specification. They were primarily opposed by four Ferraris, of 4.1 and 4.5 litres, while Alfa Romeo made their first post-war appearance with three 3.5 litre 'Disco Volante' coupés, fresh from Mille Miglia; so were the Lancias – four of the new Jano designed D.20 coupés, the model which had won the Targa Florio. No mere souped-up Aurelia GT this – with a supercharged 2.7 litre V6 engine, inboard brakes front and rear and a tubular space frame.

Among the other contenders there were three Cunninghams, and Aston Martin had three of the new DB.3 S models. France was represented by the Talbots and the Gordinis; one of the latter was now a full 2½ litre car. The remaining cars over two litres all bore the name of Healey: two 4.1 litre Nash-Healeys, and two of the new 2.6 litre Austin-Healeys – or, if you like, this was Austin's first Le Mans entry since 1937. In the two-litre class two Frazer-Nashes were joined by two Bristol 450 coupés, with their exceptionally aerodynamic but not very attractive bodywork; also a Fiat 8-V coupé, a rare appearance for Italy's biggest car manufacturer, but not a successful one: the car retired almost immediately after the start.

Jowett, in their last year of manufacture, did not go to Le Mans, leaving the 1½ litre class to Porsche and a German newcomer, Borgward, with dohc engines; there was also a single Osca, a 1½ litre Gordini, and the Constantin-Peugeot. One Osca and one Porsche were the only entries in the 1,100 cc class, and five Renaults shared the 750 cc class with seven Panhards. The exciting Spanish Pegasos had been seen in practice, but following a bad crash they were withdrawn from the race itself.

Winner of Index and Biennial Cup in 1953, the Panhard of Chancel and Chancel.

With so many potential winners, there was no particular favourite, but most people were probably expecting at least an Italian victory – Ferrari, Alfa or, just possibly, Lancia. The main Anglo-American challengers would be Jaguar and Cunningham. As it turned out, the main battle of the race was the Jaguar–Ferrari duel; Stirling Moss took the lead for Jaguar first, pursued by Villoresi in the Ferrari 4.5 litre; then followed the Rolt/Hamilton Jaguar, another Ferrari and the three Alfa Romeos. The Cunningham C5R was eighth, and the two big Gordinis ninth and tenth after the first hour. The Aston Martins, Talbots and Lancias were trailing behind and never constituted a serious threat, while both the Bristols provided entertaining displays of pyrotechnics which put them out of the race.

Of the other British teams, both the Allards retired; one Nash-Healey was lost almost immediately with failing oil pressure, while the Johnson/Hadley car was driven carefully up through the diminishing field and eventually finished in eleventh place. Both of the Austin species of Healey completed the race, and did comparatively better by finishing twelfth and fourteenth, which equalled second and third in the three-litre class. They bracketed the winner of the two-litre class, a Frazer-Nash in thirteenth place. Finally, all four Aston Martins retired; the longest surviving car of this make, driven by Poore and Thompson, got no higher than fourteenth place before retirement.

Mike Hawthorne, driving for Ferrari, was disqualified when his brake fluid was replenished too soon; another Ferrari overturned at White House early on Sunday morning, and its driver, Tom Cole, was killed. The Ascari/Villoresi car was lying second for a long time before its clutch gave out, so only one Ferrari, of the Marzotto brothers, finished – in fifth place. All the Alfa Romeos and all the Lancias were eliminated with mechanical breakdowns while French honours were defended by the 2.5 litre Gordini, driven into fifth place by Trintignant and Schell, and the Talbot of Levegh and Pozzi which finished eighth. This year Levegh had to hand the wheel over to his co-driver; a new regulation for 1953 stipulated that any one driver could only drive for 80 laps consecutively, and 18 hours in total.

But it was Jaguar's – and Cunningham's – race in 1953. In a race where so many teams had only one car – if any – finish, all the Jaguars and all the Cunninghams came through to the end. The three works C-types were first, second and fourth, while the privately entered car came ninth; the American cars were third, seventh and tenth. Duncan Hamilton and Tony Rolt drove the winning Jaguar, Moss and Walker were second and Whitehead/Stewart fourth. Apart from anything else, this was a record-breaking Le Mans like never before; the winner's average was over 100 mph for the first time, at 105.841 mph – and the total distance was 2,540.2 miles, breaking the 2,500 mile (4,000 km) barrier. Furthermore, the following six cars also finished at speeds over 100 mph. There were new records in all classes except Class A (unlimited capacity over 8,000 cc) and a new

Small fry getting away at the tail end of the field in the 1953 race. Mainly Renault and Panhard but also Constantin's Peugeot Special (no. 66).

lap record, set by Ascari in the Ferrari, at 112.866 mph.

The class winners were Cunningham (to 8,000 cc), Jaguar (to 5,000 cc), Gordini (to 3,000 cc), Frazer-Nash (to 2,000 cc), Porsche (to 1,500 cc), Osca (to 1,100 cc) and DB-Panhard (to 750 cc). A Panhard also took the Index of Performance and the Biennial Cup. Of 60 starters, 26 finished.

A memorable year, not only for the Jaguar success, but for the quality and variety of the entries, for the eventful racing, for the punishing pace that demanded so many retirements and for the triumph of the disc brake.

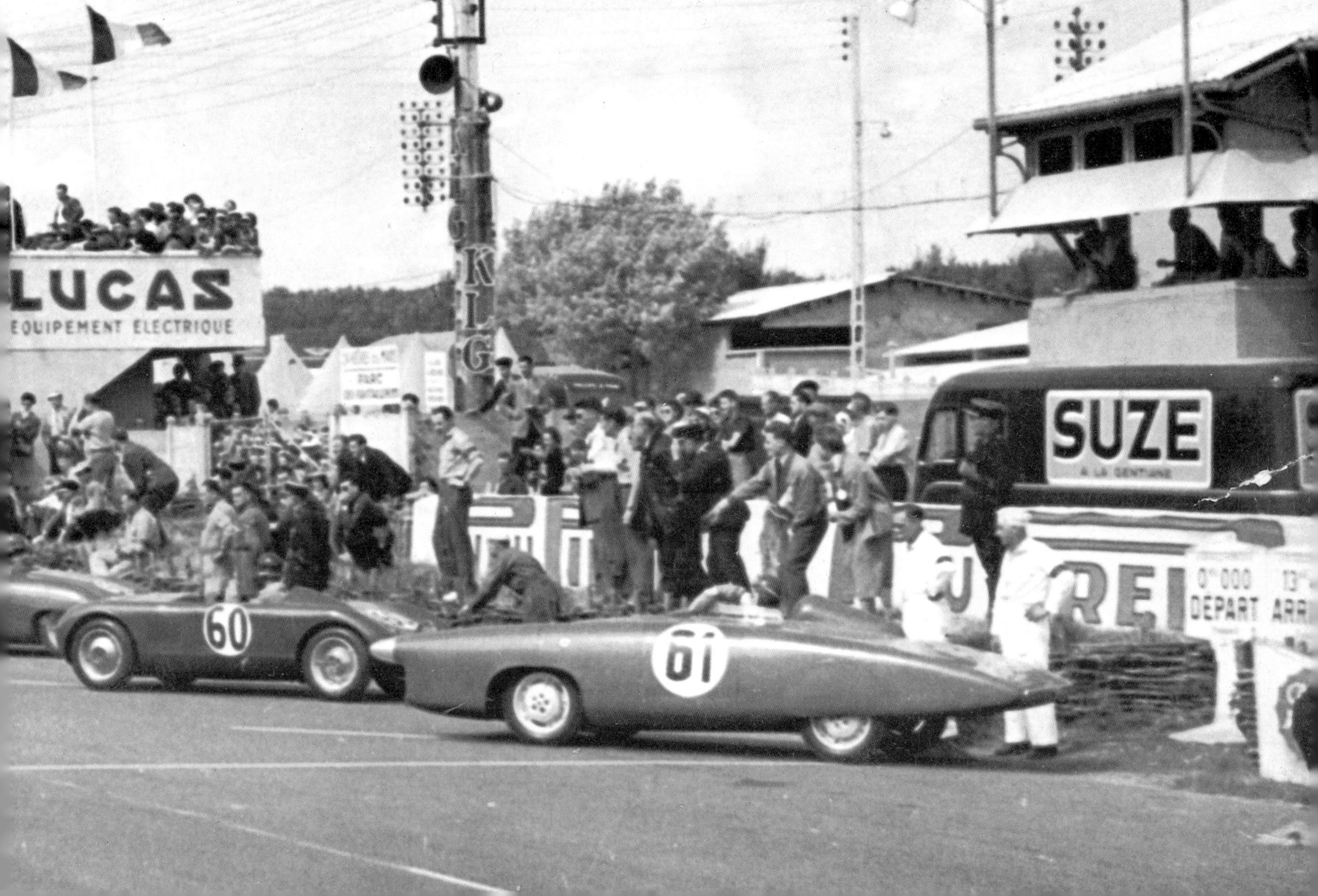

LE MANS 1954

This year's Le Mans was notable as much for those absent as for those present. Expected entries which failed to materialise included Lancia, Mercedes-Benz, Austin-Healey (this team was withdrawn after protesting about the continued policy of allowing prototypes to take part) and the works Maseratis which met with an accident on the way to Le Mans. However, Jaguar had their new D-types, of which three were entered together with a Belgian owned C-type; their main opponents were the three big Ferraris, 375 'Plus' models disposing of no less than 4.9 litres each. There were two other Ferraris in the race one of which was entered by the American Cunningham team, although they still had two of their own C-4 R models as well.

There was a notably strong Aston Martin entry, comprising five cars plus a sixth running under the hallowed name of Lagonda, and even with a 4.5 litre V12 engine under the bonnet; but that was as far as the similarities to the 1939 entries of that make reached, as the 1954 Lagonda was based on the Aston DB.3 S and its engine was, in effect, a doubled-up Aston Martin DB engine. Other works entered Astons included two closed and two open DB.3 S models, one of the open cars fitted with a supercharger, and finally there was a privately entered DB.2/4 coupé. Possible French opposition came from three privately entered Talbots, and among four Gordinis was not only a 2½ litre six but also a new three-litre straight-eight fitted with disc brakes.

Aston Martin follows sister make Lagonda through Tertre Rouge in 1954.

Despite valiant digging, the Baggio/Rubirosa Ferrari stayed in the Tertre Rouge sandpit for the rest of the 1954 race.

The three Bristol 450 coupés were of somewhat improved aesthetics compared to the previous year's entries and were backed up by three Frazer-Nashes also using the 1,970 cc Bristol engine. Among their opponents in the two-litre class was a single privately entered Maserati A6G, and a Triumph TR2. In the smaller classes Porsche had four cars, covering both the $1\frac{1}{2}$ litre and the 1,100 cc classes, and Osca also divided their efforts between the two, with one 1,100 cc and two $1\frac{1}{2}$ litre cars. The Peugeot based Constantin special was back; there was a new British contender for the 1,100 cc class in the shape of two Kiefts; and the 750 cc class attracted no less than 15 entries, of which most were small French cars based on either Renault or Panhard, such as the DB or the Monopole, but they were joined by an Italo-American cross-breed, a Crosley engined Nordi.

The race turned out to be completely dominated by the Jaguar–Ferrari duel; the other important factor was the weather which varied from drizzle to downpour for most of the time, with only short periods of dry weather which barely permitted the road surface to dry out completely. While the Jaguars probably had the edge over the Ferraris in terms of road holding in the wet, it was obvious that the extra power of the Ferraris gave them a definite advantage when the road was dry. From the start, the Gonzales/Trintignant Ferrari took the lead, followed by its team mate driven by Maglioli and Marzotto; they were pursued by the D-type Jaguars of Moss/Walker and Rolt/Hamilton, who both succeeded in getting in front of the third Ferrari of Rosier/Manzon.

An early retirement was the Lagonda which spun at the Esses and had to be withdrawn as its rear lights could not be repaired, while the Maglioli/Marzotto Ferrari was out of the race by mid-evening with gearbox trouble; but not before Marzotto had set a new lap record at a resounding 117.53 mph. Among other retirements in the first twelve hours of the race were two of the Aston Martins, two of the Talbots, the big Gordini and the Jaguar D-type of Moss/Walker. But the Gonzales/Trintignant Ferrari still retained the lead, followed by the Rolt/Hamilton Jaguar D-type, and the Rosier/Manzon Ferrari. At half time these were followed by a Cunningham driven by Spear/

French contender, the Gordini 2.5 litre of Guelfi/Pollet which finished sixth in 1954.

The 1954 winners, Trintignant and Gonzales – with Ferrari somewhere underneath.

Johnston and the supercharged Aston Martin of Parnell/Salvadori. But this was not Aston Martin's race; the Parnell/Salvadori car lasted until midday on Sunday when it blew a gasket and was withdrawn as the last Aston Martin in the race. It had, however, outlasted the Rosier/Manzon Ferrari which fell victim to gearbox troubles similar to those suffered by the Maglioli/Marzotto car.

By early afternoon on Sunday the order was as follows: Ferrari (Gonzales/Trintignant), Jaguar (Rolt/Hamilton), Cunningham (Spear/Johnston), the Belgian C-type Jaguar and the other Cunningham followed by the six-cylinder Gordini. This became the finishing order, but not without some last-minute drama as a prolonged pit stop of the leading Ferrari permitted the Jaguar to all but catch it up, especially as it was raining again – but within the last half hour of the race the rain stopped, and the Ferrari speeded up as the road dried out. Gonzales won at a margin of $2\frac{1}{2}$ miles; his total distance was 2,523.476 miles, at an average of 105.145 mph. The six leading cars were followed home by the team of three Bristols, and in tenth place was a DB-Panhard which won the Index as well as the Biennial Cup. A total of 18 cars finished, and Porsche was victorious in both the 1,100 cc and $1\frac{1}{2}$ litre classes. If Britain was robbed of victory, at least the impressively regular performance of the Bristols was a consolation, and the Triumph TR2 which finished in fifteenth place was perhaps that entry closest in spirit to the old Le Mans regulation which demanded that entries should be standard touring cars.

LE MANS 1955

The year of disaster. Pierre Levegh and 80 spectators were killed when Levegh's Mercedes hit the barrier opposite the pits and disintegrated. Its engine went flying over the barrier into a crowd of spectators, with dreadful results. This was the single worst accident in the history of motor racing, and was to have far-reaching effects on the Le Mans race and on the sport as a whole.

The entry list had promised a more than usually interesting race. Mercedes-Benz made their comeback with a team of three 300 SLR models with fuel injected straight eight engines and the novel air brake – the tonneau panel behind the seats could be raised on hydraulic rams activated by the driver. This innovation was hoped to offset the advantages held by Jaguar and other disc brake users. Mercedes had assembled an international team of drivers – Levegh was partnered by the American Fitch, another Frenchman Simon shared a car with the German Kling, while the third car was entrusted

Lots of Panhards at the start of the 1955 race, while no. 62 is the Porsche of Glockler/Juhan which came sixth.

The 1955 disaster: the wreck of Levegh's Mercedes burning.

The Bristol team finished intact in 1955; this is the Wisdom/Fairman car.

to an Anglo-Argentine alliance: Stirling Moss and Fangio. The closest rivals for victory were the Jaguars; of five D-types, three were works entries with the new long nosed bodywork, with drivers including Mike Hawthorn/Ivor Bueb, and the 1953 winners, Rolt/Hamilton. Ferrari's works team had three 121 LM models with 4.4 litre six-cylinder engines; in one of these a young American driver called Phil Hill had his first experience of Le Mans. Two further Ferraris were entered privately, one of these coming from the Briggs Cunningham stable.

Aston Martin had three DB.3 Ss and the Lagonda V-12; Maserati's works team made it this year with a pair of three-litre cars, while there was also a two-litre car of this make. In addition to the Ferrari entry, Cunningham had a single car under his own name, a C-6 roadster with a three-litre Offenhauser engine in place of the usual big V8. Talbot was absent this year, so the main French contender was a two-litre Gordini – the sole car of this make to compete

in 1955. There was renewed British interest in this year's race; among British newcomers was Cooper with two entries, one with a Jaguar engine, the other a Climax engined 1,100 cc car. MG made their return to racing with the first official works entry since 1935 – three EX.182 prototypes, based on the soon-to-be introduced MGA. There was a single Austin-Healey 100 S and three Triumph TR2s. Kieft came back for their second (and last) Le Mans entry, and were joined by Connaught (the only time a Connaught raced at Le Mans).

A more important newcomer was a Lotus IX Climax, driven by Ron Flockhart and no less than Colin Chapman himself – one of the few occasions when a constructor has driven his own car at Le Mans, although others who have done so include Sidney Allard, Briggs Cunningham, Amedee Gordini and Jean Rondeau. Bristol's three cars were open this year – open cars far outnumbered closed cars in 1955 – and finally, there were two Frazer-Nashes. The total number of British starters was 27.

The strong Porsche contingent comprised four 1½ litre cars and two 1,100 cc models; Osca fielded a single 1½ litre car; and the Constantin-Peugeot special made its positively last appearance. For the first time since 1933 a Salmson was entered; a 2.3 litre four-cylinder car with twin overhead camshafts in the classic manner of this make. In the 750 cc class French makes were dominant again, with four DB-Panhards, two Panhard Monopoles (two further Monopoles had 850 cc engines and therefore competed in the 1,100 cc class) and a single VP-Renault; but two Italian entries challenged the smallest class this year, a Stanguellini and the remarkable twin boom bodied Nardi which looked like a stray from some Monza record attempt. For the last time in Le Mans history the field held the full number of 60 cars; and some of the starters were in fact reserves who had been pulled in at the last minute after a series of accidents had occurred during the practice session.

The initial stages of the race fully confirmed the expectations from the entry list. First to lead was the Castelloti/Marzotto Ferrari, while Fangio in the Mercedes and Hawthorn in the Jaguar fought for the number two spot. The leaders were followed by the Maglioli/Hill Ferrari, the Cunningham entered Jaguar and the Mercedes of Kling/Simon. At the end of the first hour, Levegh in the third Mercedes was number seven, followed by the two other works Jaguars; a Maserati in tenth place was, at that early stage of the race, the highest placed car which was not either a Ferrari, a Jaguar or a Mercedes. The lap record was broken several times and finally went to Hawthorn at 122.386 mph.

The first pit stops were being made soon after 6 pm and it was then that disaster struck. Before pulling into his pit, Mike Hawthorn had just passed the Austin-Healey driven by Lance Macklin; Macklin swerved to the left to avoid Hawthorn crossing his bows, but in doing

The Glockler/Juhan Porsche 550 in the wet.

so he put his car in the path of Levegh's Mercedes which was approaching at high speed. Levegh hit the Austin-Healey's tail and was deflected across the track, hitting the safety barrier. He was killed instantly; but the engine and other parts of the wreckage were flung across the barrier, in amongst the crowd. In the first moments after the disaster confusion was total and it was only later as the death toll mounted that the full horrors became apparent; but the decision had already been taken to let the race continue, as it was feared that the rescue work would be seriously impeded if the 200,000 spectators were to leave the circuit while the ambulances were still ferrying casualties to the hospitals.

Nevertheless, the disaster had a decisive effect on the outcome of the race; after prolonged consultation between Mercedes-Benz team manager, Neubauer, and the hastily assembled board of Daimler-Benz back in Stuttgart, it was decided at 2 am to withdraw the two

The winning Jaguar of Hawthorn and Bueb.

Another British team which finished intact in 1955: the Triumph TR2s.

remaining Mercedes cars as a mark of respect to the victims of the disaster. At the time, the Fangio/Moss car was leading the race. In the meantime, two of the works Ferraris as well as the two privately entered cars had had to retire, and the last works Ferrari – the Trintignant/Schell car – went out with engine trouble soon after the Mercedes withdrawal. This gave Jaguar a 1–2 lead with Hawthorn/Bueb in front of Rolt/Hamilton. One of the works Maseratis moved into third place, the Collins/Frere Aston Martin was fourth and was followed by another D-type Jaguar.

The remainder of the race was fairly predictable. Rolt and Hamilton had to retire when their gearbox seized, and the transmission also proved the Achilles heel of the Maserati. Hawthorn and Bueb won the race, at an average speed of 107.067 mph for a total distance of 2,569.601 miles – a new record so, despite the lack of competition, this was no hollow victory. The Aston Martin was second, and the Belgian Jaguar D-type third. The next three places all went to 1½ litre Porsches which had edged ahead of many larger cars in an unobtrusive but most convincing manner; they were followed by the three Bristols and a Frazer-Nash. The Porsche of Polensky and von Frankenberg in fourth place also won on Index and took the Biennial Cup; the first time since 1949 that these awards had not gone to a Panhard or Panhard-based car.

The three Triumph TR2s all finished in good order, but were beaten by one of the MGs; another MG finished but the third car had crashed, landing Dick Jacobs in hospital for a prolonged period. The Lotus had been disqualified – Colin Chapman landed in a sandbank and, while he got free, he restarted without waiting for permission from a marshal to do so. Altogether 21 cars finished the race and among other non-finishers were the two other Aston Martins as well as the Lagonda, the Cunningham and the Gordini, and all the Ferraris and Maseratis. The only Italian car to finish was the Osca, and of the French entries only two of the DB-Panhards. The Nardi had been literally swept off the track when caught in the slipstream of a faster car – so much for aerodynamics.

The aftermath of the 1955 Le Mans was a temporary ban on all motor racing in France, and a prolonged enquiry into the cause of the disaster; Hawthorn, who initially had been stamped by the Continental press as the culprit, was completely exonerated and it was established that no single factor, and no individual driver, could be blamed. But the A.C.O. decided that drastic changes were required to the race as well as the circuit at Le Mans.

LE MANS 1956

New regulations, and new facilities marked the first post-disaster Le Mans. The pits were completely reconstructed, and a sunken road was laid opposite the pits, separating the circuit proper from the safety barrier of the grandstand enclosure. The construction work took time and in consequence the race was delayed to the last weekend of July – 28 and 29 July. The number of entries was reduced to 52 – in fact 49 cars started – and a new set of regulations was brought in which was so stringent that the Le Mans race could not qualify for the sports car championship. The new rules were intended to demonstrate the A.C.O.'s concern for safety by making every effort to 'tame' the performance previously achieved by the large capacity prototype cars. Prototype cars were restricted to a maximum capacity of 2½ litres, and all cars were allowed to carry only 130 litres of fuel while the minimum distance before re-fuelling was increased to 34 laps, putting a limit on the fuel consumption of 26 litres per 100 km (less than 11 mpg). Full width windscreens of a minimum depth of 200 mm were required, as was proper seating wide enough for two people.

Mercedes-Benz had made another strategic withdrawal from racing although the make was represented by a privately entered 300 SL coupé. Another absentee was the Briggs Cunningham team, which fielded neither any of their own cars nor any of any other make. Of the stalwarts, Jaguar and Ferrari dominated with six entries each; Jaguar's works team had three D-types, while two further D-types were entered by the Scottish Ecurie Ecosse and the Belgian Ecurie Francorchamps respectively. It is interesting to note that the D-types qualified as production rather than prototype cars as more than 50 had been made. There was also a Jaguar XK 140 coupé. By contrast, the Ferrari works team had three type 625s with 2½ litre four-cylinder engines following their current Grand Prix design; the remaining Ferraris were all two-litre cars.

Aston Martin had one prototype – the DBR 1/250 – and two production DB.3 S models; two 2½ litre Gordinis were both in the prototype class, and there was also a 1½ litre car of this make. Talbot made a return with two Maserati engined prototypes; Maserati proper also had two entries but both were 1½ litre cars. Salmson again fielded a 2.3 litre car (their last Le Mans entry) whereas Bristol had retired gracefully, but there was still one Frazer-Nash – the only two-litre car apart from the three Ferraris. Lotus had three entries, of which one was a 1½ litre car, the other two were in the 1,100 cc class which also comprised a Cooper and an Osca engined RB – a French make which seems to have been specially created for this occasion. With the ill chosen cylinder capacity of 845 cc, a Renault based VP was also in the 1,100 cc class. In the 750 cc class there were three Panhards, four DB-Panhards and, from Italy, two Stanguellinis, an Osca and two Morettis – apart from the RB, the only new make in 1956. Finally, perhaps rather more important than all the other small cars, six Porsches which were all in the 1½ litre class.

The race began badly when on the second lap Paul Frere spun his works D-type Jaguar on the wet road at the Esses; he hit the barrier and Fairman, in another works D-type, spun trying to avoid Frere's car and was hit in turn by the Marquis de Portago in a works Ferrari. All three cars were so damaged that they had to be withdrawn. Almost immediately after this debacle, Hawthorn brought the surviving works Jaguar into the pits with a bad mis-fire which turned out to be caused by a cracked fuel pipe; Hawthorne did eventually re-enter the race but had dropped right to the bottom of the scoreboard.

This sequence of events seemed to have eliminated the Jaguars completely, except for the Ecurie Ecosse D-type driven by Sanderson and Flockhart; this car, and the Aston Martin DB.3 S of Moss and Collins, took turns to lead for the rest of the race. Of the other works Ferraris, the Simon/Phil Hill car was eliminated with transmission trouble while lying fourth, but then the Gendebien/Trintignant car went into third place after five hours and stayed there until the finish. No less than 13 cars met with accidents, most serious was that of Louis Hery who overturned his Panhard at White House and died on the way to hospital; but there were also two cars disqualified under the new refuelling regulations, including the Jaguar XK 140.

The Sanderson/Flockhart Jaguar was the winner, at an average of 104.465 mph and a distance of 2,507.183 miles; their lead over the Moss/Collins Aston was just 10 miles and the duel between these two cars provided most of the interest in an otherwise uninspiring race. The Ferrari was third, and was followed by the Belgian D-type Jaguar; fifth was a Porsche ahead of the Hawthorn/Bueb works Jaguar which had been driven brilliantly up through the field, Hawthorn putting in the fastest lap of the race at 115.812 mph – but well below his 1955 record. A Lotus was seventh – winning the 1,100 cc class. A DB-Panhard in tenth place was winner of the 750 cc class and also won on Index as well as the Biennial Cup. Porsche won the 1½ litre class but no two-litre car finished. Indeed, only 14 cars altogether did finish this race.

D-type Jaguar of Sanderson and Flockhart, winners in 1966.

LE MANS 1957

The regulations were somewhat relaxed for the 1957 race – prototypes of unlimited capacity were again admitted, and there was no limit on fuel tank capacity, while the distance between fuel stops was reduced to 30 laps. A complete break with tradition was that spares and tools need no longer be carried in the car but could be left at the pit. Certain aspects of the rules were, however, tightened up; open cars had to have two doors and a hood, and the passenger seat had to be identical with the driver's. The Le Mans race was once again part of the championship, and the C.S.I.'s new sports car regulations (appendix C) took some heed of the A.C.O.'s Le Mans rules. The number of entries was fixed at 55, and 54 cars came to the start.

The Italian manufacturers made serious efforts to swamp Le Mans – there were no less than ten Ferraris, ranging from the new four-litre type 412 V-12s in the hands of Peter Collins/Phil Hill and Hawthorn/Musso, to a row of privately entered two-litre Testa Rossa cars. Then there were five Maseratis, including new 450 V 8 models – a Costin designed aerodynamic coupé driven by Stirling Moss/Schell, and a Spyder by Behra/Simon – a three-litre six and two two-litre cars. While there were also five Jaguar D-types – including for the first time new 3.8 litre engined versions – none of these was entered by the factory which had retired from racing at the end of 1956; instead two of the Jaguars were entered by Ecurie Ecosse, the others were privately entered.

Other British entries came principally from Aston Martin with four cars – two DBR 1s with three-litre engines, a 3.7 litre DBR 2 and a three-litre DB.3 S. There were single representatives of Frazer-Nash and AC – both using the two-litre Bristol engine; this was AC's first entry at Le Mans, apart from a non-starting car in 1925. Another British newcomer was an 1,100 cc Climax engined Arnott; this Coventry built engine was gaining in popularity on the racing scene and was also found under the bonnets of the 1,100 cc Cooper and the four Lotus entries, three 1,100 cc cars and a single 750 cc model.

Competitive big French cars were virtually a thing of the past; Gordini had two entries, one three-litre and one two-litre model, while the sole Talbot – with a $2\frac{1}{2}$ litre engine – broke down on the starting line. Six Porsches – part works cars, part private entries – had the $1\frac{1}{2}$ litre class to themselves in the absence of a $1\frac{1}{2}$ litre Lotus. In the 1,100 cc class competition for the assorted British entries came from a Stanguellini and a most unusual entry of the German DKW make: a 1,000 cc two-stroke three-cylinder front-wheel drive coupé with plastic bodywork. The smallest class, up to 750 cc, contained the usual DBs and Panhards – seven of them altogether – a VP-Renault, an Osca and two Stanguellinis in addition to the Lotus.

A very fast and very competitive race unfolded. The big works Ferraris and Maseratis set up a fantastic pace at the sort of speed normally associated with Grand Prix racing; Peter Collins in one of the Ferrari 412s touched the lap record on his first lap from a standing start. He was out of the race within the hour with a seized piston. Then Hawthorn in the sister car took over the lead, followed by the two big Maseratis and the Ferrari 312 driven by Gendebien/Trintignant. In the early stages of the race the highest placed Jaguar was that of Flockhart and Bueb which was lying fifth. Inevitably, the pace took its toll; the open Maserati 450 broke its back axle when in the lead in the third hour, the coupé lasted a few hours more (giving Stirling Moss a most uncomfortable ride) before succumbing to the same trouble. It was all too soon followed by the Ferrari of Hawthorn and Musso but not before Hawthorn had set up a new lap record of 126.147 mph – the first lap in less than four minutes. Next to go was the three-litre Maserati, and to complete the Italian debacle, the Ferrari 312 of Gendebien/Trintignant retired soon after midnight.

The British contenders had also suffered setbacks, however; two of the Aston Martins had gone out before midnight with transmission trouble, and the surviving works DBR 1 of Brook and Cunningham-Reid crashed at Tertre Rouge (a Porsche fetched up against the wreckage). Only the DB.3 S was left to represent Aston Martin; this was an elderly car entered by a French team. Taking stock at half time, there were Jaguar D-types in the first four places, followed by a Ferrari 290 and a Porsche. The Porsche, which at times was placed as high as fifth, ran out of fuel in the last hour of the race but there was no other change among the leading cars; Flockhart

1958: Ferraris pursuing the Salvadori/Evans Aston Martin through the Esses.

and Bueb in an Ecurie Ecosse D-type led a magnificent procession of Jaguars home in first, second, third, fourth and sixth places. The winning average was a new record of 113.845 mph and the distance 2,732.230 miles. Ferraris filled fifth and seventh places and the only surviving Porsche was eighth, followed by an 1,100 cc Lotus. The close-to-standard AC did well to finish tenth, ahead of the Aston Martin DB.3 S.

Jaguar was not the only British make to triumph; all four Lotuses also finished, the 750 cc in fourteenth place winning its class and – much to the chagrin of the French competitors – the Index of Performance. A special award was given to Lotus driver Masson who finished in sixteenth place after having had to push his car four miles back to the pits when he ran out of fuel. In total, there were 12 British cars among the 20 finishers.

This was the 25th Grand Prix d'Endurance to be held since the inception of the race in 1923, and was the subject of special festivities; including a run of *les ancetres* – actual veteran cars rather than historic Le Mans competitors – and, on a more contemporary note, a demonstration lap of Renault's experimental turbine car *L'Etoile Filante*.

LE MANS 1958

The C.S.I. decreed a limit of three-litres capacity for the sports car championship in 1958 and the Le Mans race followed suit. There were 55 starters; Ferrari again numerically dominant with 11 cars, of which ten were three-litre 250 TRs – works cars and privately entered – the odd man out being a two-litre car entered privately by the Rodriguez brothers from Mexico. As Ricardo Rodriguez was refused entry – being of tender years – his but slightly older brother

Pedro was partnered by Jose Behra in the race. By contrast Maserati seemed to have lost interest as there were only two privately entered cars of this make – one three-litre and one two-litre model. Again there were five Jaguar D-types entered by various teams, including two from Ecurie Ecosse, while Duncan Hamilton and Ivor Bueb shared a third. They all used the new short stroke versions of the XK engine, with carburettors rather than fuel injection. Similar engines were found in a pair of Lister-Jaguars, the first Le Mans appearance of this make. The final important contender in the three-litre class was Aston Martin with three works entered DBR 1s and a single DB.3 S driven by the Whitehead brothers, Peter and Graham.

Lotus this year entered six cars, led by their first ever entry in the two-litre class, a Climax engined model XV which had proved very fast in practice. Otherwise, they had one $1\frac{1}{2}$ litre car and two each in the 1,100 cc and 750 cc classes. Having found Le Mans to their liking, AC came back with two two-litre cars, and also in this class was a very sturdy touring Peerless GT; the only Le Mans race for this Triumph TR based fibreglass bodied 2+2 which later changed its identity to become the Warwick. Porsche fielded five entries including two cars with 1.6 litre engines which therefore had to compete in the two-litre class; the remaining three were $1\frac{1}{2}$ litres. Alfa Romeo made their second post-war comeback, more modestly than in 1953, with a pair of Zagato bodied Giulietta coupés which ran in the $1\frac{1}{2}$ litre class. Apart from the two Lotuses, the only other 1,100 cc car was a Climax-engined Tojeiro (another British newcomer to Le Mans); and again apart from the two Lotus entries, the 750 cc class was given over to the usual bunch of French and Italian cars, including four DBs and four Monopoles (all Panhard based), three Stanguellinis, two Oscas and a VP-Renault.

As in 1954, the 1958 race was largely decided by the weather; a number of thunderstorms causing numerous accidents and retirements. However, there were also other factors contributing such as the too weak fuel mixture which burned pistons on both the Ecurie Ecosse Jaguars soon after the start. The two-litre Lotus was another early retirement. Stirling Moss (whose co-driver was Jack Brabham) had taken the lead from the start in one of the works Aston Martins, but in less than three hours a con rod broke, ending another unlucky

Who said production touring car? The Peerless GT.

The Ferrari 250 TR of Hugus/Ericksson finished seventh in 1958.

Le Mans race for Moss. Soon after one of the Lister-Jaguars and another works Aston Martin dropped out of the race. These setbacks inevitably reduced the chance of a British win; meanwhile the works Ferrari of Oliver Gendebien and Phil Hill took the lead, pursued by other Ferraris while the Brooks/Trintignant Aston Martin and the Hamilton/Bueb Jaguar were still in the running. Mike Hawthorn, who shared a works Ferrari with Peter Collins, put in the fastest lap at 121.416 mph before retiring with a worn out clutch; but he failed to break his own 1957 record. This was Hawthorn's last Le Mans; within a few months he had been killed in a road accident. Ironically, Peter Collins was also killed soon after the 1958 Le Mans race.

At half time the Gendebien/Hill Ferrari was still in the lead, followed by the Brooks/Trintignant Aston Martin; but now one of the 1.6 litre Porsches had moved into fourth place, while the Aston Martin DB.3 S was fifth. There were only two other Ferraris left in the race, and no other Aston Martins or Jaguars; a French entered

The Index-winning Osca of de Tomaso/Davis takes the flag.

1956: The crushed two-litre Ferrari of Tavano and Meyrat.

Jaguar had overturned on the Tertre Rouge section, and its driver 'Mary' (whose real name was Brousselet) was killed. Early Sunday morning saw the retirement of the Books/Trintignant Aston Martin, and when Duncan Hamilton went off the road at Arnage at noon the Ferrari was left with a comfortable lead over the following cars. Phil Hill and Oliver Gendebien drove to victory at an average of 106.2 mph for a total distance of 2,548.813 miles – rather less than the 1957 record figures. They were followed home by the Whitehead brothers in the privately entered Aston Martin DB.3 S, and Porsche filled third, fourth and fifth places. The two other surviving Ferraris were sixth and seventh, and an AC eighth, another Porsche ninth, and tenth place went to a 750 cc Osca which also won on Index. It was co-driven by Colin Davis – son of Sammy Davis, the 1927 winner – and the Argentinean Allessandro de Tomaso, car manufacturer to be. A total of 20 cars finished, but three failed to qualify on the minimum distance for their respective classes; these included the other AC, and the Peerless. The double triumph for Italian entries completely reversed the 1957 results.

The DB-Panhard team of 1958 – untypically cheated of Index victory.

The Aston Martin of P. and G. Whitehead which came second in the 1958 race crosses the finishing line.

LE MANS 1959

While the three-litre limitation on prototypes was still in force, a new idea was to divide the entries into two categories – Sports Prototypes and Grand Tourisme cars – picking a winner from each; the Biennial Cup was revived after having missed out two years, while another innovation was the introduction of an Index of Thermal Efficiency in addition to the Index of Performance. The new Index took not only speed but also fuel consumption and the car's weight into account. Of the 53 starting cars, 31 were classified as sports prototypes and 22 as GT cars. Ferrari again fielded the largest number of entries; in the prototype class, six 250 Testa Rossa models with three-litre V 12 engines, and a single 'Dino' V 6 model in the two-litre class; complemented by four 250 GT coupés in the GT class. A single Jaguar D-type, two Lister-Jaguars and a Tojeiro-Jaguar were all in the prototype class; Aston Martin had four DBR 1 prototypes, and a Swiss entered DB.4 coupé in the GT class. As Maserati was absent for the 1959 race, these completed the entries over two litres.

Cooper had a two-litre 'Monaco' in the prototype class; Lotus

The Index winner of 1959, DB-Panhard of Cornet and Cotton.

also had a two-litre prototype as well as two prototypes in the 750 cc class, and three Elite coupés (with 1,216 cc engines) in the GT class. Remaining British entries were all in the GT class, and included an AC Ace and a Frazer-Nash (both still with the venerable Bristol two-litre engine), three Triumph TRS Models with the dohc Sabrina engines, and an MGA Twin-Cam which was sponsored by the MG Car Club. Of the six Porsche prototypes, four were in the $1\frac{1}{2}$ litre class and two in the two-litre class; seven DB-Panhards were split between the prototype and GT classes, one car in each class had an 850 cc engine, the remainder were all 750 ccs. Two Oscas and three Stanguellinis were all in the 750 cc prototype class. All the way from Trollhattan in Sweden came two very innocent looking SAAB 93 saloons; they started in the 750 cc GT class, and had three-cylinder two-stroke engines driving the front wheels.

For the first time, a practice day was held in April and the results of this seemed to favour the Ferrari V 12 prototypes yet again; the Testa Rossa models were now fitted with disc brakes, six years after these brakes had first appeared at Le Mans. However, in the race itself, it was the Aston Martin DBR 1 of Stirling Moss and Jack Fairman which first took the lead, probably deliberately baiting the Ferraris, on the instructions of Aston Martin team manager Reg Parnell – himself a seasoned Le Mans driver. Sure enough, the Ferraris of Gendebien/Hill and Behra/Gurney followed Moss in second and third places in the initial stages of the race; a third Ferrari was fourth and the D-type Jaguar was fifth. None of these cars were to finish the race.

First to retire of the leading cars was the Ferrari of Allison and da Silva Ramos; but then the Moss/Fairman Aston went out with engine trouble. The D-type Jaguar broke a con rod while lying second, and the Behra/Gurney Ferrari which had taken the lead from Moss dropped to fourth place before being put out with transmission failure. The Aston Martin of Roy Salvadori and Carroll Shelby had taken the lead by now but was constantly challenged by the Gendebien/Hill Ferrari. The two cars changed places several times, and were followed by the Aston Martin DBR 1 of Trintignant/Frere which occupied third place for most of the race. With the depletion of the Ferrari ranks – at half time only one of the prototypes, the Gendebien/Hill car, was still in the race – the next four

1959: The Aston Martin of Trintignant/Frere, which came second, here appears to get some assistance from Oliver Hardy.

cars were amazingly enough all 1.6 and 1.5 litre Porsches, and they were followed by the four Ferrari 250 GTs, in eighth to eleventh places.

However, none of the small Porsches lasted for very long; the Hugus/Ericksson car had crept into fourth place by midday on Sunday when its engine finally gave up, about the same time a sister car retired with clutch failure – and all the Porsches were out of the race. The next drama came when the Gendebien/Hill Ferrari overheated, stopped at the pit, re-started and completed two very slow laps before being withdrawn. It was then that a Le Mans victory came within Aston Martin's grasp, after 30 years of dogged persistence – the result was a 1–2 victory, the Salvadori/Shelby car (average 112.569 mph, distance 2,701.654 miles) leading Trintignant/Frere; both had a comfortable margin over the four Ferrari GTs which had gradually moved up as the Porsches dropped out, and which defended Maranello's honour by finishing third, fourth, fifth and sixth; the leading car also winning the GT class.

The Biennial Cup was won by the DB-Panhard of Cornet/Cotton; they also won the Index of Performance, while the new Index of

Shelby (at the wheel) and Salvadori with the winning Aston Martin in 1959.

Thermal Efficiency went to another DB-Panhard, the Consten/Armagnac car; it is perhaps of interest to note that at an average speed of 86.4 mph this car returned better than 25 mpg. By contrast the winning Aston Martin's fuel consumption was a shade worse than 10 mpg. The fastest lap was recorded by Jean Behra in one of the Ferrari prototypes at 124.995 mph but Hawthorn's absolute record from 1957 was still untouched. Only 13 cars of 53 starters finished this race, and one of the SAABs was twelfth.

Perhaps the closest parallel to the 1959 result was that of the 1935 race: in both cases the winner was a British car favoured by luck, though admittedly there was less of the fluke about Aston Martin's 1959 victory than there had been about the 1935 Lagonda win. For Aston Martin, it was a reward for persistent dedication since their first Le Mans race in 1928, and participation in every race since 1931. But it was also the last time before 1975 that a purely British car won the Le Mans 24-hour race – although Britain is not placed badly on the overall scoreboard of 50 Le Mans races, with a total of 13 victories – the same as Italy, and more than either France, Germany or the USA has achieved.

Getting there, 1959: Shelby passes the time-keepers' box.

The 1960 start. Six Ferraris head the line-up and would, almost, head the result list as well.

LE MANS 1960

Porsche RS of Barth and Seidel.

New C.S.I. regulations were introduced from 1 January 1960 which also applied to the Le Mans race. These were the Appendix C covering sports cars up to three litres, and Appendix J for Group 3 Grand Touring Cars of unlimited capacity. Some of the new regulations were aimed at making the sports cars more 'realistic' – such as the 10 inch depth of screen and the requirement for luggage space – and with the new regulations came a new set of sub-divisions. No longer did the time honoured Classes A to J apply, instead there were 15 new capacity classes, of which class 15 was unlimited above 5,000 cc; going down the scale, 14 was up to 5,000 cc, 13 to 4,000 cc, 12 to 3,000 cc, 11 to 2,500 cc, 10 to 2,000 cc, 9 to 1,600 cc, 8 to 1,300 cc, 7 to 1,150 cc, 6 to 1,000 cc, 5 from 701 to 850 cc. Smaller cars were not seen at Le Mans after 1960, indeed already in 1960 the smallest permitted GT entries were class 7 cars.

Of 55 starting cars, 37 were sports cars and 18 GT cars. Ferrari, as usual, fielded the largest entry – five Testa Rossa sports cars, together with six 250 GT models, all with three-litre engines. The only other makes to cover both classes were Austin-Healey, with a 996 cc Sprite in the sports car class and a 3,000 GT car; and Alfa Romeo with a Conrero modified 1,147 cc Giulietta sports car and a 1,290 cc SZ GT car. The GT class also attracted two Bristol engined ACs and four Lotus Elites. Rather more unusual was the entry of four Chevrolet Corvettes by Briggs Cunningham and the Camoradi racing team. With massive 4.6 litre V 8 engines they were in the GT class.

The sports car – for which one might substitute 'sports prototype' class was better supported. There were two Aston Martin DBR 1/300s, an Ecurie Ecosse entered Jaguar D-type, but more interestingly a Cunningham entered E-type prototype which put in the fastest practice lap. Maserati made a return to Le Mans, with three Tipo 61 models – the notorious 'Birdcage' – which were all entered by the Camoradi team. This completed the three-litre class; there were no $2\frac{1}{2}$ litre cars, and the two-litre class contained two Porsches, three Triumph TRSs, a single Lola and the MGA Twin-Cam which had been entered in 1959 and which now had an engine of 1,762 cc. The 1,600 cc class was a Porsche preserve with four entries. Next, in descending order came three DB-Panhards with 851 cc engines which just put them in the 1,000 cc class; and in the smallest class there were another two DBs, three Fiat based Abarths, two Oscas

Chevrolet Corvette of Thompson and Windridge.

and a Stanguellini. Abarth, Lola and Chevrolet were all newcomers to Le Mans.

The first car to take the lead was a Maserati Birdcage, driven by Masten Gregory; he was followed by five Ferraris, with the Jaguar D-type in seventh place. While two of the pursuing Ferraris ran out of fuel on the circuit (there was no minimum distance to be covered between fuel stops with the new regulations and presumably the Ferrari team had just miscalculated the cars' consumption), the Maserati gradually fell back permitting the Ferrari Testa Rossa of Paul Frere and Olivier Gendebien to take the lead. There it stayed for the rest of the race, almost equalling the performance of Gonzales and Trintignant in the Ferrari when they led the 1954 race from start to finish. The 1960 race was marked by the lack of effective competition for the Ferraris; the new Jaguar E2A driven by Dan Gurney and Walter Hansgen did not live up to its practice record and was well down the field until it eventually retired, and the D-type broke its crankshaft. Only the Aston Martin driven by Roy Salvadori and Jim Clark kept pace with the Ferraris and in the end finished third after the winning car of Frere/Gendebien and the number two Ferrari driven by Pilette/Rodriguez. Fourth, fifth, sixth and seventh places were all occupied by Ferrari 250 GTs which were followed home by a Chevrolet Corvette and the Baillie/Fairman Aston Martin.

Frere and Gendebien had covered 2,620.644 miles at an average speed of 109.193 mph; fastest lap, however, had been made by Masten Gregory in the Maserati Birdcage at 123.407 mph – before he retired, as did all the Maseratis. The Ferrari in fourth place also won the GT class. Porsche won the 1,600 cc class, the MGA Twin-Cam driven by Lund and Escott the 2,000 cc class and there were other British class victories: Lotus Elite in the 1,300 cc class and Austin-Healey Sprite in the 1,000 cc class. A DB-Panhard won the Index of Performance and also won the 850 cc class as well as the Biennial Cup, while another Lotus Elite won the Index of Thermal Efficiency. A total of 25 cars finished this Le Mans but five failed to cover the minimum distance and were therefore not classified – this included the entire team of three Triumphs.

The Camoradi-entered Birdcage Maserati of Gregory and Daigh in 1960.

LE MANS 1961

Arguably, the modern Le Mans racing car was born in 1961. There was nothing new about rear or mid-engined cars – indeed, up to 1961 and for many years afterwards, Porsche had never built or raced anything else – but the presence at Le Mans in 1961 of a new breed

Ferrari 250 GT of Stirling Moss and Graham Hill.

Rear-engined Maserati, the Tipo 63 of Scarfiotti/Vaccarella in 1961.

of mid-engined sports racers from Ferrari, Maserati and other makes was an important pointer to future developments. The regulations were largely unchanged from 1960 and 35 sports cars came to the start together with 20 GT cars. Jaguar was a notable absentee, for the first time since 1950. Ferrari again entered 11 cars; four were works entries in the sports car class and included two V 12 three-litre Testa Rossas, the mid-engined $2\frac{1}{2}$ litre six and (just to confuse matters) a prototype 250 GT. There was also an American entered Ferrari

The Ferrari 250 TR of Mairesse and Parkes finished second in 1961, after the similar car of Gendebien and Hill.
Opposite top: The Mairesse/Parkes Ferrari at Arnage.
Opposite bottom: The Rodriguez brothers' Ferrari being re-fuelled.

Esso
BP
ENERGOL
Firestone
ASTON MARTIN
FRANCE
ASTON MARTIN 2
MARTINI
11
17

A Ferrari-dominated scene at the Esses in 1961 – no. 10 is the winning car, of Olivier Gendebien and Phil Hill.

Testa Rossa driven by the Rodriguez brothers and, in the GT class, six 250 GT coupés, one of which was driven by Stirling Moss and Graham Hill – Moss' last Le Mans; he retired from racing following his accident at Goodwood at Easter 1962.

Maserati had no works entries but entrusted three new mid-engined Tipo 63s with three-litre V 12s to Scuderia Serenissima (one car) and Briggs Cunningham (two cars) – Cunningham also entered a two-litre Birdcage which he co-drove. Aston Martin had two DBR 1/300s; also a DB.4 and two Zagato bodied DB.4 GTs with 3.7 litre engines which ran in the GT class. The last cars with engines over two litres were an Austin-Healey 3000 (GT class) and a Cooper Monaco $2\frac{1}{2}$ litre (sports class). The two-litre class was much better supported: apart from the Birdcage Maserati, it contained three Porsches, three Triumph TRSs and the MGA Twin-Cam appearing for the third time at Le Mans. All of these ran in the sports car class but there were also two AC Ace GTs among the two-litre cars.

There were two 1,600 cc Porsches and two Sunbeam Alpines, entered by Rootes, a late return to Le Mans for a famous name – had not the three-litre Sunbeam come second in 1925? – even if the name was the only similarity between the 1925 and the 1961 entries. Of the Alpines, one was open and the other a fastback coupé by Harrington. Four Lotus Elites were the only cars in the 1,300 cc class, and the one-litre class was not well supported with two Austin-Healey Sprites and a single Osca. By contrast, there were no less than 13 cars in the 701–850 cc class: six DB-Panhards, five Abarths, an Osca and a Lotus which had a 750 cc engine in an Elite body.

Winners and constructors in 1961. Left to right: Mairesse and Parkes (second), Gendebien and a bedraggled Hill (winners), Bouharde, Paul Panhard, (unknown), Laureau, Rene Bonnet. Bouharde and Laureau won on Index in a DB-Panhard; Bonnet was the B in DB.

Ferrari was again the dominant force in the race; this might have led to a relatively uninteresting Le Mans, but this was not so due to two factors: the spirited performance of the Rodriguez brothers driving in opposition to the works entries, and the appearance of the 2.4 litre mid-engined car driven by Ginther/von Trips. These two cars, together with the works Testa Rossas of Gendebien/Hill and Mairesse/Parkes regularly filled the first four places on the scoreboard throughout the race, with the Ferrari GTs yapping at their heels. The Aston Martin DBRs were not effective challengers; the clutch of the Flockhart/Jim Clark car gave in, although the Salvadori/Maggs car was lying fourth when the fuel tank split. The GT Astons did not fare any better; the two Zagato bodied cars were among the earliest retirements with blown gaskets due to overheating, while the third DB.4 had to stop in the last hour of the race when the electrics failed. Nor were the mid-engined Maseratis able to break Ferrari's hold over the race; two of the Tipo 63's had retired early on, and only one of the Cunningham entered cars (driven by Pabst and Thompson) survived the race.

As the mid-engined Ferrari ran out of fuel and the Rodriguez brothers blew up their engine (though not before Ricardo had put in a lap at 125.020 mph), it was a second victory for Gendebien and Phil Hill (it was in fact Gendebien's third) with the Mairesse/Parkes Testa Rossa in second place, followed by the first Ferrari GT in third place (this car also won the GT class). Pabst and Thompson drove their Maserati up through a depleted field to finish in fourth place, followed by the first of the Porsches which also won the two-litre class. In addition Porsches won the 1,600 cc class, while among British successes was a win for the Lotus Elite in the 1,300 cc class, and the team prize was awarded to the three Triumphs which finished ninth, eleventh and fifteenth. There were no finishers in the one-litre class, and an Abarth took the 850 cc honours.

The Index of Performance went to a DB-Panhard, but the Index of Thermal Efficiency was won by the Sunbeam Alpine Harrington, mainly because it was 50 per cent heavier than most of the other contenders for this Index. This fastback coupé version of the Sunbeam Alpine was immediately re-named Le Mans. A total of 22 cars finished the race, and the highest placed British car to finish was the Triumph in ninth place. Ferrari, celebrating the fifth victory for the make, had equalled the record of Bentley and Jaguar.

1962: The Porsche of Buchet and Schiller.

LE MANS 1962

Another complete change of regulations banned sports cars but promptly substituted a new category of 'Experimental' cars – if the intention had been that these should be GT prototypes, the outcome was instead some 'bigger and better' sports prototypes, especially as the capacity limit was increased to four litres for the experimental class. The Italian manufacturers were quick to exploit the new rules and Ferrari had two 330 models with four-litre V 12 engines – an open 330 LM model driven by past winners Hill and Gendebien, and a closed 330 GT driven by Parkes and Bandini. Maserati countered with three Tipo 151 V8 four-litre coupés, entered by Briggs Cunningham and Maserati France. Ferrari were out in force with one of their biggest ever entries totalling 15 cars; apart from the two four-

The Abarth team in 1962.

Panhard's last Le Mans triumph came in 1962. The Index-winning C.D.Panhard of Bertaut and Guilhaudin.

litre cars, works experimental entries included two mid-engined cars, a 2.6 V 8 and a 2.4 V 6 (the latter in the hands of the Rodriguez brothers). There were also two Testa Rossas, an experimental 'bread van' coupé and in the GT class eight 250 GT models.

Aston Martin had the 212 GT prototype driven by Graham Hill and Ritchie Ginther, backed up by two DB.4 GT Zagato bodied cars. Jaguar made a return to Le Mans with three privately entered E-type coupés and there was a single Chevrolet Corvette with a 5.3 litre engine. Ecurie Ecosse fielded a Tojeiro coupé with a Coventry Climax Grand Prix 2.5 litre engine in the experimental class, and the only remaining big car was an Austin-Healey 3000 run in the GT class. There were a mere three cars in the two-litre class, all GTs: an AC Ace (the final appearance at Le Mans of the venerable Bristol engine), Chris Lawrence's Morgan Plus Four (which had been

The start of the 1959 race, seen from the tail end of the field with the small cars getting under way. In the foreground, a Lotus XV (54) still stationary; a team-mate (53) is well away, and so is the Stanguellini (55). Most of the cars are D.B.-Panhards but note the two SAAB saloons further up the line (43 and 44).

The Aston Martin DBR 1 of Jim Clark and Roy Salvadori finished 3rd in the 1960 race – here snapped at Mulsanne corner.

Two views of the Alfa Romeo SZ, with the characteristic 'Kamm-Heck' profile, driven by Foitek and Ricci in the 1962 race – after 22 hours they were lying in 20th place when the clutch went.

The Ferrari 250 GTO of 'Elde' and 'Beurlys' which finished 3rd in 1962.

Not quite Jaguar's last appearance – the marque had another two Le Mans races to come. This E-type coupé in the American racing colours (white and blue) was driven by Briggs Cunningham and Roy Salvadori into 4th place in the 1962 race.

10

‘ – and *that* is the engine’. *That* being a gas turbine, in the Rover-B.R.M. – here with its pretty coupé bodywork before the 1965 race in which it finished a creditable 10th, driven by Graham Hill and Jackie Stewart.

This Ferrari 275 LM, driven by Langlois and 'Elde' in the 1965 race, has just passed the pit straight and is now heading towards Tertre Rouge. Compare this picture with the 1935 photo on page 61, which was taken from almost the same vantage point.

The one that didn't: The Matra 650 of Servoz/Gavin/Muller was the only one among four Matras that did not finish the 1969 race.

rejected by the Le Mans scrutineers in 1961 as 'old fashioned') and finally there was a T.V.R. (Blackpool's only Le Mans entry) with an MG engine of the unsuitable capacity of 1,622 cc.

In the smaller classes, Abarth had four 1,300 cc cars with Simca based engines and three with 701 cc Fiat engines. Alfa Romeo fielded two 1,300 cc coupés, and Lotus had two Elites, also in the GT class. Lotus would have entered the 850 and 1,000 cc experimental classes with two Type 23s but these were rejected by the scrutineers under the infamous 'contrary to the spirit' clause, causing a lot of bad feeling in the British camp against what was seen as French favouritism for their own small cars. These were divided among two makes as the long-running DB partnership had been dissolved – Charles Deutsch had three 702 cc Panhard based cars, while Rene Bonnet in a change of allegiance used Renault Gordini engines in his cars, one of 706 cc and two of 996 cc. The total number of cars was 55, of which 25 were GTs and 30 experimental.

As expected, the main battle was between the experimental Ferraris and the Maseratis; the only other car that kept pace with the leaders was the Aston Martin 212. In a virtual repeat of the 1961 race, the Hill/Gendebien car took turns to lead with the mid-engined Ferrari of the Rodriguez brothers, until the latter was forced to retire with transmission failure around half time. It turned out that neither the Aston Martin nor the Maseratis had the stamina to last the race; the Aston was out after six hours with engine trouble and by half time the last of the Maseratis had also retired. For most of the rest of the race Ferraris filled the first four or five places on the scoreboard; it was only in the last few hours that the E-type Jaguars of Cunningham/Salvadori and Sargent/Lumsden managed to squeeze past into fourth and fifth places, helped by the retirement of the other mid-engined Ferrari.

The result was victory for Hill and Gendebien, their third together and Gendebien's fourth. Their total distance was 2,765.876 miles at an average speed of 115.244 mph; and lapping at 126.884 mph, Hill finally broke Hawthorn's 1957 lap record. They were followed home by the GT class winners, Guichet/Noblet in a Ferrari 250 GTO, a similar car was third and then came the two Jaguar E-types. Porsche took the 1,600 cc class, but Britain could score two class wins: the Morgan (which was the thirteenth car home) in the two-litre class and the Lotus Elite in the 1,300 cc class. Small car honours went to France, Bonnet in the 1,000 cc class and Panhard-CD in the 850 cc class; this car also won the Index of Performance, while the Index of Thermal Efficiency went to the class winning Lotus Elite which combined an average of 100 mph with a fuel consumption of 20 mpg. A total of 18 cars finished the race.

LE MANS 1963

The experimental cars now became unashamedly prototype again, but were still divided from the GT cars; restrictions on engine size were, however, removed from both classes. A great number of pre-race withdrawals gave a small field of 48 cars to which was added the experimental Rover-B.R.M. gas turbine car which ran outside competition. Ferrari was in a virtually unassailable position with 11 cars entered; four four-litre 330 LM prototypes, but more interesting,

1963: First of a new breed – the one-litre Alpine Renault of Richard and Frescobaldi.

Innes Ireland and Bruce McLaren drove this Aston Martin DB4GT in 1963.

three mid-engined 250 P prototypes with three-litre engines and finally, four 250 GTs with three-litre engines. Maserati had a single five-litre version of the Tipo 151 entered by Maserati France; Aston Martin tried to contend with the 215 prototype with a full four-litre engine, as well as three DB.4 GTs. Three lightweight Jaguar E-types were entered by Briggs Cunningham in the GT class, and there was a Jaguar engined Lister prototype as well. The last big engined cars all used American Ford V 8 engines of 4.7 litres capacity but were otherwise widely different; they were two front-engined A.C. Cobras and a mid-engined Lola prototype.

Porsche was back in force in the two-litre class with their flat-eights, of which two were entered in the prototype category, together with two four-cylinder two-litre examples in the GT class. The only other entry in this class was a solitary MGB driven by Paddy Hopkirk and Hutcheson and looking very ordinary. Nor was there much support for the 1,600 and 1,300 cc classes; two Sunbeam Alpines and an Alfa Romeo in the former, another two Alfas and a pair of Lotus Elites in the latter. All these ran in the GT category. An Austin-Healey Sprite countered two Bonnets in the 1,150 cc prototype class. There was more interest among the smallest cars; in the 1,000 cc class two Bonnets, an Abarth, a new British name – Deep Sanderson with a BMC based engine – and the first appearance of a famous French name – three Alpine Renaults. Among the 850 cc cars was another Abarth, the last Bonnet and a C.D. which this year forsook the Panhard engine in favour of DKW power. The total field was made up of 26 prototypes and 22 GTs.

And then there was the Rover-B.R.M. Since 1953 there had been a formula equating gas turbine with piston engined cars, and the A.C.O. had created a special prize to be awarded to the first turbine car to complete Le Mans. Rover had run the world's first gas turbine car in 1950 and by 1963 were confident enough about the future of the gas turbine to enter a car for Le Mans, in collaboration with B.R.M. – the resulting car could be described as a Rover turbine engine in a B.R.M. chassis. The reason why the car ran outside classification at Le Mans was that without a heat exchanger, the fuel consumption of the turbine car was so great that it would have been impossible to run with a regulation size fuel tank. But under the equating formula, the turbine car was set a minimum average speed of 150 kph (93.2 mph). The drivers were Graham Hill and Ritchie Ginther.

The big Maserati soon took the lead but was only able to retain it for a few hours before going out with transmission problems; it just outlasted the Aston Martin 215 which succumbed to the same trouble. From then on there were no further threats to the Ferraris. The Parkes/Maglioli 250 P briefly took the lead but was soon replaced by the sister car of Surtees/Mairesse; when this caught fire and burned out in the Esses on Sunday morning, the Scarfiotti/Bandini 250 P which had been lying second for a long time, simply took

Wheel change for the Ferrari 330 of Sears/Salmon.

The rear-engined Ferrari of Surtees and Mairesse which had led the race for so long burns out at the Esses.

over the lead to finish. For the first time a rear-engined car had won at Le Mans; furthermore it was Ferrari's seventh win, and their fourth in a row. While it was the eleventh time an Italian car had won, it was the first time that both drivers had been Italian. The winning car averaged 118.104 mph for a total distance of 2,834.509 miles – which was a new record; another new record was Surtees' fastest lap at 129.067 mph. The Scarfiotti/Bandini car also won on Index; the first time since 1950 that a big car had won the Index, and not since 1949 had the same car won the race both on distance and Index.

Apart from anything else, the next five places in the finishing list were also occupied by Ferraris; the GTO in second place won the GT class. Only from seventh place did other makes get a look-in; an A.C. Cobra was seventh, followed by a Porsche prototype (which won the two-litre class), an E-type Jaguar, a Lotus Elite (winner of the 1,300 cc class), a Bonnet which won the Index of Thermal Efficiency in addition to the 1,150 cc class, while twelfth and last was the MGB. Many of the retirements had been caused by accidents, particularly after oil was spilt on the track; the worst accident claimed the life of Bino Heinz when his Alpine Renault crashed and burned.

1963's winner, the Ferrari of Scarfiotti and Bandini, under the Dunlop bridge near Tertre Rouge.

Heinz lost his life in this 1963 disaster when his Index-leading Alpine crashed and burned.

The Rover-B.R.M. finished too, and at an average of 107.71 mph (distance covered 2,592.92 miles) handsomely exceeding the minimum required of it. This performance would have placed it eighth had it been running in competition with the other cars, and would have won Le Mans as late as 1958. The result of the 1963 race was one of the most convincing demonstrations of the superiority of one make ever witnessed at Le Mans; many contemporary pundits were however convinced that the Rover-B.R.M. performance was more important in heralding a new era, and only with the benefit of hindsight 20 years after is it possible to understand why there was no wholesale revolution after the introduction of the gas turbine in the world of motor racing.

LE MANS 1964

In many ways this was a watershed in Le Mans history: 1964 saw the last entry of a Jaguar, and the first entry from Ford. While it was also the last entry of an Aston Martin, this make would return to Le Mans many years later, in contrast to Jaguar. The rules were as before but there was now a minimum engine size of 1,000 cc, instead of 700 cc which had been the previous limit. The Rover-B.R.M. had been expected to return, with sleek coupé bodywork designed by Bill Towns and fitted with a heat exchanger to reduce its voracious appetite for paraffin; but the car was damaged in transport on the way back to Solihull after the April practice session, and could not be ready in time for the race itself.

The number of starting cars was back up to 55 and again Ferrari filled the lion's share of places with 12 cars entered: three four-litre and five 3.3 litre prototypes as well as four three-litre GTs. The biggest engine on the track was found in another Italian car, a new make that made its appearance, the Iso Rivolta which disposed of 5.3 litres – courtesy of Chevrolet. This car ran in the prototype category, as did a five-litre Maserati. If a Chevrolet V 8 was found in the Iso, Ford V 8 engines were favoured by no less than three competitors: the four AC Cobras in the GT category had 4.7 litre Ford engines, while the Sunbeam Tiger prototypes used the 4.2 litre size; slightly bigger than the engines used in Ford's own trio of GT 40 prototypes. These in fact used dohc engines originally developed by Ford for the Indianapolis race, and were conceived in Anglo-American collaboration between Ford and Lola. The first GT 40 had been

1964: The Cobra of Gurney and Bondurant at Arnage.

1964: The Alpine Renault of Delageneste and Morrogh.

completed less than three months before Le Mans and there had only been one race appearance (at the Nürburgring) prior to the 24-hour race.

Aston Martin fielded one car, and Jaguar two; they shared a common engine capacity of 3.8 litres and all ran in the GT category. As the $2\frac{1}{2}$ litre class did not attract any entries there was quite a gap down to the Porsches – two prototypes with eight-cylinder engines and five plastic bodied 904 GT coupés – which shared the two-litre class with the MGB of Andrew Hedges and Paddy Hopkirk. A Lotus Elan ran in the 1,600 cc prototype class while three Alfa Romeos of a similar capacity qualified as GT cars; in the 1,300 cc class, there was a Lotus Elite GT, a Deep Sanderson prototype and two Panhard engined C.D.s; their capacity was only 851 cc but they had been fitted with superchargers which under the current correction factor (1.4) took them up to a theoretical 1,191 cc. The smallest class was the 1,150 cc class; five Bonnets and four Alpine Renaults were kept company by a single Austin-Healey Sprite, and three Triumph Spitfires with special fastback coupé bodywork which formed the pattern for the later GT 6 model.

As it turned out, the new and untried Fords were worthy challengers of Ferrari's supremacy. The Ginther/Gregory car took the lead after the start but had to give way to the Surtees/Bandini Ferrari 330 P; while Phil Hill in another Ford set a new lap record at 131.375 mph. However, one of the Fords went off the road, and the Ginther/Gregory car retired with gearbox failure; the gearboxes apparently could not stand up to the sheer power of the engines. The only other Ferrari-challenger, the Maserati, which had been driven into third place, bowed out around midnight with electrical trouble. By then the remaining Ford GT 40, driven by Phil Hill and Bruce McLaren, was fifth after three Ferraris and an A.C. Cobra, until early Sunday morning when this Ford suffered gearbox failure as well. This left the Ferraris in control of the race.

The final result was a 1–2–3 Ferrari victory; the winning 3.3 litre 275 P model driven by Guichet and Vaccarella had covered 2,917.524 miles at an average of 121.563 mph. It was followed home by two four-litre 330 P models; in fourth place came the A.C. Cobra Daytona, entered by Carrol Shelby and driven by Dan Gurney and Bob Bondurant, and this car won the GT category as well as the five-litre class. Ferrari took the four- and three-litre classes, while the Iso Rivolta won the unlimited (over five-litre) class; a Porsche 904/4 in seventh place was best among the two-litres, and the 1,600 cc class went to an Alfa Romeo TZ. The only British win came from a Lotus Elite in the 1,300 cc class, and the smallest class of 1,150 cc cars went to an Alpine Renault which also won the Index of Thermal Efficiency; whereas the Index of Performance went to the winning Ferrari. A total of 24 cars finished, including the MGB, one Triumph Spitfire and with the Austin-Healey Sprite hindmost, but neither the Aston Martin nor the Jaguars stood the distance.

LE MANS
1965

The last year for two seasoned Le Mans marques: Maserati and MG. And the year when Ford attempted to bulldoze Le Mans but at the end of the day had nothing to show for their pains, but the Rover-B.R.M. returned and did much to uphold Britain's honours.

The number of cars was slightly down this year to 51; these were split into 31 prototype cars and 20 GTs. Ferrari put most of their efforts into the prototype class with ten cars of varying engine sizes – 3.3, 4.0 and 4.4 litres – entered by the works but also by American and Belgian teams. In addition there was a single Ferrari 275 GTB,

Italo-American newcomer for 1965, Iso Grifo with Chevrolet V8 engine.

1965 was second time for the Ford team. This is the GT 40 of Trintignant and Ligier.

The start of the 1965 race. No. 8, the Maserati of Siffert and Neerpasch, was first away only to leave the road almost immediately.

The Porsche 904/6 of Linge/Nocker which surprised everybody by finishing fourth.

a new model with a 3.3 litre engine. The opposition, meaning Ford, had six prototype cars; four GT 40s with either 4.7 or 5.3 litre engines, but topping even these, a pair of Mk II models with monstrous seven-litre engines – among the biggest ever seen at Le Mans. Maserati had a single five-litre mid-engined car; but most punters probably gave the five Cobras (née A.C.) more of a chance, considering their fourth place the previous year. They used the same Ford V 8 4.7 litre engines again. The last big car was a Chevrolet engined 5.3 litre Iso Grifo.

Unusually, there was not a single car between two- and three-litres; a class which had so often in the past been the most important one at Le Mans, and the emerging split between 'big bangers' on the one hand, and on the other a group of small cars mainly chasing the Index, may have caused the organisers some concern. Leading the two-litre class was Porsche with seven entries, four- and eight-cylinder cars but also two 911 six-cylinder models. They were countered by a single Elva-B.M.W.; while the Rover-B.R.M. was now classified as the equivalent of 1,992 cc and therefore ran in the same class. So did the MGB which had returned to the fray for the third time.

The 1,600 cc class was strictly Italian territory; four Alfa Romeo TZ IIs entered by the Scuderia Autodelta, and a Dino (a Ferrari by

1965: Ferrari 275 LM of Bianchi and Salmon.

Ferrari 330 P2 of Surtees and Scarfiotti.

any other name) with a V 6 engine amidships. In the smaller classes, there was a notable absentee: the air cooled flat twin Panhard engine which had been present at every Le Mans since 1950, and often as not had won the Index of Performance and its class. But with a new one-litre minimum rule also applying to supercharged engines, even the ingenuity of Charles Deutsch failed to find a solution. In consequence there were no C.D. entries this year; and his erstwhile partner Rene Bonnet was also absent from Le Mans in 1965, but engaged on staging an eventual comeback in Matra's regie. In the absence of these two stalwarts, French hopes for Index wins centred on the Alpine Renaults; a single 1,108 cc GT, and five prototypes – two in the 1,300 cc class and three in the 1,150 cc class. British opposition came from two 1,293 cc Austin-Healey Sprites, and four 1,147 cc Triumph Spitfires which now ran in the GT class.

Bearing the events of the 1964 race in mind, the big question was whether the Fords were reliable enough to stand the distance. No one doubted that they had the power; Phil Hill had made the fastest practice lap in a seven-litre Mk II, and would indeed put in the fastest

Ferrari 275 LM of Spoerry and Buller.

lap of the race – a new record of 138.443 mph. As it turned out, the Ford troubles were not over. Although the McLaren/Miles car took the lead soon after the start (whereas the Maserati left the road almost immediately) none of the Fords lasted very long; their retirements were due to either blown head gaskets or to recurring gearbox and clutch problems which put out both the seven-litre cars. Phil Hill and Chris Amon lasted longest but even they were out before midnight.

The race then became another Ferrari procession; but with frequent changes in the leading positions it proved more interesting than some past Le Mans races. Surtees/Scarfiotti and Guichet/Parkes took turns to lead in their works entered 330 P2 models, but eventually both were forced out of the race with mechanical trouble. This allowed the Belgian entered 275 LM into the lead but in the closing hours of the race on Sunday afternoon this had to give best to the N.A.R.T. (North American Racing Team) 275 LM driven by Masten Gregory and Jochen Rindt. They became the winners at an average of 121.092 mph and a total distance of 2,906.215 miles. The Belgian Ferrari was second, followed home by the GT category winner, the lone Ferrari 275 GTB. Fourth and fifth were two Porsches, a 904/6 prototype and a 904/4 GT which took the two-litre honours in their categories; the 904/6 also won the Index of Performance and the 904/4 the Index of Thermal Efficiency.

French hopes of Index wins came to nothing, nor were there any French class wins and not a single Alpine finished the race. The 1,300 cc class went to an Austin-Healey Sprite, and a Triumph Spitfire won the 1,150 cc class. However, the highest placed British car was the Rover-B.R.M. which finished tenth, although at an appreciably lower average than in 1963. It was followed home by the MGB in eleventh place, MG's highest position at Le Mans in the post-war period. There were only 14 finishers. With a total of nine wins, of which six were in a row, Ferrari had built up a unique record in the annals of Le Mans; but 1965 marked the end of Ferrari's dominance, and thus the end of an era. It was also effectively the end of the era when British cars were among the most numerous entries at Le Mans; from 13 British cars in 1965 it dropped to 3 in 1966, and it was to be a long time before there was again a British car with a chance of winning the 24-hour race.

Out of Tertre Rouge and towards the Mulsanne straight; compare this 1965 photo with the illustration on page 13. Cobra in the foreground.

Inset: The 1965 winners, Masten Gregory and Jochen Rindt . . . and (above) setting out on the lap of honour. A nine-seater Ferrari?

Jules
Jules
BOSCH

5. 1966-1981 FROM RECORDS TO RECESSION

Bell driving the 1981 winning Porsche 936

LE MANS 1966

A new set of C.S.I. regulations meant that the Le Mans entries changed in character yet again. The GT class which had been popular since its inception in 1959 was now reduced to a mere two entries – a Ferrari 275 GTB and a Porsche 911 – as the minimum production run for cars in this class was increased from 100 to 500. The prototype class was left as before but a new Sports Car class was added, for cars of which at least 50 examples had been built. This now became the qualifying class for the championship. There was, however, little sign that manufacturers paid much heed to the new categories; apart from the two GT cars, the entry consisted of 11 sports cars and no fewer than 42 prototypes, for a total field of 55 cars.

By way of a change, Ford had the most cars entered – eight Mk IIs with seven-litre engines which ran as prototypes, backed up by five 4.7 litre GT 40s in the sports car class. There were eleven Ferraris; apart from the 3.3 litre GT car, these consisted of three 3.3 litre sports cars, three four-litre prototypes (330 P3) and four 4.4 litre prototypes (365 P2). Next came Porsche with seven cars; the GT 911, and six variations on the 906/6 theme, six-cylinder two-litre cars of which three ran as sports cars, three as prototypes.

The remaining cars were all entered as prototypes. Apart from Ford the American stakes were raised by a Chaparral, the Texas built sports-racing car with a Chevrolet 5.3 litre V 8 and automatic transmission. A sister under the skin – as far as the use of a Chevrolet engine was concerned – was the Italian Bizzarini, based on the Iso

Ford was third time lucky in 1966. The Mark 2 of Bucknum and Hutcheson during a pit stop; it eventually finished third.

Impudence and dignity. The Mini-Marcos leads Ford and Ferrari through the Esses.

Grifo; two of these were entered. Another Italian newcomer was the 3.4 litre Serenissima. In the two-litre class, opposition to Porsche came from three Dino-Ferraris with V 6 engines and a trio of French Matras with B.R.M. V 8 engines; the first appearance of this important new make which had an ancestry going back to the D.B. and Rene Bonnet cars. There were no entries in the 1,600 cc class but a

Mixed bunch at Tertre Rouge, with 1.3 litre Alpine Renault in the lead.

Power and glory – the Ford Mk 2 of Miles and Hulme which was placed second.

good spread of marques among the 1,300 cc cars: two Austin-Healey Sprites, five Alpine-Renaults, as well as two new makes – a single Marcos, with a 1,300 cc BMC engine, originally based on the Mini and the only front-wheel drive car in the race and two Italian Asas, in effect small Ferraris born out of wedlock with Bizzarini as mid-wife. The 1,150 cc class was by contrast all-French territory: one 1,000 cc Alpine and three C.D. Peugeots, entered by Charles Deutsch after a year's absence, their aerodynamic bodywork hid 1,130 cc Peugeot 204 transverse powerpacks mounted amidships.

The race started badly with one of the Bizzarinis skidding into the barrier on the starting line. The Fords soon demonstrated their supremacy; at the end of the first hour, Ford Mk IIs were leading 1–2–3, with the best Ferrari (a 330 P2 driven by Rodriguez and Ginther) in fourth place. Dan Gurney in the leading Ford set a new lap record at 142.979 mph. The Chaparral was initially seventh but was the first of the top contenders to retire, with a flat battery. The Gurney/Grant Ford and that of Hulme/Miles took turns to lead for most of the race; the Rodriguez/Ginther Ferrari got past the Fords once but eventually retired with gearbox failure, while the sister car of Scarfiotti/Parkes had already withdrawn, following a crash which

The 1966 winner, Ford Mk 2 of Bruce McLaren and Chris Amon.

The winning Ford again, with the Index-winning Porsche 906 of Siffert/Davis.

Three little maids from school are we: 1966 was first outing for Matra, with these three B.R.M.-engined cars.

also involved a C.D. Peugeot and a Matra.

There were, however, numerous retirements in the Ford camp, including that of a young Belgian driver, who had his first Le Mans drive in a GT 40 at the age of 21: Jacky Ickx; and with only a few hours to go, the Gurney/Grant Mk II retired with a blown gasket. But the rest of the race was a procession of the Mark IIs of McLaren/Amon, Hulme/Miles and Bucknum/Hutcheson which finished in that order. Their procession over the finishing line was one of the most memorable sights in Le Mans history, the first two cars being so close that it caused the timekeepers no little head scratching. Both were deemed to have achieved the same average speed of 125.389 mph but the distance of the McLaren/Amon car was worked out at 3,009.350 miles and that of the Miles/Hulme car 3,009.338 miles – the closest finish ever in Le Mans history. For the first time the 3,000 mile/125 mph barrier had been broken.

It was a sadly depleted field of 15 cars which finished this race; after the three Fords came four Porsche 906/6s, the leading car driven by Siffert/Davis won the Index of Performance in addition to the two-litre class. The Porsches were followed home in eighth place by the leading Ferrari, the 275 GTB which won the GT class; the sports car class had gone to the Porsche which came seventh. One other Ferrari finished, as did the Porsche 911; also four Alpine Renaults of which the car in eleventh place won the Index of Thermal Efficiency. Fifteenth and last to finish was the Marcos, the only British car of three to finish the race. After 41 years – as a Chrysler had been the first American car entered at Le Mans, in 1925 – there was an American victory and although it was a very decisive victory in its own right, it would merely serve as a curtain opener for the next Le Mans.

LE MANS 1967

If Ferrari had their new P4 model with four-litre engines, Ford had another 'four', the Mk IV with seven-litre engines. It was obvious that Le Mans would be a clash of the titans. The categories were the same as the previous year and the prototype group still attracted by

1967: 1.3 litre Alpine Renault of Delageneste and Chinisse . . .

far the most numerous entries: 41 out of 54 starting cars were defined as prototypes, as against six sports cars (of three different makes) and seven GT cars of four different makes.

Ford were again leading contenders, with four of the Mk IV prototypes and three Mk II Bs, all with seven-litre engines said to develop around 550 bhp; the back-up team were three GT 40s, 4.7 litre sports cars. Ferrari concentrated efforts on the prototype group, with seven P.4 models (some were strictly speaking P.3/4s) which were all of four-litres capacity; there was a single 4.4 litre P.2 and in the GT class, a 3.3 litre 275 GTB. Porsche fielded a wider range of cars than any other manufacturer; they supported all three categories, but a common bond between their entries was that all were two-litre flat sixes. In the GT class, there were four 911 S models; in the sports car class, two 906/6s and among the prototypes, two 907/6s and two 910/6s.

Chaparral entered two cars, still with Chevrolet V 8 engines – this year, however, boosted to seven-litres and with automatic gearboxes, but a distinct novelty was a movable aileron high over the back of the car which was expected to help aerodynamics; the driver could move it into a braking position, shades of the Mercedes air-brake of 12 years earlier. The Chaparral's practice times confirmed that there

. . . and the sister car of de Cortanze/Leguellec, at the April test day.

49

Two Ferraris in 1967: Rodriguez leading Amon.

was definitely something in it; thereafter it did not take long for the powers that be in the racing world to ban movable spoilers. There were two new British contenders in the race – after his interlude with Ford, Eric Broadley had re-started his Lola company and was now back at Le Mans with two prototypes, fitted with Aston Martin V 8 engines which displaced just over five litres. It was, however, the first Le Mans for John Wyer's Mirage; the two cars were in effect light-weight versions of the Ford GT 40 and used Ford V 8, 5.8 litre engines. Two big American cars were found in the GT class – a seven-litre Chevrolet Corvette and a Shelby GT which was a Ford Mustang with a 4.7 litre Ford-Shelby-Cobra engine under the bonnet. Shelby and Ford made almost 15,000 of those. These two Americans were two of five front-engined cars in the race; a good measure of how much things had changed since the beginning of the 1960s.

Apart from the multitude of Porsches, there were only two other two-litre cars, both Matras with B.R.M. engines, and the 1,600 cc class was extremely badly supported with just two cars, an Alpine Renault which had grown to 1,470 cc and a rare reappearance of the marque Lotus, a type 47, the Europa with the Ford based dohc 1,588 cc engine. The 1,300 cc class could boast of no less than five

1967: Ford Mk 2 of Hawkins and Bucknum.

1967: The winning Ford Mk IV of Dan Gurney and A. J. Foyt.

A. J. Foyt and Dan Gurney, winners of the 1967 race.

Alpines, the perennial Austin-Healey Sprite, the Mini-Marcos and an Abarth which, alone among the small cars, ran in the sports car category. The 'little ones' below 1,150 cc comprised another two Alpines, two Peugeot engined C.D.s and a British entry, the Costin-Nathan which featured a Hillman Imp based engine in a plywood chassis.

The Fords initially took the lead, with the Gurney/Foyt Mk IV leading the race from the second hour. For many hours the Chaparral of Phil Hill/Spence was a strong challenger and the Ferrari P4 of Scarfiotti/Parkes gradually worked its way up the field, followed by the sister car in the hands of Mairesse/Beurlys. The big British cars did not last long; the Surtees/Hobbs Lola Aston retired with piston failure soon after the start and its team mate had followed within four hours, at about the same time that the Mirage of Jacky Ickx/Muir broke a con rod. The other Mirage lasted an hour longer; none of the British cars had ever been in a position to challenge the race leaders. By half time numerous retirements had included both the Matra-B.R.M.s and, while the Gurney/Foyt Ford was still in the lead, the two Ferraris were second and fourth, separated by the Chaparral. The Ford team was still relatively intact with only three retirements of ten starting cars when a multiple accident at the Esses put out three Fords, including the Mark IV of Mario Andretti/Bianchi, fortunately without injury or loss of life.

However, this did not change the leading positions; but when the automatic gearbox of the Chaparral gave in it became a straight Ferrari–Ford battle to the finish. But Dan Gurney and A. J. Foyt were unassailable; they scored the first all-American (car and both drivers) victory at Le Mans, at an average of 135.482 mph for a total distance of 3,251.567 miles – breaking the 5,000 kilometre barrier for the first time. A new lap record was set by Denis Hulme and Mario Andretti who both recorded speeds of 147.894 mph in their Ford Mk IVs. The Ferrari P.4s of Scarfiotti/Parkes and Mairesse/Beurlys were in second and third places, followed by the Ford Mk IV of McLaren/Donohue; the next four places were all filled by Porsches. The Siffert/Herrmann 907/6 in fifth place took the Index of Performance, and the two-litre prototype class; the best sports car was the Porsche 906/6 in seventh place and the GT class was won by a Ferrari 275 GTB in eleventh place behind a pair of Alpine Renaults. The winning Ford also took the Index of Thermal Efficiency. Of 16 finishers, the only British car was the Austin-Healey Sprite in fifteenth place. So ended a memorable Le Mans with all records broken and the biggest engined winner ever at the Sarthe circuit.

LE MANS 1968

How easily this year might have been a repeat of 1936 when the race was cancelled due to civil unrest in France; but General de Gaulle proved to have a firmer grasp of the political situation in the Fifth Republic of the 1960s than his predecessors had 30 years earlier. As it was, the political situation in France was enough to delay Le Mans until the autumn; the race was held on 28 and 29 September. Two rules were amended in deference to the season – a change of battery was permitted during the race and the start was an hour earlier at 3 pm, owing to the longer period of darkness. There were many other changes, however, an artificial chicane had been constructed at the approach to the pits, named the *Virage Ford* after the company which provided the funds, in an effort to reduce the speed past the pits. Then the C.S.I. decided that the capacity of sports prototypes would be limited to 3,000 cc, although sports cars built in at least 50 examples would still be allowed to use larger engines. This may have been intended to exclude the seven-litre cars from Ford and Chaparral, but it also meant that the four-litre Ferraris were on the wrong side of the barrier. In consequence there were no works Ferraris, no Chaparrals and Ford's entries were the Anglo-American GT 40s.

But the entry list of 54 cars was not by any means devoid of interest. Of the five Ford GT 40s, three had 4.9 litre engines and were entered by the Gulf-Ford team managed by John Wyer. They shared the sports car class with four (privately entered) Ferrari 275 LMs and two Lolas which, for 1968, tried Chevrolet V 8 engines of five-litres capacity. The only other car in this category was a two-litre Porsche 906. The GT category was retained but was not much better supported than in previous years: four Porsche 911s, two Chevrolet Corvettes, two Alpine Renault A 110s and a single Ferrari 275 GTB. A total of 12 sports cars and nine GTs; more variety was found among the 33 prototypes.

Alfa Romeo came back to Le Mans with a full-blown prototype – the Tipo 33 with a two-litre V 8 engine. Six of these cars were entered by Alfa Romeo subsidiary Autodelta. Porsche was, naturally, represented in force; the works entry consisted of four 'Langheck' 908 models with three-litre flat eight engines, backed up by

The Alfa's return: Tipo 33/2 of Giunti and Galli which finished fourth in 1968.

The Lola-Chevrolet of Norinder and Axelsson was disqualified when it ran out of fuel in the 1968 race.

private entries of three 2.2 litre flat eight 907s and a single two-litre flat six 910. Porsche had suddenly emerged as a serious contender for a Le Mans win. There were also some important new French cars under the three-litre formula, a single Matra 630 with the V 12 three-litre engine also found in Matra's Grand Prix racers, and Alpine Renault's entry was headed by four of their A 220s with three-litre V 8 engines. Another five Alpines competed in the prototype classes below 1,600 cc.

A new British name was among the other prototype entries – Chevron, with a single car fitted with a three-litre Repco Formula One engine; while a return was staged by Healey as a marque in its own right, with a Climax engined two-litre car. There were two two-litre prototypes with the name Dino, one a Fiat, the other a Ferrari; both used V 6 engines but in the Fiat it was in the front, in the Ferrari in the back. There was also a 1,600 cc Deep Sanderson, a 1,300 cc Austin-Healey Sprite which featured fuel injection but this was the last Le Mans for this make, and a 1,200 cc Moynet with a Simca based engine in a Nathan chassis. The two final entries were American Howmet turbine cars which were deemed to be the equivalent of three litre petro-engined cars.

The new formula, and the absence of the Ferrari works team, had combined to throw this Le Mans wide open; there was no particular favourite. The Porsche 908s soon proved that they were the fastest cars on the circuit and after an hour's racing they had established a 1–2–3–4 lead, followed by a gaggle of other makes and not a Ford in sight before tenth place. This was the Pedro Rodriguez/Bianchi car which then gradually moved up the scoreboard while three of the Porsche 908s succumbed to mechanical and electrical defects within

Alpine Renault joins the big bangers – the 1968 three-litre A 220 model, this is the Bianchi/Depailler car –

– but the little ones were more successful: 1.3 litre Alpine Renault A 210 of Nicholas and Andruet.

The Stommelen/Neerpasch Porsche 908/8 finished third in 1968.

1968: The Ferrari 275 LM of Vestey and Pike.

a few hours, leaving just the Stommelen/Neerpasch car in the running and that had dropped back to fifteenth place by the time the Ford went into the lead. The Matra of Pescarolo/Servon Gavin was then in second place and was being challenged by one of the Alfa Romeos. The surviving Porsche 908, meanwhile, regained some of the lost ground and fought a private battle with a Porsche 907 for fourth place.

This was the position for most of the rest of the race. Early retirements had included the Healey and the Chevron Repco, while the three-litre V 8 Alpines were not fast enough to challenge the leaders seriously; the Bianchi/Depailler car was doing best and was in sixth place when Bianchi lost it at Tertre Rouge; he was badly burned in the subsequent fire. Indirectly, this accident cost Pescarolo and the Matra a possible second place; some of the debris from the Alpine punctured one of the Matra's tyres and a second puncture put Pescarolo out. Other victims of accidents included one of the Howmet turbine cars which had already shown a most disappointing performance.

With the Matra out of the running, the Rodriguez/Bianchi Ford was a clear winner at an average of 115.286 mph and a total distance of 2,766.886 miles. In second place came the privately entered Porsche 907, while the three-litre works car was relegated to third, although Rolf Stommelen in this car had made the fastest lap at 138.143 mph. Alfa Romeos were fourth, fifth and sixth, followed by a Ferrari 275 LM and the only surviving three-litre Alpine. The GT class was won by a Porsche 911 in twelfth place and both the Index of Performance and the Index of Thermal Effieicncy went to small Alpine Renaults. The fifteenth and last car to finish – and again, the only British car to do so – was the Austin-Healey Sprite.

LE MANS 1969

The year of the big argument over spoilers: to move, or not to move? – it was also the year when advertisements started to spread all over the cars; when the Mulsanne straight was lined with Armco barriers; it was the first year of the Porsche 917 but the last year of the traditional Le Mans start. And it was the first win for Jacky Ickx.

While the race was back where it should be, on 14 and 15 June, the starting time was brought forward to 2 pm. Withdrawal of a number of teams – including Autodelta Alfa Romeo – meant that the number of cars was reduced to 45, of which no fewer than 16 were Porsches. The three categories were as before – prototypes, sports cars and GT cars, but the production figure required for sports cars was reduced to 25. Porsche immediately laid down 25 examples of their new $4\frac{1}{2}$ litre flat twelve 917 model and three of these came to the start. In the prototype category, there were four 908 three-litre models and two 910 two-litre cars; seven 911s contested the GT category. By contrast, even the eight cars entered by Alpine Renault seemed modest; these were all in the prototype category and included four of the three-litre V 8s and four small cars in the classes below 1,600 cc. The five Ford GT 40s all ran in the sports car category and included three 4.9 litre cars of John Wyer's Gulf-Ford team. The number of Ferraris entered was down to four, a 275 GTB in the GT category, a 275 LM in the sports car category and two 312 P prototypes.

Most of the remaining entries were, naturally enough, prototypes; in the absence of Autodelta, two Alfa Romeo Tipo 33s were entered by a Belgian team. One had a two-litre and the other a 2.5 litre engine. Matra was out in force with four three-litre V 12s, the 630/650 models. Apart from the Anglo-American Fords, British entries were a Lola with a five-litre Chevrolet engine in the sports car

Ickx's first win, with Oliver in the Ford GT 40 in 1969.

class and three two-litre prototypes: a Chevron with a BMW engine, a Nomad with a B.R.M. engine and the Climax engined Healey. The smallest car in the race was a 1,001 cc Fiat Abarth (and, apart from the four Alpines, this was the only entry in the classes below 1,600 cc) while the biggest was a Chevrolet Corvette of 6,996 cc. The total was 25 prototypes, lined-up against 11 sports cars and nine GT cars.

From the outset the race was marred by bad accidents – on the first lap John Woolfe crashed his Porsche 917 near White House and was killed. While the 917 thus confirmed its reputation for bad road-holding in a somewhat sinister way, the sister cars (which both had long tails, whereas Woolfe's car had been 'short') driven by Stommelen/Ahrens and Elford/Attwood went into a 1–2 lead, with 908 works cars in the next three positions. However, after a brief spell in the lead the Siffert/Redman 908 went out with gearbox failure; the Elford/Attwood 917 took over the lead and, while Porsches still filled the first four positions on the scoreboard, the Matras and the Ford GT 40 of Ickx/Oliver moved into position just behind the German cars.

But other Porsches were to retire with mechanical trouble; the Stommelen/Ahrens 917 went out with a broken oil pipe and clutch failure, leaving the Elford/Attwood 917 and the Links/Kauhsen 908 in a 1–2 lead which they held for eight hours, while the Ickx/Oliver GT 40 went into third place, followed by another Porsche 908 and the Hobbs/Hailwood GT 40. This pattern continued until almost noon on Sunday; then, with less than three hours to go, the two leading Porsches withdrew from the battle. A sick clutch on the 917 finally gave in, while the gearbox on the 908 failed. Suddenly, Ickx and Oliver in the Wyer Gulf-Ford GT 40 found themselves leading, if only by a very small margin, over the only surviving works Porsche, a 908 driven by Herrmann and Larrousse. Ickx and Oliver won, scoring Ford's fourth victory in a row but at the narrowest margin in Le Man's history except for the dead heat of 1967. Their average speed was 129.400 mph for a total distance of 3,105.607 miles; the Porsche had covered 3,105.532 miles at an average of 129.397 mph. Ickx and Oliver also won the Index of Thermal Efficiency. Remarkably, their GT 40 was the same car which had won the 1968 Le Mans. The Hobbs/Hailwood GT 40 was third, followed by two Matras. If Porsche was cheated of overall victory, at least a 911 S took the GT honours; while a 1,000 cc Alpine Renault won the Index of Performance, as the sole finisher of this make. It came in twelfth of 14 finishing cars, which did not include a single all-British entry.

LE MANS 1970

A very rainy Le Mans and in many respects a very confusing one. Not, let it be said, because of the A.C.O. which for once decided to run the race in accordance with all F.I.A. regulations! New regulations permitted up to three drivers in each car and the possibility of changing drivers came in – the same driver might now be behind the wheel of two different cars in the same team during the race. The use of safety harnesses became compulsory and the traditional Le Mans start was abandoned – while cars were still parked diagonally with engines stopped, drivers now had to be seated in the cars with harnesses fastened when the flag fell.

Alpine and Ford were absent; works entries from Ferrari and Alfa Romeo were back – on the other hand, there were no Porsche works cars, although 24 of 51 starters were of this make. Instead 'official' Porsche entries were made by two stables: the Austrian Porsche-Konstruktionen KG of Salzburg and the British John Wyer-Gulf team. A total of seven 917 models were entered in the sports car category, with long- or short-tailed bodywork and 4.5 or 4.9 litre engines. Then there were five prototype entries – two 908 three-litre cars, a 2.2 litre 907 and two two-litre 910s; and no less than a dozen GT category Porsches, with one exception, all of them 911s with two- or 2.2 litre engines; the one that was not was a VW-Porsche 914/6 with a two-litre six-cylinder engine.

Ferrari had by now followed Porsche's example and built 25 examples of their 512 S model so it could be entered as a sports car; there were no less than eleven of these five-litre machines in the race, together with a single 312 P three-litre prototype. Apart from Porsches and Ferraris, the only other sports car entry was a five-litre Lola-Chevrolet; while in the GT category, there were two seven-litre Chevrolet Corvettes in addition to the surfeit of Porsches. At least there was a more equal split numerically between the three categories, with fourteen GT entries, while for the first time there were more sports cars than prototypes – 19 against 18.

The remaining entries were all prototypes; the four Alfa Romeo Tipo 33s were now full three-litre cars, while the three Matras were now Matra-Simcas, following a merger in the French motor industry which effectively brought Matra under the control of the American Chrysler corporation. Their Le Mans entries were three-litre V 12s as before. However, their arch rival Alpine Renault was a notable absentee; the company had retired from racing at the end of 1969 in order to concentrate on rallying. Instead there was a new French make, Ligier – a pretty little coupé with a 1.8 litre Ford-Cosworth engine, co-driven by its designer Guy Ligier. In addition to the Lola, there were four other British entries – the Healey for the third (and last) time, now fitted with a three-litre Repco-Brabham engine and three Chevrons with a diversity of engines: a two-litre BMW, a 1.8 litre Ford and a two-litre Mazda rotary – the first appearance at Le Mans of a car with a Wankel type engine.

As in 1969, the Porsches took an early lead, with five Porsche 917s in the first five places, followed by Jacky Ickx/Schetty in a Ferrari 512 S. However, the bad weather caused several accidents; three Ferrari 512 Ss were put out after a shunt at White House and many more cars were to go the same way, including the Porsche 917s of Hailwood/Hobbs and Piper/van Lennep. Meanwhile, after just six hours of racing, the entire Matra-Simca team was withdrawn with defective piston rings which effectively put paid to any French hopes of a Le Mans win. Ickx's Ferrari crashed at the Ford chicane and halfway through the race, the Siffert/Redman Porsche 917 which had been race leader for several hours, went out with engine problems.

The Attwood/Herrmann 917 then moved into the lead and the Porsche position seemed as impregnable as ever, with 917s leading 1–2–3, followed by a 908; an Alfa Romeo Tipo 33 was in fifth place, followed by three Ferraris. There was some place swopping among the leading Porsches but the situation was not affected before Sunday morning when the Elford/Ahrens 917 retired from fourth place with a failed distributor. The highest placed Alfa Romeo had then been disqualified when its starter failed; this left just one of the

In the 1970 race the Porsche 917 of Elford and Ahrens was second for a long time but did not finish.

Tipo 33s in the race, the de Adamich/Courage car which lasted for another two hours before the engine gave up; by then the finishing order had been established. The Porsche 917 (short-tail) of Attwood/Herrmann which came in the winner at an average of 119.298 mph for a total distance of 2,863.154 miles, followed by the Porsche 917 (long-tail) of Larrousse/Kauhsen and the three-litre Porsche 908 of Lins/Marko in third place which also won the Index of Performance, while the Larrousse/Kauhsen 917 took the Index of Thermal Efficiency. Ferraris were fourth and fifth, the VW-Porsche 914/6 was sixth and won the GT class; seventh and last to finish was a Porsche 911. Although another nine cars finished, they did not qualify as they did not complete the minimum distance required of them.

The rain was responsible for the small number of finishing cars and for the comparatively low average speeds attained; a new lap record was, however, set by Vic Elford in the Porsche 917 'Lang-Heck' at 149.896 mph. The only other records were the record low number of finishing cars and the fact that one make won all categories and classes. In the 20th Le Mans in which Porsche had been represented, they were at last awarded with victory and they had made their mark in no uncertain manner.

LE MANS 1971

A remarkable year – the fastest Le Mans on record so far. The year when it seemed that Le Mans was a glorified outing for the Porsche Club with 33 out of 49 starting cars of this make and for the first time, there was a rolling start behind a pace car (a Porsche, what else?), Indianapolis style. However, the Alfa Romeo and Ferrari works teams were absent and Matra-Simca ran only a single car. In the circumstances, the result was perhaps fairly predictable but with two competing official Porsche teams, Gulf-Porsche and Martini Racing Team, there was still some interest attached to the race itself.

The Porsche onslaught was led by seven 917s in the sports car category with one exception; they all had five-litre engines and it is worth noting that Pedro Rodriguez put in a practice lap at 155 mph in one of the Gulf-Porsche cars. On the other hand, their Martini opponents had a 917 with a lightweight magnesium chassis. The car that most people noticed was perhaps the 917 Can-Am model painted pink and decorated like a butchery chart of a pig. The 'back-up team' consisted of six prototype cars – five 908/02 models with three-litre engines and a single two-litre 907. The remaining 20 Porsches were all in the GT category; 18 of these were 911s with various engine sizes – 2.2 or 2.4 litres – while there were two of the two-litre VW-Porsche 914/6 models.

Of ten Ferraris entered, nine were 512 models with five-litre engines – the British driver Alain de Cadenet experienced his first Le Mans as co-driver in one of these – while the tenth was a 365 GTB/4 'Daytona' coupé with a 4.4 litre engine; by rights a GT car but it was then still a new model and not enough had been built for it to be homologated. In consequence it started in the sports car category with the other Ferraris. It was one of only three front-engined cars in the race; the other two were seven-litre Chevrolet Corvettes which started in the GT category. There were only four other cars entered – two Lolas, a sports car with the five-litre Chevrolet V 8 engine and a prototype with a 1.8 litre Ford-Cosworth engine (which was the smallest car in the race!) and two French three-litre prototypes: the Matra-Simca V12 and a new Ligier which marked the first appearance at Le Mans of the Ford-Cosworth three-litre V8 engine – highly successful in Formula 1 but not a constantly dominating force at Le Mans.

For the third year in succession the Porsche 917s took the lead in the early stages of the race, with the Ferrari 512s as the main challengers. The Rodriguez/Oliver Porsche 917 led for eleven hours with one short break when it was second after the Siffert/Bell 917, while the highest placed Ferrari in the first part of the race was the Donohue/Hobbs 512 LM which, however, retired with engine failure. When Pedro Rodriguez' chances of a second Le Mans win were scuttled by a broken pipe half way through the race, the Vaccarella/Juncadella Ferrari 512 LM led briefly before the gearbox gave up. Only then did the Martini Racing Porsche 917 K of Marko and Gijs van Lennep come into the lead, followed by the rival Gulf team's 917 driven by Attwood and Müller. Again repeating the pattern of 1969–70, the ultimate winners had emerged from among those cars lying further down the field in the first half of the race, while the early leaders had all gone out with mechanical trouble.

For the entire second half of the race the Marko/van Lennep car stayed ahead of that of Attwood/Müller; the lone Matra-Simca of Beltoise/Amon which had been lying third, stopped when its fuel injection failed. Instead the North American Racing Team Ferrari 512 M, driven by Posey/Adamovicz, moved into third place, followed by a similar car which was shared by British driver Chris Craft. This was the finishing order. When the winning Marko/van Lennep car crossed the finishing line, it had covered a total distance of 3,315.203 miles at an average of 138.133 mph – Le Mans records then as now. The fastest lap in the race was put in by Jackie Oliver in the 917 he shared with Rodriguez; his speed was another record, at 151.854 mph. Marko and van Lennep also won the Index of Performance in the last year this method of judging the result was used. Fifth place went to the Ferrari 365 GTB/4 which also won the Index of Thermal Efficiency; it was followed by the first GT car, a Porsche 911 and only then was there a prototype car in the list: the two-litre Porsche 907. Another six cars finished – all Porsche 911s. The Ligier did not cover a high enough mileage to qualify.

With the second win of the Porsche 917 the era of the 'monster' sports cars ended. With a new set of regulations, they went the way the 'monster' prototypes had gone after the win of the seven-litre Ford in 1967.

LE MANS 1972

The regulations were completely overhauled and brought into line with C.S.I. rules; some thought the new rules strengthened the position of Le Mans as the premier sports car race; others were of the opinion that it was all a plot to ensure a French victory! The most important new rule limited sports cars (Group 5 cars) to a maximum engine size of 3,000 cc – making the Ferrari 512s and Porsche 917s redundant at one stroke, but conveniently enough still allowing the Matra V12 to race. The new limit also coincided with the Formula 1 engine size, and in consequence the Ford-Cosworth engine gained a certain following also among Le Mans entrants. The previous GT category was now defined as Group 4 Grand Tourisme Special – GTS for short – and in a partial return to the original 1923 Le Mans regulations, a category was created for Group 2 Special Touring, or TS cars. There were no upward limitations on the GTS and TS categories but both had a lower limit of 2,000 cc. The Index of Performance was discontinued, and the Index of Thermal Efficiency now applied only to GTS and TS cars.

The Sports car category attracted 24 entries; Porsche was still a major supporter with eight cars, of which six were 908s with three-litre engines, while there was also a 2.4 litre 910 and a two-litre 907. Matra fielded four cars, of the 660 and 670 types; all were three-litre V12s. The other French contender, Ligier, by contrast used an Italian engine; their three JS 2 models had three-litre Maserati V6 engines. All-Italian were the trio of Alfa Romeos, as in the 1970 Le Mans three-litre versions of the Tipo 33 V8. The Ford-Cosworth V 8 three-litre engine was used by two British makes: Lola, for their two T.280 models; and Duckham-Ford, a new car so-called after the sponsoring oil company, and partially designed round Brabham F.1 components. A third Lola and two Chevrons used 1.8 litre Ford-based engines, and were the smallest sports car entries.

'Big bangers' were henceforth relegated to the GTS category, which for the second year running attracted the majority of entries: 26. The list was headed by five Chevrolet Corvettes, with their massive seven-litre engines; American V8s were also the motive power in the four de Tomaso Panteras, but their 5.7 litre engines were made by Ford. Although the de Tomaso is an Italian make, the man behind the car Allessandro de Tomaso, is an Argentinean; he himself was a Le Mans competitor in 1958–59, winning the Index of Performance at the wheel of an Osca in the former year. Porsche had seven cars in the GTS category; 911s with varying engine capacities around the 2.4–2.5 litre mark. Finally, all Ferraris in the 1972 race were in this category; nine were the 4.4 litre 365 GTB/4 models, the odd man out a 2.4 litre Dino 246 GT.

The new Touring car class attracted only five entries; both of them from makes staging a come-back at Le Mans. The BMW 2800 CS, a coupé model with an engine just short of three litres, was the first car of this make to run at Le Mans since the remarkable performance of the 328s in 1939. By contrast, Ford had been absent only since 1969, although their 1972 cars were very far removed from the GT 40s: a team of four Capri RS models, with three-litre V6 engines.

The circuit had been considerably modified for 1972; a completely new section with several bends sweeping past the old White House corner and into a re-designed Ford chicane. Apart from being safer than the old White House corner, the new section was expected to be more interesting from the drivers' point of view and was named the 'technical' section. It also helped to slow the cars even more as they came into the pit area and past the grandstands. President Pompidou was given a complete tour round the circuit before the race, in a motorcade of Citroën SMs.

There was no doubt that Matra-Simca had come to Le Mans this year with every intention of winning. One of the three-litre Lolas briefly took the lead early in the race but after the first hour, it was one of the Matra 670s which led; either the Pescarolo/Graham Hill car, or that driven by Cevert/Ganley. The third 670, the Beltoise/Amon car was eliminated very quickly with piston failure; so the main battle of the race became the struggle for third place, behind the two leading Matras. The Lola briefly held onto third before falling farther down the field prior to eventual retirement; leaving the position open for the de Adamich/Vaccarella Alfa Romeo, but halfway through the race, the Matra 660 C driven by Jabouille/Hobbs came up from behind and overtook the Alfa. It was then a Matra 1–2–3, until the gearbox of the Jabouille/Hobbs car gave in with less than an hour to go. A possibly rather surprised crew (Joest/Weber/Casoni) of a Porsche 908 then found themselves placed third, ahead of the Alfa Romeo. But the two Matras leading the race were unassailable; Pescarolo and Hill drove to victory, at an average of 121.460 mph and a total distance of 2,915.059 miles. The Cevert/Ganley Matra followed, for a 1–2 victory; France's first since the Rosiers in the Talbot in 1950.

The Porsche 908 was third, and the Alfa Romeo Tipo 33 fourth; fifth was the first of the Ferrari 365 GTBs, winning the GT category and also the Index of Thermal Efficiency. Then another four Ferraris followed, before the first Ford Capri in tenth place which was the fastest Touring car. The Duckham-Ford, driven by Alain de Cadenet and Chris Craft, was best British car, in twelfth place; a total of 18 cars finished. One fatal accident marred this year's Le Mans; the Swedish driver Joachim Bonnier was killed, when his Lola T 280 left the circuit and crashed in the woods. Ironically, his co-driver Gijs van Lennep – the 1971 winner – had earlier set the lap record for the race at 134.472 mph.

With a new winner, and a well-deserved French victory, together with the most varied Le Mans field for many a year, it really did seem that the classic race had been sufficiently re-juvenated to celebrate its half-centenary in style.

LE MANS 1973

The fiftieth anniversary of the first 24-hour race at Le Mans was celebrated with, among other events, the first parade of historic Le Mans competitors: as yet without an actual historic race. The entry promised an interesting race, in the best traditions of Le Mans – a piece of 'living history' with renowned names such as Porsche, Ferrari, Alfa Romeo, BMW, and Ford apart from the previous year's winner Matra. The Alfa Romeo works team was regrettably withdrawn but the make was still represented by a private entry. Another bit of history in the making was the first Japanese car at Le Mans; but it is sad to note that the British entries, although not uncompetitive, were not, either in terms of number or of quality up to the standards previously achieved by British cars.

Ferrari, however, was back in the Le Mans business, with a team of three three-litre 312 models, competing in the sports car category primarily against the four Matra-Simcas. The third make with a winning chance was of course Porsche, their three-litre sports car entries were divided between three 908s, and two silhouette specials, looking like mutant 911s, Carrera RSRs with 2.8 litre engines and incorporating many parts from the 908 and 917 racers. A single Tipo 33, privately-entered, defended Alfa Romeo's honours; and the Franco-Italian Ligier-Maserati team was back with three cars. The remaining three-litre sports cars were all British, and all subscribed to the Ford-Cosworth school of thought: Lola, with two cars; a single Duckham-Ford; and finally, two cars on which the name Mirage re-appeared for the first time since 1967 – developed by

Hat-trick for Matra-Simca and Henri Pescarolo who together with Larrousse drove this Matra 670 to victory in 1974.

John Wyer, and sponsored by Gulf.

The two-litre Sports car class was not well supported, with just seven entries; including a Porsche 910, a 1.8 litre Lola-Ford, three Chevrons using similar Ford-based engines and a fourth car with a BMW two-litre engine; while the final two-litre entrant was a Japanese Sigma with two Japanese (and one French) driver. Its engine was a two-litre Mazda rotary.

Three makes entered the GTS category – Chevrolet Corvette, three cars; Porsche, nine cars – all the 911-derived 2.8 litre Carrera models but in Group 2 homologated form as opposed to the similar-looking hybrids in the Sports Car category; and finally, Ferrari, also with nine cars, all of the 4.4 litre 365 GTB/4 model. In the Touring category, only six cars were entered, three each of the makes BMW and Ford; the BMWs were 3.0 CSL coupés with 3.3 litre engines, while the Fords were three-litre Capris.

As it turned out, the race was a splendid and dramatic 24-hour battle between Matra and Ferrari; Porsche hardly got a look in, and the best of the British contingent, the Gulf-Mirage of Hailwood/Watson/Schuppan, was eliminated in an accident, after having been as high as third position. By contrast the Alfa Romeo was a more constant challenger until it dropped back in the field in the second half of the race, and eventually finished as low as fifteenth. Nor were the Ligiers in luck; one car was disqualified, one broke down and the sole survivor finished in nineteenth place.

The Matra–Ferrari battle began with the Merzario/Pace Ferrari 312 pulling into the lead from the start. After two hours, it was replaced by the Beltoise/Cevert Matra, which in turn was overtaken by the sister car of Depailler/Wollek. Theirs was a short-lived triumph; the car suffered from failing oil pressure and in the sixth hour of the race, a Ferrari – this time the Reutemann/Schenken car – was back in the lead. At half-time that had retired with engine trouble, and the Ferrari of Jacky Ickx and Redman took over. Then, finally, the Pescarolo/Larrousse Matra edged past; Ickx/Redman might have had a chance to regain the lead and ultimately victory, but the engine of their Ferrari gave up in the last hour of the race. Pescarolo repeated his 1972 win; he was followed home by the Merzario/Pace Ferrari, and in third place, the Matra of Jabouille/Jaussaud. The winning Matra's average was 125.670 mph, and the distance 3,016.095 miles.

The best Porsche was the experimental Carrera (Sports car category) which finished fourth, ahead of the first 908 in fifth place. Sixth, and winning the GT category, was again a Ferrari 365 GTB/4, while the Touring category went to a BMW 3.0 CSL in eleventh place. The Index of Thermal Efficiency went to Porsche, a GT category Carrera which was driven into eighth place. A total of 21 cars finished – a relatively high number; but although there were British drivers in the list, notably Vic Elford who shared the GT-winning Ferrari, there was not a single British car among the finishers.

LE MANS 1974

In the absence of important works teams such as Ferrari (who were developing a new three-litre sports prototype which could not be ready in time for Le Mans) and Alfa Romeo (who withdrew their flat-12 engined Tipo 33TT12s) Matra-Simca was the undoubted favourite in a reduced field of 49 starting cars. The Group 5 sports car prototypes accounted for the majority of entries – 25, of which 20 were in the three-litre class and five of less than two litres; this compared with 21 GT cars and a mere three Touring cars. Both BMW and Ford had stopped entering works teams in the Touring car category, and the few entries were privately made.

All the Matras were three-litre V12s; three 670 models, and a single example of the new 680 model. Their competition included two Ligier JS2s, the Maserati-engined cars; two Ferraris, both entered by the American N.A.R.T. team – an elderly (1969) 312 model, and a brand-new Dino 308, modified to Group 5 specification. Four British cars all used the DFV (Ford-Cosworth) F.1 engine: John Wyer's two cars were now plain Gulfs rather than Gulf-Mirages, while on the other hand the Duckham-Ford had shed its sponsor's name and was re-named De Cadenet after its chief protagonist. The British quartet was completed by a Lola-DFV. But the strongest challenge to the French cars probably came from Porsche; for the first time, the Martini racing team fielded a pair of turbocharged Carreras, with 2.1 litre engines. In addition, there was a three-litre Carrera hybrid which had been entered in 1973, and of less consequence, four privately-entered 908s.

The smaller sports cars included the Japanese Sigma-Mazda (2.3 litre rotary engine) and five two-litre cars: a Porsche 910, two Chevrons, and two cars with engines based on the Chrysler-Simca 180 – a Lola T292, and a French Grac-Gotti MT 20.

The GT category was well supported if lacking in variety: no less than 14 Porsche 911 Carreras, with 2.8 or three-litre engines, with the Ferrari 365 GTB Daytona being the next most popular model – five were entered. Finally, there were single examples of the seven-litre Chevrolet Corvette and the 5.7 litre De Tomaso Pantera. The Touring category contained two BMW CSLs, and one Ford Capri three-litre; a Mazda RX-3 failed to qualify.

Although the Gulfs had recorded good practice times which put them in third and fourth position on the starting grid – sandwiched between the four Matras – the Matras initially established a 1–2–3–4 lead. But when the 680 Matra of Beltoise/Jarier had an argument with a Porsche in the pit lane and dropped back down the field while repairs were being made, the Bell/Hailwood Gulf got into fourth position, followed by the two Porsche Turbos, and the De Cadenet. While the Pescarolo/Larrousse Matra remained in the lead, there were setbacks to other members of the Matra team: two cars retired before midnight with engine failures, including the luckless Beltoise/Jarier car.

The De Cadenet rear suspension broke on Sunday morning, with the car spinning dramatically in front of the pits; the end of the race for a promising contender. Meanwhile the van Lennep/Muller Porsche Turbo edged into second place; and then the most dramatic part of the race began, as first the leading Matra went into the pits with gearbox failure, and soon after, the Porsche lost all gears but third and fourth. While a hectic gearbox rebuild was being performed by Matra's mechanics, the Porsche slowly gained lap after lap; after a 47-minute pit stop, the Matra was back on the road, but had only four minutes in hand over the Porsche. It was enough, Pescarolo and Larrousse were able to extend their lead and won the race comfortably – Matra's, and Pescarolo's, third win in a row.

Their average was 119.266 mph, and the total distance 2,862.38 miles; the van Lennep/Muller Porsche Turbo was placed second, followed by the other surviving Matra, of Jabouille/Migault. A British car came fourth; the Bell/Hailwood Gulf-DFV, and in fifth place came the first GT car, winner of this category and of the Index of Thermal Efficiency, the Ferrari 365 GTB Daytona of Grandet/'Bardini'. The best touring car, the BMW CSL of Auriet/'Depnic', finished in fifteenth place; there were 21 finishers, but the Sigma-Mazda which was last home had not covered enough ground to qualify – it had spent four hours in the pits having its engine rebuilt. The fastest lap had been driven by Jarier, in the Matra 680 before this car was withdrawn, at 137 mph.

The 1974 race was remarkable for the hat-trick of Matra and Pescarolo; three victories at Le Mans is a fine achievement for any manufacturer or driver. It was not entirely unexpected that Matra-Simca decided to rest on their laurels after their successes of 1972–74; they were absent from the 1975 race and have not returned to Le Mans since, leaving the responsibility of defending France's honour to other contestants.

LE MANS 1975

By common consent, a perhaps less interesting Le Mans; the favourite description was 'The Economy Le Mans'. Perhaps the after-effects of the fuel crisis, and the talk about waste of fuel in motor sport, had got through to the Automobile Club de L'Ouest;

they decided to run Le Mans according to a fuel-consumption formula – a minimum number of 20 laps between re-fuelling, and limited size of fuel tanks; in consequence the minimum fuel consumption necessary to qualify was above 7 mpg. They were rewarded for their initiative by the C.S.I. withdrawing the world championship status of Le Mans – which in turn meant that the works teams of Matra, Alpine, Ferrari and Alfa Romeo three-litre prototypes all stayed away. Yet one wonders what the fuss was about as after all, every Le Mans race prior to 1960 had been run according to similar regulations restricting fuel consumption, and nobody complained then. Another historical parallel was the 1956 Le Mans race, run under safety-inspired restrictions after the 1955 disaster, as these restrictions also cost the race its championship status then.

Among the makes entered, Porsche was numerically in by far the strongest position; of 55 starting cars, no less than 24 were 911s or Carreras running in the GT categories. In addition there were other Porsches running in the Sports car prototype category; these were three elderly 908 three-litre cars entered by the German Joest-team which were the Porsches with the best chance of a high place among the finishing cars. Otherwise the three-litre class was dominated by the Ford-Cosworth DFV engine which was fitted to six important contenders: John Wyer's two Gulf-Fords (ex-Mirage); two Lolas, of which one was entered and driven by Alain de Cadenet; and two of the Gitane-sponsored Ligiers, while this French team's third car retained the Maserati engine used by Ligiers in previous years.

Among the two-litre prototypes, a V6-engined Alpine-Renault driven by Lombardi/Beaumont attracted attention as the fastest car in practice in this class and was the first Alpine-Renault at Le Mans since 1969; other entries included a Moynet-Simca, four Lolas with Simca-based engines, a BDA-engined Lola, a Tecma and a March-Cosworth. The Japanese Sigma had for the 1975 race forsaken the Mazda rotary engine in favour of a turbo-charged Toyota engine.

As mentioned the GT classes were completely dominated by Porsche Carreras, but there were two Ferrari Daytonas, a Chevrolet Corvette, a Datsun 240 Z and two De Tomaso Panteras. A Porsche Carrera Turbo was the only starter in a new category, the GTX class created for limited-production, non-homologated GT cars; it should have been kept company by three Ferraris entered by Luigi Chinetti and the American N.A.R.T. team but these were withdrawn at the last moment after an argument over qualifying times. The Touring car category was badly supported; an eye-catching BMW CSL decorated by artist Alexander Calder put in the fastest practice times, and a model not previously seen at Le Mans was a two-litre BMW 2002 saloon. Finally, a Ford Capri and a Mazda.

The Gulf driven by Schuppan/Jassaud went into the lead from the start but after the first pit-stops was overtaken by its team-mate driven by Jacky Ickx and Derek Bell. But the Gulfs retained a 1–2 lead, followed by the Joest Porsche 908; Chris Craft in the Lola he shared with de Cadenet; and the first Ligier-DFV, driven by the triple winner Henri Pescarolo together with Migault. Among the first cars to retire was the two-litre Alpine which ran out of fuel, and the artistic BMW coupé which had been favourite to win the Touring category. Then the Ligier-Maserati was destroyed in a collision with a Ferrari Daytona; fortunately without injury to either driver.

As the evening wore on, the Schuppan/Jaussaud Gulf was delayed with electrical trouble, and a peculiar accident delayed two of the most important entries: the rear bodywork of de Cadenet's Lola fell off without the driver realising what had happened, and Migault in the Ligier struck the debris at 150 mph. Both cars were delayed while repairs were made, and the damage eventually caused the retirement of the Ligier, while the Lola was able to finish the race, albeit in a lowly position. The Bell/Ickx Gulf was still leading, and by early Sunday morning the Schuppan/Jaussaud car was back in second place; only to slip down the field when its ignition was affected by a rainstorm. Nor was the leading Gulf free of problems; with less than two hours to go, it was in the pits with a cracked exhaust system. While a replacement was being fitted the surviving Ligier of Lafosse/Chasseuil steadily reduced the gap between the two cars – but the Gulf was back on the track with one lap in hand, and came home the winner. The average of Ickx and Bell was 118.98 mph and their distance 2,855.55 miles – virtually the same as the 1974 result. The Ligier was second, and the Schuppan/Jaussaud Gulf third, a 1–2–3 victory for the DFV engine. Fourth was the Joest Porsche 908, and this was followed by the GT winner, the first of many Porsche Carreras. The Craft/de Cadenet Lola was fifteenth; a remarkable 31 cars finished the race, with the Moynet-Simca first in the two-litre class, and the BMW 2002 took the Touring car honours.

For the first time since 1959, an all-British car had won at Le Mans – even if sponsored by an American multi-national company – and it was an outstanding triumph for John Wyer as it was his fourth win as entrant – Aston Martin in 1959, Ford GT 40 in 1968 and 1969, and now Gulf-DFV. The fastest lap was put in by another British entry: Chris Craft in the Lola, at 130.5 mph.

LE MANS 1976

Was Le Mans re-born in 1976? With a new set of categories the race was thrown open to a much wider variety of cars than before; the A.C.O. welcomed Group 6, Group 5 and Group 4 cars, together with some specially-invented categories like GT prototypes, and even Le Mans prototypes . . . and a special invitation was made to American entrants, so categories were reserved for I.M.S.A. (International Motor Sport Association) specification sports cars, and N.A.S.C.A.R. (National Association for Stock Car Auto Racing) stock cars, as part of a tie-in with the world's other 24-hour race, at Daytona.

It was also the year of the turbo-charger; while turbo-charged cars had been seen at Le Mans before, it was the first time that several of the leading Group 6 entrants had turbo-chargers. Such cars were subject to an equalisation formula; the capacity of a turbo-charged engine was multiplied by 1.4 for classification purposes. The engine of for instance the Alpine-Renault, of two-litres capacity, was thus deemed to be 2.8 litres. The equalisation factor was no new invention and in fact, the formula existed ready-made in the Le Mans rule-book as a hang-over from the heyday of the supercharger.

Porsche-Martini works entries were back; with two Group 6 2.1 litre turbos, the 936 Spyders driven by Jacky Ickx/Gijs van Lennep (both past winners) and Joest/Barth; in addition to a Group 5 2.9 litre 935 turbo, a Carrera-lookalike 'silhouette' car. A similar 935 turbo was privately entered, and there were two 908s: a 2.1 litre turbo, and a normally-aspirated three-litre. In the Group 4 GT category, there were no less than 20 Porsches, split between the 934 turbos and the 911 Carrera RSRs.

An economy Le Mans it may have been but the winning Gulf-Mirage of Jacky Ickx and Derek Bell did not look like an economy car (1975).

Apart from the Porsches, Group 6 included the two-litre V6 Alpine-Renault A442 which was seen at Le Mans for the second time, but now fitted with a turbo; it was driven by Jabouille/Tambay/Dolhem, and started in pole position, having put in the fastest practice lap. Among the DFV-supporters were the Gulfs which had come first and third in 1975, now under new American sponsorship and running as plain Mirage-Ford-DFVs; and a pair of Lolas, including the car of Chris Craft/Alain de Cadenet. Remaining Group 6 cars were all in the two-litre class, including three Chevrons, three Lolas, a Lenham and a Cheetah-BMW; apart from the last-mentioned, using either Simca or Ford-Cosworth engines.

The final categories were the special prototype classes which contained some particularly interesting cars. Running under the main sponsor's name Inaltera, two elegant coupés with three-litre Cosworth-DFV engines were the brainchildren of Le Mans-based constructor Jean Rondeau who himself drove one of the cars together with Jaussaud and Beckers, while the other was manned by past winner Pescarolo and Beltoise. Another new French contender was the WMP, with a 2.7 litre Peugeot V6 engine; the first Peugeot-engined car to appear since the Constantin of 1955. The lion of Sochaux is a reluctant racer; Peugeot's previous Le Mans entries were in 1926, 1937, 1938 apart from the Constantin's lacklustre career of 1952–55. Finally, there was a turbo-charged 2.4 litre Lancia Stratos, the first Lancia at Le Mans since 1951–53; and a Japanese newcomer, a French-entered Datsun 260 Z. But notably not a single Ferrari.

The Alpine-Renault went into the lead from the start, but was soon overtaken by the Ickx/van Lennep Porsche 936. They then stayed firmly in the lead; at one stage they were as much as 16 laps ahead of the number 2 car, although a half-hour pitstop on Sunday at midday to change a broken exhaust system cut this in half. But they were still unassailable, and cruised home to an easy victory; van Lennep's second, Ickx's third and Porsche's third. So most of the interest in the race was in the battle for second place; for two-thirds of the race, the other Martini-Porsche 936 of Joest/Barth had been lying second, but then went out with transmission failure. The Alpine-Renault had held on to third place for a while but had retired much earlier, soon after midnight, when a piston broke.

The two Mirage-Fords had been fairly regularly running in fourth and fifth places, and with the retirement of the two higher-placed cars, moved up; the Lafosse/Migault car held on to its advantage and eventually finished second, but the Bell/Schuppan Mirage had fuel pump troubles and dropped back to finish fifth, while Craft and de Cadenet in the Lola went past them into third place, followed by Stommelen and Schurti in the Group 5 Porsche in fourth place. A Porsche Carrera – the first Group 4 car to finish – was sixth. Both the Inalteras finished, the Pescarolo car eighth after a Porsche 908, the other in twenty-first place. The big disappointment of the race had been the American cars – the stock cars proved to be far too slow, and while the Greenwood Corvette showed a spirited performance, a puncture resulted in a holed fuel tank, and that was that. None of the American cars finished. The Datsun crashed through the barriers at the Mulsanne straight, and its driver, Andre Haller, was killed in the ensuing fire.

The average speed of Ickx and van Lennep had been 123.49 mph, for a total distance of 2,968.88 miles; while the fastest lap was recorded by Reinhold Joest, in the Porsche 936, at 134.076 mph. The first win of a turbo-charged car began the present era at Le Mans; though for van Lennep, this win also marked his retirement from racing. Jacky Ickx by contrast, had not quite finished with Le Mans.

LE MANS 1977

Alpine-Renault staged their first major attack on Le Mans, with three works-entered, and a fourth privately-entered but works-supported, cars; all were the two-litre V6 turbo model A442s, running in Group 6. Martini-Porsche countered with two 936 turbos in Group 6, supported by a 935 Group 5 car in addition to the four privately-entered 935s, of the Loos and Kremer teams. Other Group 6 entries included the two Mirages from the 1975 and 1976 races, but now re-vamped with Renault turbo engines. The DFV brigade included two Inalteras, now running in Group 6; a Lola; and a Lola-based but much-modified car entered by Alain de Cadenet under his own name.

Among the two-litre cars were three Chevrons, two with the ROC-Chrysler-Simca engines; two Lolas; and three cars with BMW-based engines, from Osella, Cheetah and Sauber. A BMW 320 saloon ran in Group 5. The various GT sports car categories, Group 4 and I.M.S.A., included two BMW 3.0 CSLs, a Ferrari Boxer entered by the N.A.R.T. team – after a year's absence by the Ferrari marque – and sundry Porsches, of the 934 turbo and Carrera models. The total number of Porsches in the race was 27. In the GT prototype class, there was a third Inaltera, two WM-Peugeots, a Lancia Stratos, an Alpine-Renault A.310, and Robin Hamilton's 5.3 litre Aston Martin V8 – the first Aston Martin at Le Mans since 1964.

The main battle was naturally expected to be between Renault and Porsche, with the possibility of a DFV-engined car joining the fray. Renault's number one car, driven by Jean-Pierre Jabouille and Derek Bell which had started from pole position, took the lead initially, with the Martini-Porsche 935 of Schurti/Stommelen acting as pursuit car in accordance with the works team's strategy. But the 935 soon fell back with various mechanical problems and eventually retired after three hours with a blown gasket. However, the 936 allocated to the old masters – the combination of two triple winners, Ickx and Pescarolo – moved into second place following the leading Alpine; the other 936, driven by Barth/Haywood was third, and then came the remaining two works Alpine-Renaults.

The Barth/Haywood Porsche pitted to have its fuel pump changed, and when it re-joined the race had dropped well down the field; that left effectively only one of the Martini team cars in the running, the Ickx/Pescarolo 936. Pescarolo briefly challenged Jabouille for the lead; but apparently, he over-revved the Porsche's engine, and the car was withdrawn after less than three hours. The Alpine-Renault works cars were now in a 1–2–3 lead, followed by a Porsche 935, the two Mirage-Renaults and the first Inaltera. Was it going to be an Alpine walkover? It certainly seemed that the odds against a Porsche victory were staggering.

But then a quick decision was taken in the Martini-Porsche camp. The Barth/Haywood 936 was called in, and Jacky Ickx put behind the wheel. This was in accordance with the regulations that three drivers per car were permitted, and the same driver might drive two cars in the same team. At the time, the 936 was lying fifteenth, but in Ickx's hands it moved inexorably up the scoreboard – according to one report, Ickx flew, and in the course of a magnificent drive not unnaturally put in the fastest lap of the race, at 141 mph. Shortly after midnight, the Porsche 936 went into fourth place, just behind the leading trio of Alpine-Renaults.

During the hours between midnight and dawn, the Porsche team played a waiting game; soon rewarded as within the space of three hours, first the Jaussaud/Tambay Alpine retired with a blown up

Anglo-French alliance or Renault's second team: the Mirages with Renault V-6 engines, 1977 race.

engine, and then the Depailler/Lafitte car went into the pits for a gearbox repair; when it got back on the track, the Ickx/Barth/Haywood Porsche was in front. Then at 9 am, the leading Jabouille/Bell Alpine expired with piston failure, and the Porsche went into the lead; the Depailler/Lafitte Alpine might still have challenged, but with four hours to go, the last Alpine-Renault engine went the way of its team-mates' engines. From then on there was nothing to touch the Porsche; after what seemed a miracle, the tables were completely turned on the Alpines, and Ickx's fourth Le Mans win seemed a reality.

But the drama of the race was not over; with less than an hour to go, the Porsche came into its pit in a cloud of smoke. A piston had broken; however, as there was no time to undertake an engine rebuild, it was decided to stay in the pit until 3.50 pm, and then Jurgen Barth eased the car round two final laps of the circuit, to take the flag as winner at 4 pm. Ickx, Barth and Haywood were winners, at an average speed of 120.95 mph, and a total distance of 2,902.81 miles.

While the Alpine-Renault team had suffered a total defeat, at least the Mirage-Renault of Schuppan/Jarier finished second; third, and winner of the Group 5 class, was the Ballot-Lena and Gregg Porsche 935. The local hero Jean Rondeau, together with Ragnotti, brought his Inaltera-DFV home in fourth place as first French car; followed by Chris Craft and Alain de Cadenet in the De Cadenet-Lola in fifth place. Sixth was a Chevron-ROC which won the two-litre Group 6 class, and seventh the highest-placed Group 4 car, a Porsche 934. Then came a BMW 3.0 CSL, as winner of the I.M.S.A. category. Among the remaining finishers were the other two Inalteras, the Ferrari Boxer in fifteenth place, and Robin Hamilton's Aston Martin in sixteenth place after a completely reliable run. A total of 21 cars finished, although the two-litre Lola last home did not classify.

1977 was one of the most exciting and dramatic Le Mans races in modern times; the victory of Jacky Ickx was hugely popular, despite the French disappointment with their national cars. At 32, Ickx with four Le Mans wins had reached a level previously only attained by his fellow Belgian Oliver Gendebien who had won Le Mans in 1958, 1960, 1961 and 1962. The major point of interest over the next few years before every Le Mans race would be, will Ickx make it his fifth victory?

LE MANS 1978

Sometimes Le Mans history seems to repeat itself, and there were many similarities between the 1977 and 1978 races. Once again, the major battle would be between the two big works teams – Porsche and Renault. Even if Le Mans was still without championship status, the A.C.O.'s 24-hour race once again asserted its pre-eminence in the world of endurance racing, in terms of its entry record, and the publicity it attracted.

Alpine-Renault first tried for an overall victory at Le Mans in 1968–69, with a three-litre V8-engined car, which was just not fast enough. They came back in 1975 with a two-litre V6, which then was fitted with a turbo-charger, blossoming out as the A442 and now the A443. Four of these cars in various models were entered; of these, the Jaussaud/Pironi car ran with a high almost all-enveloping windscreen known as the bubble top which proved in practice to be worth another 10 mph down the Mulsanne straight. The Alpine-Renaults all ran on Michelin radial tyres.

Against the Alpine-Renault team, the other main contender was the Martini-Porsche team which had three 936 Spyders – one of

Renault's moment came at last in 1978. The winning car of Pironi and Jaussaud in the pit.

A car that has achieved virtual dominance over Le Mans in recent years – the Porsche family of 911 look-alikes. This is a Carrera RSR, the Kremer/Koob/Huber car in Porsche's annus mirabilis of 1971: 33 of 49 starting cars were of the Stuttgart make, and all category wins fell to Porsche in addition to 1st and 2nd places.

Before the fall: The Renault-Alpines for the 1977 race, the Depailler/Lafitte car (8) in front of the Jaussaud/Tambay car (7) with the car of Jabouille/Bell (9) half-hidden on the right. All three blew their engines.

By 1976 the rolling start was standard practice. The pace car has just pulled in and the race is under way. No. 19, in pole position, was the Jabouille/Tambay Renault-Alpine which was an early retirement; next to it, the ultimate winner, no. 20: The Porsche 936 of Ickx and van Lennep.

The Ickx/Pescarolo 936 in 1977. This car retired but Ickx found himself another drive sharing the Barth/Haywood sister car which went on to win.

After six years of disappointment, Matra scored their first victory in 1972 – this was the winning car driven by Pescarolo and Graham Hill.

Take the bodywork off a modern Le Mans car and the similarities to a Grand Prix racing car become obvious. A two-litre Group 6 Lola photographed during a pit stop in the 1979 race.

Porsche drivers do it in the wet. Two 935's raise a cascade of spray in the rain-sodden 1980 race.
Inset: Rondeau, Jaussaud and Moet on the balcony after the Rondeau's historic win, 1980.

AUTOMOBILE
AUTOMOBILE

The business end of a Porsche 935 K.3 – the Wood/Cooper/Bourgoignie car which finished 4th in 1981, winning Group 5.

Jules, Jacky and Derek: The Porsche 936 of 1981 winners, Jacky Ickx and Derek Bell.

For the record Jules is an aftershave and Derek Bell is driving.

which was driven by Jacky Ickx and Pescarolo – with a supporting 935 in Group 5. Apart from the Renaults and Porsches, the other Group 6 cars consisted of a new Lola for Alain de Cadenet and Christ Craft, and de Cadenet's old car in the hands of Faure, Philips and Beasley; a third British contender, also using the Cosworth-DFV engine, was the Ibec-Hesketh-Ford with a Postlethwayte-designed chassis and driven by Grob, Edwards and Bracey. Finally, the two Mirage-Renaults which had been seen in 1977.

The majority of the two-litre Group 6 cars were British-made if not necessarily British-entered; there were no less than seven Lolas, of the 294, 296 and 297 types; four Chevrons, with Chrysler-Simca or Ford engines; and finally, one each of Cheetah, Osella-BMW and Sauler-BMW. By contrast both Group 5 and Group 4 were entirely Porsche-dominated; Group 5 was made up of eight Porsche 935s, including the Martini-Porsche entry, while Group 4 consisted of four Porsche 934s and three Carrera RSRs.

The GT prototype class held one Inaltera, together with Jean Rondeau's newest design which also used a Cosworth-DFV engine but which ran under the constructor's own name; in addition there were three WM-Peugeots, with their 2.7 litre turbo-charged V6 engines – one was a new car and the other two had been seen at Le Mans in previous years. Finally the I.M.S.A.-category held five Ferrari 512 BB Boxers, two Porsche 935s, a single Porsche Carrera and the only American car in the race, a Chevrolet Monza. If Porsche still dominated the field with 21 cars, there was at least a lot of variety among the other 34 cars.

Apart from the 24-hour race itself there was a half-hour race on Saturday morning for historic Le Mans cars; won by Stirling Moss in a not-quite-appropriate Maserati 250 F single-seater Grand Prix racing car entered by JCB, with Willie Green and Martin Morris coming second and third, both in D-type Jaguars. After ten entries at Le Mans in the period 1951–61, with the best results two second placings, Moss had the satisfaction of winning a race at Le Mans, after 16 years in retirement.

Although Ickx had set the fastest lap time in practice and started from pole position the race began badly for Porsche; within a few laps two of the 936s were in the pits, Ickx's own car and the Haywood/Gregg car. So the Alpine-Renault of Pironi/Jaussaud went

The 1978 winners, Pironi and Jaussaud, in the traditional balcony scene – the champagne spraying is obviously over.

into the lead, followed by the Jarier/Bell sister car, while the Barth/Wollek Porsche 936 held on to third place followed by the remaining two Renaults. For most of the early part of the race, Alpine-Renault had a 1–2–3 lead with the Barth/Wollek Porsche in fourth place. Then the Ickx/Pescarolo Porsche went into its pit again with a serious gearbox problem; and in a repeat of the 1977 race, the Martini-Porsche team leader decided to put his best driver into the highest-placed Porsche. Ickx joined Barth and Wollek, and with his assistance, that car had gone into second place by midnight, after the Jabouille/Depailler Alpine-Renault which was now race leader. Soon after, the Jarier/Bell Renault had to be withdrawn with a broken differential.

On Sunday morning, the Ickx/Wollek/Barth Porsche lost its fifth gear as had the original Ickx/Pescarolo car the previous evening but it took little more than half an hour to rebuild the gearbox. Similarly, the Pescarolo car had had its gearbox rebuilt and had rejoined the race with Jochen Mass co-driving; but he crashed the car on Sunday morning. Then disaster overtook the Renault team when the Jabouille/Depailler car blew its engine after twelve hours as race-leader; however, the Pironi/Jassaud car which had gained second place while the Porsche gearbox was being rebuilt, now moved back into the lead. And although the Ickx Porsche was able to reduce the leader's margin in the final hours of the race, Jaussaud and Pironi drove home to Renault's first victory in the 24-hour race. Their distance was 3,134.51 miles at an average of 130.6 mph. The fastest lap in the race was driven by Jean-Pierre Jabouille in the other Alpine-Renault, at 142.44 mph.

Second and third places were taken by the Porsche 936s, of Ickx/Barth/Wollek and Haywood/Gregg/Joest, while the only other surviving Alpine came fourth. The next four places were filled by Porsche 935s, of which the Redman/Barbour car in fifth place won the I.M.S.A. category and the Busby/Cord/Knoop car in sixth place was the first Group 5 car home. Ninth place, and victory in the GTP category, went to the Rondeau. The first two-litre car was a Chevron-Chrysler-Simca in eleventh place, followed by a Porsche Carrera in twelfth place which won the Group 4 category. Of the British contingent, the de Cadenet/Craft Lola succeeded in finishing in fifteenth place after a host of problems, while the Ibec-Hesketh blew its engine on Sunday morning. A total of 25 cars finished but only 17 classified under the minimum distance rules.

So Renault had achieved their ambition; winning the most prestigious French race. Immediately after the race, Renault's managing

The Mirage-Renault no. 10 also finished tenth in the 1978 race, driven by Jacques Lafitte and Vern Schuppan.

director Bernard Hanon made known that the team was retiring from sports car endurance racing, in order to concentrate on Grand Prix racing. Porsche, having suffered defeat at the hands of an arch-rival, went home and began thinking about next year's Le Mans.

LE MANS 1979

In the absence of the Alpine-Renaults or indeed any other works-supported Group 6 team, Porsche was the undoubted favourite; their two 936 cars were entered in co-operation with Essex Motorsport. Additionally, the two 935s entered by the German Kremer organisation were supported by the Porsche company; one of these was a very special K3 type with 'ground-effect' aerodynamic bodywork, driven by the German Klaus Ludwig and the American Whittington brothers. The 936s were in the hands of experienced Le Mans veterans, no one more so than Jacky Ickx who shared one car with Brian Redman, while an international complement of drivers crewed the other car – Wollek, Haywood and Barth.

This year, all of the other Group 6 entrants favoured the Cosworth-DFV engine; there were three Lolas entered by various equipes; Alain de Cadenet's own car which he shared with a new co-driver, Francois Migault; three examples of the Le Mans-built Rondeau M379s; the two Mirages which had shed their Renault engines and returned to Cosworth-DFV power getting sponsorship from the French Ford company and therefore racing as Ford M-10s. Finally, two Japanese cars, Dome-Zeros, with four British drivers – Craft/Spice and Evans/Trimmer. An Anglo-German entry which despite the use of a 3.5 -litre turbo-charged engine had been given special dispensation by F.I.S.A. to run as a Group 6 car was an exciting lightweight BMW M.1, prepared by March engineering for Guy Edwards; but it failed to qualify, proving disappointingly slow in practice.

The two-litre cars were as usual a mixed bunch of five Chevrons, six Lolas, two Cheetahs and a Toj, using either Chrysler-Simca, Ford or BMW engines. Group 5 numbered nine cars – all Porsche 935s – and Group 4 consisted of five Porsche 934s. The I.M.S.A. category held another five Porsche 935s, four Ferrari Boxers and a BMW M.1 which did make it into the race; driven by Winkelhock/Poulain/Mignot and painted by Andy Warhol. It was however *not* sponsored by Campbell's Soups. Apart from this the I.M.S.A. car getting most media attention was a Porsche 935 entered by Dick Barbour, and driven by himself together with Stommelen and 53-year old Hollywood star Paul Newman. Finally, the GT prototype category held four cars – three WM-Peugeots, and the turbo-charged Aston Martin V8 of Robin Hamilton which had first come to Le Mans in 1977. Among the non-qualifying entrants had been a Mazda RX-7 rotary-engined coupé which the Mazda company had entered in the I.M.S.A. category, and a SAAB turbo entry in the GT prototype category failed to materialise.

As there was going to be the election for the European Parliament on Sunday 10 June, the time of the race was brought forward two hours to allow the French time to vote after the finish of the race at 2 pm Sunday afternoon. The circuit had been slightly shortened and was now 8.47 miles long; the alteration was a newly-laid out Tertre Rouge corner, leading into the Mulsanne straight.

Porsches filled the first four positions on the grid: the two 936s, followed by the 935s of Ludwig/Whittington and Schurti/Heyer. Then came the Schuppan/Jaussaud Mirage-Ford, a Rondeau, another Porsche 935, the Bell/Hobbs Mirage-Ford, a second Rondeau and the De Cadenet. The race sorted itself out soon after the start, the two Porsche 936s took the lead with the Mirage-Fords in third and fourth places. But none of the favourites were to last out the race. The first car to hit trouble was the Ickx/Redman Porsche 936; a tyre blew out, and there was considerable damage to bodywork and one of the radiators. The car got going again after a pit stop of 80 minutes but was later stranded on the circuit, and was disqualified when Ickx accepted outside assistance. The Wollek/Haywood/Barth 936 similarly had to spend a long time in the pit in the early stages of the race; although it got going again and at one stage had re-captured second place, it had to retire with further engine problems.

After the initial Porsche troubles set in the Bell/Hobbs Mirage-Ford took the lead while the Schuppan/Jaussaud car had the gearbox break. But the Bell/Hobbs car also ran into trouble and had to have its exhaust system replaced; and after a quarter of the race had been run, the Group 5 Porsche 935 of Ludwig/Whittington went into the lead, followed by the similar car of Schurti/Heyer. At one stage, there were five Porsche 935s leading the first Group 6 car. This set the pattern for the rest of the race; with the fastest Group 6 cars either out of the race, or seriously delayed, the Porsche 935s retained their grip on the race. Then Sunday morning brought a spell of wet weather with it; as so often before, rain was the great equaliser at Le Mans, effectively reducing the advantages of the fastest cars.

The Ludwig/Whittington Porsche 935 led for most of the rest of the race and came home a comfortable winner, albeit at the slowest speed for a Le Mans winner since 1958, 108.10 mph for a distance of 2,590.928 miles. They were followed by an I.M.S.A. Porsche 935, the Barbour/Newman/Stommelen car – and naturally, the fact that Paul Newman came second in his first Le Mans was the biggest Le Mans story for years; *Motor*'s headline 'The Day the Winner Came Second' spoke for itself. But with a third 935 in third place, and a Group 4 934 in fourth place, the 1979 Le Mans was a notable triumph for Porsche; their fifth win elevating the Stuttgart sports car manufacturer to the same level as Bentley and Jaguar in the Le Mans history.

In this year of debacle for the Group 6 cars, the best-placed Group 6 car was the Rondeau which came fifth, followed by the BMW M.1, another three Porsches and a second Rondeau. A total of 22 cars finished. Of the British entries, the De Cadenet had been forced to abandon within the first hour of the race with gearbox failure, and the Aston Martin broke its engine in a big way, after suffering loss of oil pressure. Two British cars were first and second among the two-litres, and one of the DFV-engined Lolas also survived, to finish in twentieth place. The lesson learned from the 1979 Le Mans race was that once again, endurance had proved more important than speed.

LE MANS 1980

The chief innovation for the 48th 24-hour race was a much revised set of regulations, drafted by the A.C.O. to encourage efficiency and reliability rather than speed. While there was not a return to the old fuel consumption restrictions as such, the maximum tank capacity was fixed at 120 litres (approx. 26 gallons) for all cars and the rate of delivery from the pumps installed at the pits was reduced to 50 litres per minute, so the length of the average pit stop was increased from 40 seconds to two and a half minutes. It is interesting to note that the *least* time spent in the pit by a car in the 1980 race was 45 minutes in contrast to the record ten minutes that the Macklin/Thompson Aston Martin DB 2 spent at its pit during the 1952 race. Then there was a ban on the replacement of major components (engine, gearbox etc) from the start of official practice to the end of the race which put a stop to the practice of using one engine for qualifying and another for the race itself, and also to those lightning engine changes that team mechanics had entertained pit-watchers with in the 1970s.

Another new regulation shortened the official practice period to two hours, and cars had to qualify on the basis of the average lap times recorded by all named drivers; if more than two drivers, the third could be dropped to improve the average speed to enable a car to qualify. One driver eliminated because of this rule was Desire Wilson who had an accident while practising in Alain de Cadenet's car; she was unhurt and the car was rebuilt for the race but the A.C.O. officially recorded a lap time which was more than twice what the team thought it should be. After this and similar episodes the atmosphere was somewhat strained in the British camp, and some teams were talking in terms of suing the A.C.O. because of the discrepancies in officially and unofficially recorded lap times, which led to a number of British teams not qualifying.

Again, there was noticeably little direct works involvement at Le Mans in 1980; only two factory teams appeared, Porsche and Lancia, and neither company fielded Group 6 cars. Porsche ran a team of three 924 Carrera turbos (in itself a major milestone: for the first time a front-engined water-cooled Porsche at Le Mans!) in the GT prototype category while Lancia concentrated efforts on Group 5 which held the world championship status – three mid-engined Beta Monte Carlo coupés, with turbo-charged 1.4 litre Fiat-based engines. Apart from the unsuccessful Stratos entry in 1976–77, this was the first Lancia entry at Le Mans since 1953.

The number of cars entered in Group 6 was reduced, with six cars over two litres and eight in the two-litre class. Heading the list was a single Porsche, a specially-built 908/936 cross-breed sponsored by Martini Racing, and entered for Reinhold Joest to drive together with Jacky Ickx who had let himself be tempted out of 'retirement' by the prospect of winning a fifth Le Mans. All the other big Group 6 cars used the Cosworth-DFV engine – two Rondeaus, the De Cadenet, a Swiss ACR based on the Lola T380 and a much-improved Japanese Dome with British drivers Craft and Evans.

In the two-litre class there were four Lolas and two Chevrons with various engines, an Osella-BMW entered by March engineering and co-driven by Mark Thatcher, and a Toj-BMW. Group 5 held seven Porsche 935s apart from the Lancias; Group 4 four Porsche 934s and a Porsche 911 SC which ran on ethanol. The GTP category had the Porsche 924s, three WM-Peugeots and an extra Rondeau. A Grand Touring Production (GTX) category was revived for the benefit of a single BMW M.1 entry although another three examples of this model ran in the I.M.S.A. category together with the modified March-BMW M.1, eight Porsche 935s, a rotary-engined Mazda RX-7 and five Ferrari 512 BB Boxers. Among those who did not get a race was a sixth Ferrari Boxer which had a holed cylinder block and had to withdraw under the rule forbidding engine replacements after the practice session. Also a second De Cadenet entered by Nick Faure, Ian Bracey's Ibec-Cosworth and a Janspeed Triumph TR7-V8 turbo which had been entered in Group 5 with the enthusiastic co-sponsorship of the TR Register. This would have been the first Triumph at Le Mans since 1965, so the failure of this car to qualify was a particularly intensely felt disappointment.

The Pescarolo/Ragnotti Group 6 Rondeau started from pole position just as a thunderstorm passed over the circuit – this was to be another wet Le Mans and many competitors suffered from misfires, damp ignition systems and similar maladies. A Porsche 935 soon went into the lead, with a challenge coming from an unexpected quarter – a BMW M.1 driven in spirited fashion by Hans Stick until he was involved in a slight collision and had to stop for repairs to bodywork. The Ickx/Joest Porsche was gaining and got briefly ahead in the early evening before stopping on the circuit with a broken fuel injection pump belt; a contingency for which the team had been prepared so Ickx was able to continue after fitting the spare carried in the car. With the delay the car had gone right down the scoreboard, but once under way again Ickx did not tarry, putting in some very quick laps including the fastest lap of the race at 138.30 mph, and before the first half of the race was over the Porsche was leading again, now followed by the Rondeau of Jaussaud/Rondeau, a Porsche 935 and the Martin/Martin/Spice Rondeau GTP car – the Pescarolo/Ragnotti Group 6 Rondeau had retired with engine failure.

Sunday morning dawned with more rain, and a further mishap for the Porsche 936 which lost its fifth gear – a recurring Porsche problem in past races – losing half an hour in the pit which permitted the Rondeau to go into the lead. The French car was to retain this position. There was some further drama when quick showers washed over the circuit in the afternoon; both the leading Rondeau and the Ickx/Joest Porsche spun and fetched up against the Armco barriers though neither car suffered much damage and both were able to continue. While many teams made hurried tyre changes, the Rondeau stayed on slicks and was rewarded when the sun came out drying the circuit in the last half hour of the race. The Rondeau won and Jean Rondeau became the first constructor to win Le Mans in a car bearing his own name, while his co-driver Jaussaud could celebrate his second victory in a French car. Their average speed was 119.30 mph and the total distance 2,863 miles.

The Ickx/Joest Porsche followed, while the Martin/Martin/Spice Rondeau was third and winner of the GTP category. Fourth was a WM-Peugeot and next came the first I.M.S.A. car, a Porsche 935, with one of the works Porsche 924s in sixth place and the De Cadenet seventh. This was the first British car to finish. A total of 25 cars finished, including two BMW M.1s but only one of the Lancias. Also among the finishers were the Ethanol Porsche, the Mazda RX-7 and the Dome which was last car home after having spent four hours in the pit.

An outstanding memory from this Le Mans was the live television coverage, broadcast via a helicopter link from a camera mounted in the WM-Peugeot which finished in fourth place. The colour pictures were shown in the press-box and also projected on a huge screen in the 'Village'. Suddenly everybody could experience the thrill of driving down the Mulsanne straight at 190 mph in the rain.

LE MANS 1981

Works Porsches were back in Group 6, with a pair of 936s; there was a notable return of a Porsche 917 built by Kremer Racing as a replica of a ten-year old car in a British museum; the hoped-for return of Ford to endurance racing was frustrated as the new C.100 with its claimed 250 mph top speed could not be ready in time; and there was universal relief when the A.C.O. gave way over the complicated qualifying rules and decided to accept the 55 fastest cars, on the basis of the fastest time achieved irrespective of individual drivers' times and without worrying about fixed quotas for individual categories. These, and Ickx's entry together with Derek Bell in one of the works Porsches, were the highlights of Le Mans previews in 1981.

The Group 6 entry was headed by the two Porsche 936s with 2.6 litre turbo-charged engines based on Porsche's abortive Indianapolis project and four-speed gearboxes which it was hoped would be more robust than the previously troublesome five-speed boxes. Then there was the 917 and for good measure a Porsche 908 as well. Against these were ranged assorted cars with Cosworth engines, some of which used the new 3.3 litre DFL engine. There were three Rondeaus, a Lola, a Lola-based ACR, two De Cadenets, a Dome-Zero and an Ibec. The two-litre class attracted precisely four cars, three Lola-BMWs and a Renard-Delmas-Simca.

In Group 5 there were six Porsche 935 turbos, four BMW M.1s and four Lancia Beta Montecarlo turbos. Group 4 held another two BMW M.1s, a Porsche 934 and a Porsche 924 Carrera. A particularly interesting new car in the GT prototype category was a Porsche 944 turbo, with Porsche's own 2.5 litre engine which was then still on the secret list. Other GTP entries included two Rondeaus in addition to their two Group 6 cars, while WM-Peugeot's entries were also divided in two categories: two GTP cars, and two in the new Group C category which was effectively a preview of the 1982 Le Mans regulations. Finally the American-style I.M.S.A. category was as usually well supported with 13 cars. Four Porsche 935s and five Ferrari Boxers were what you would expect but they were kept company by a Porsche 924, a Chevrolet Cameo and two Mazda 253s based on the RX-7 with 320 bhp 2.6 litre rotary engines. These cars were entered by Tom Walkinshaw racing.

Porsche had come back with a vengeance. The grid was headed by the two 936s with the Ickx/Bell car in pole position; the 908 was third, then came the two Group 6 Rondeaus followed by two Porsche 935s. The start was at 3 pm – as had happened before to allow sufficient voting time in the following day's election. Ickx and Joest in the Porsche 936 and the Porsche 908 respectively went into a 1–2 lead while the other 936 in the hands of Jochen Mass went almost straight into the pit with a misfire which was eventually traced to a faulty plug. After the first pit stops the 908 took the lead but in the third hour was overtaken by a Porsche 935. Both of these cars were to retire soon afterwards while the Ickx/Bell Porsche 936 went into the lead in the fourth hour of the race – a lead it was never to relinquish. The sister car of Mass/Schuppan/Haywood kept pace and for a long time was in second place only to drop back in the second half of the race when it was delayed for an hour while a new clutch was fitted. The car eventually finished thirteenth, and Haywood put in the fastest lap of the race at 142.47 mph.

With the second Porsche 936 dropping back the two Rondeau three-litre cars which for a long time had been shadowing the leaders moved into second and third places. The margin of the Ickx/Bell 936 was so great that little short of wholesale mechanical disaster there was no hope for any other car to snatch victory; and this year the Porsche 936 behaved faultlessly, without any of the niggling mechanical problems that had proved Ickx's undoing in the previous three years. When Jacky Ickx and Derek Bell finished the race as winners, the crowd was delighted – the Belgian driver became the first driver to win at Le Mans five times and went straight into the record books. For his British co-driver it was a second win – Bell had shared Ickx's victory in the Gulf-Mirage-Ford in 1975. And for Porsche it was a notable sixth win – the German make now had the second greatest number of Le Mans wins, after Ferrari's nine. The winners' average was 124.9 mph and the total distance 2,998 miles.

The two GTP Rondeaus followed in second and third places with the number two car winning the GTP category. A Porsche 935 was placed fourth and won Group 5. A fifth place, and a win in the I.M.S.A. category, was achieved by a Ferrari Boxer and was this

The 1981 winner – Porsche 936 of Jacky Ickx and Derek Bell.

marque's best showing at Le Mans for a number of years. A further Porsche 935 followed and the works Porsche 944 was seventh, with a Lancia Montecarlo in eighth place. Although there was a British driver in the winning car the best British car was Guy Edwards's Lola T600 with a 3.3 litre Cosworth-DFL engine which finished sixteenth. The best Group 4 car was a Porsche 934 in eighteenth place and the two-litre class was won by a Lola which came nineteenth. The total number of finishers was 21, but this did not include either of the De Cadenets, nor the Ibec.

Two tragedies marred the 1981 Le Mans. After an hour's racing the Belgian driver Boutsen lost control of his WM-Peugeot near the end of the Mulsanne straight when he was travelling at around 220 mph. The car hit the barrier and disintegrated partially; while Boutsen was unhurt, three marshals were hit by debris and one died from his injuries. An hour later, just after 5 pm about a mile further back from the Mulsanne straight the other accident happened to the Rondeau of Jean-Louis Lafosse which went out of control while accelerating. The car first hit the barrier on the right and then rebounded across the road into the barrier on the left; the second impact virtually broke the car in two and Lafosse was killed.

Le Mans 1981; the 49th race possessed many of the qualities of a classic Le Mans race but with the prospect of the new Group C regulations and increased works support, many commentators preferred to look forward to the 50th race in 1982.

The Porsche 956Ts finished first, second and third driven by Jacky Ickx/Derek Bell, Jochen Mass/Vern Schuppan and Hurley Haywood/Al Holbert/Jurgen Barth.

6. 1982 THE YEAR OF REVIVAL

Much was expected of the 1982 Le Mans race but not all expectations were to be fulfilled. The new classification and the Group C regulations had attracted much interest – the hoped-for factory entries had materialised – and the accent was on fuel consumption as the regulations restricted maximum tank capacity to 100 litres and the maximum number of fuel stops permitted during the race was 25. So even if there was no limit on engine capacity in Group C, the fuel consumption restriction would effectively keep down speed in the interests of economy.

Le Mans was open to the Group C cars, and also to the new production sports car category Group B – in the event there was only a single Group B entry, a Porsche 930 which failed to qualify for the race. But 1982 was an interim year, and the old categories were still permitted entry, including Groups 4 and 5 with their American equivalents, I.M.S.A. GT and I.M.S.A. GTX, and also Group 6 but only for cars of less than two litres' capacity. As the Group C regulations stated that the name of the engine manufacturer must be quoted before the name of the chassis constructor, the official entry list seemed to contain a lot of Fords; for Ford read Cosworth. But make no mistake about it, this was the year when Ford returned to Le Mans in their own right, with the promise of a Ford-Porsche duel as spectacular as the Ferrari-Ford-Porsche battles of the late 1960s.

Of 59 entries, 29 were in Group C, 11 in the I.M.S.A. GTX class, seven in Group 5, six in the I.M.S.A. GT class, four were two-litre cars in Group 6 and there was one entry each in Group B and Group 4. By the usual process of exclusion based on practice times this was brought down to the maximum permitted number of 55 starting cars; the unlucky ones were the Group B Porsche, a BMW M1 from Group 5, a BMW-engined R.D. two-litre in Group 6 and finally, the American-entered Ford-Cosworth engined Group C Mirage which was driven by the father and son team of Mario and Michael Andretti. This was not disqualified because it was too slow in practice – as it had returned the ninth best time; but with more than a touch of the sort of scandal that Le Mans is famous for, it was disqualified literally on the starting line because the gearbox oil cooler was mounted behind, rather than above the gearbox, thereby infringing one of the rules in the book. Some frantic re-designing took place in the paddock but the organisers had already allowed first reserve car to start instead. A modified and now legal Mirage was wheeled into the pit lane an hour after the start of the race, only to be parked in front of the marshals' box where it sat forlornly for some time while team manager Harley Cluxton lodged an unsuccessful protest.

So of the 55 cars on the grid, 28 were Group C cars. Porsche had three of their new 956s, with monocoque bodywork and twin-turbo flat-six engines similar to the 'Indianapolis' engines of the previous year's 936s. There was also a single Porsche 936, modified so it conformed to Group C regulations and entered by Team Belga and Joest Racing whereas the three 956s were works entries by Porsche System, with Rothman as the main sponsor. These four cars were given start numbers 1 to 4 and three of them occupied the first three places on the grid – the 956s of Jacky Ickx/Derek Bell and Jochen Mass/Vern Schuppan, together with the Martin/Wollek/Martin 936, while the Haywood/Holbert/Barth 956 was further down the line.

No less than 16 cars in Group C relied on Ford-Cosworth power, with the newer DFL engine in 3.3 and 3.9 litre forms far outnumbering the old three-litre DFV. Ford's own pair of C.100s, entered by Ford and run by the German tuning firm Zakspeed, and driven by Surer/Ludwig and Winkelhock/Niedzwiedz, obviously caught the public fancy more than most other cars in the race. The French Rondeau marque defended its home territory with no less than six cars of which three were Otis-sponsored works entries, drivers apart from Jean Rondeau himself including French aces such as Pescarolo, Jaussaud, Migault and Ragnotti but also British driver Gordon Spice. In addition there were two Saubers from Germany, a Cougar from France and five British cars all with Ford engines: two Lola T610s, the De Cadenet-Lola, the Grid-Plaza and the Japanese-sponsored Dome-Amada.

The remaining Group C entries used a wide variety of engines. The two WM-Peugeots were Le Mans regulars with their turbocharged 2.8 litre PRV-Peugeot V-6 engines but were in the running with a better chance than before, thanks to their straight line speed; besides, the Esso-sponsored cars were among the prettiest on the track. A U.R.D. had a 3.5 litre BMW straight six engine while the German Kremer company continued their association with Porsche by entering their own Group C car fitted with a Porsche engine. The biggest engines at Le Mans were the 5.8 litre Chevrolet V-8s fitted to the two March cars; although the Nimrods did not give them much away, with Aston Martin V-8s of 5,340 cc.

Nimrod's begetter Robin Hamilton normally runs an Aston Martin dealership in Burton-on-Trent but is no stranger to Le Mans, having run a specially prepared Ason Martin V-8 in the 24-hour race in 1977 and 1979. His desire to enter – and possibly win – Le Mans with a competitive, all-British car led to the formation of Nimrod Racing Automobiles in 1979, when Eric Broadley began the design of a chassis which would comply with the forthcoming Group C regulations and was to be fitted with the Aston Martin engine. The Aston Martin company supported the venture wholeheartedly, particularly after the enthusiastic and patriotic Victor Gauntlett of Pace Petroleum became Aston Martin Lagonda's chairman.

The Nimrod was first unveiled to the public at the end of 1981, attracting much attention from Fleet Street and other mass-media, while many motor racing insiders watched with no little scepticism – after all, the Nimrod was big and heavy and many wondered if the Aston engine really could develop enough power to make the car competitive in endurance racing, let alone down the Mulsanne straight. Nimrod's racing debut came in May 1982 in the Silverstone Six Hour Race; of two cars entered one retired but the other finished a creditable sixth. Two cars were again entered for Le Mans – the works car in silver and British racing green, driven by Geoff Lees, Bob Evans and Tiff Needell, and Viscount Downe's car sponsored by Pace Petroleum in the Pace colours of white, red and blue, driven by Simon Philips, Ray Mallock and Mike Salmon. The Pace-entered car was faster in practice and was twenty-third on the grid, the works car twenty-sixth.

Apart from the Group C cars, the other entry reckoned to be in the race with a chance of winning were the two Lancia-Martini Group 6 cars with 1.4 litre Fiat-Abarth turbo-charged engines – just scraping in under the two-litre limit with the current 1.4 equalisation factor for turbo engines. The team came fresh from wins at Silverstone and Nürburgring, where the low weight, nimbleness and good fuel economy of the Lancia had paid off, especially on a sicrcuit like Silverstone which is scarcely fast enough for a big-engined Group C car to flex its muscles. The Lancias were among the few open cars in the race – as

The WM Peugeot of Raulet/Pignard/Theys.

was the only other Group 6 entry, a Ford-Cosworth Chevron B36B.

Group 5 held six cars – three Porsche 935s, a BMW M1 and two Lancia Beta Monte Carlos with engines similar to the Group 6 Lancias but bodywork like Lancia's most recent homologation special rally car, with an ungainly high-lipped rainwater-retaining rear spoiler. The closely related I.M.S.A. GTX class was better supported, with four Porsche 935s, another BMW M1, four Ferrari Boxers for the traditionalists and two Mazda 254s – silhouette racers based on the RX-7 road cars, with 2.7 litre rotary engines. In a spirit of Anglo-Japanese co-operation, they were entered by Tom Walkinshaw Racing and Mazdaspeed, with sponsorship by Nikon.

The relatively tamest cars in the race were those entered in the I.M.S.A. GT class, together with the single Group 4 car, a British-entered Porsche 934. The I.M.S.A. GT cars were three Porsche 924 GTRs, with turbo-charged versions of the road-going 924's four cylinder two-litre engine; one of these had been the first reserve car, the Canon Camera-sponsored, GTI Engineering-entered car driven by Richard Lloyd and Andy Rouse which had been permitted to start after the disqualification of the Andretti Mirage. The team was given rather less than ten minutes' notice that they were in the race and started from the pit lane rather than the grid itself. There was also a BMW M1 in the GT class, and finally a a pair of Chevrolet Camaros entered by an American team. These had the distinction of being perhaps the noisiest cars in the race – no mean feat! – with a parti-

Ford Rondeau M382 driven by Jaussand.

cularly earth-shaking rumble.

There were two practice sessions in the days before the race, on Wednesday and Thursday evenings; the second session was cut short by a brilliant thunderstorm whereupon the heavens opened. The weather on the Friday before the race was characterised by intermittent heavy showers; there had not been a wet Le Mans since 1979 but it began to look as if this was a distinct possibility. However, Saturday dawned dry, if windy and cloudy; the weather remained like this for the rest of the day, while Sunday turned out to be sunny and pleasantly warm.

The practice sessions put the Ickx/Bell Porsche in pole position, followed by two others of the same make, while the little Lancias confounded the sceptics by running them a close fourth and fifth, ahead of the fastest Ford C.100. A mixed bunch of Group C cars followed – Sauber, Kremer, the Mirage which was subsequently disqualified and Guy Edwards' Lola which was timed at 220 mph through the speed-trap on the Mulsanne straight; only 1 mph slower than Ickx in the Porsche who was fastest of all. The second Ford was in eleventh position; followed by the two WM-Peugeots, the remaining Porsche 956, another Sauber, the first of the Rondeaus, the Grid-Plaza, the second Lola and then in nineteenth position, the first Group 5 car – a Porsche 935. Practice was interrupted by a spectacular accident in which German driver Harald Grohs suffered a blown-out tyre on his Porsche 935, doing 190 mph down Mulsanne; the car rolled and upon coming to rest caught fire. Amazingly, Grohs escaped unharmed – as the door was torn off the Porsche he was able to make a quick exit. In direct contrast to the strict rules of 1980 when engine changes from the start of the practice sessions to the end of the race were not permitted, such changes were by now commonplace, with even a few well-documented examples of cars qualifying on bigger engines than eventually used in the race – exploiting an interesting loophole in the Group C unlimited capacity regulations.

In addition to the Wednesday and Thursday practice sessions there was a 45-minute warming-up session Saturday morning, prior to the parades which precede the 24-hour race and help to pass the time for the spectators who have croweded into the grandstand and other public enclosures since 8 am Saturday morning. As 1982 was the fiftieth race the pre-race parade had a special historical content; not an historic race such as had been seen in earlier years but a dignified cavalcade of past Le Mans winners, from the Chenard et Walcker which won the first 24-hour race in 1923 to the Porsche which won in 1981. Bentleys and Jaguars featured strongly, with Victor Gauntlett enjoying life at the wheel of a Bentley Speed Six, but there were also examples of Alfa Romeo, Lagonda, Talbot, Aston Martin, Ferrari and Ford GT 40 – the latter disgraced itself and had to return on a lorry. As 1982 by coincidence saw not only the fiftieth Le Mans 24-hour race but also the fiftieth Monte Carlo Rally, there were also representatives of Monte Carlo Rally winners past and present in the cavalcade. These historic cars then went on display near the motor museum which is situated in the 'Village' behind the paddock area. A few modern cars such as the official Mercedes-Benz pace cars and examples of the new Bentley Mulsanne Turbo also took part in the pre-race parade.

The last hours before the start are spent in arranging the cars on the grid, and at six minutes to four the 55 cars start on the pace lap following the official car of the clerk of the course. At 4 pm exactly the pace car re-crosses the starting line and pulls in, and the race is under way.

The pattern which so often emerges at Le Mans is that the first few hours become almost a sprint race – a mad dash which provides a lot of the excitement in the race, for drivers and spectators alike. Perhaps there is an impish streak in even the most professional and mature driver which makes him put his foot down and join the fray – like a schoolboy who rushes off the moment the bell goes at the end of a tedious lesson. However, some teams may coolly calculate and plan to send one car off as hare to the hounds, deliberately baiting other drivers who may then run out of fuel or blow their engines in the pursuit. Or other teams may, pessimistically, consider that they have little chance of getting through the twenty-four hours anyway, and decide to have their fun – and give the sponsor his money's worth – by playing to the gallery for as long as they are in the race. It is during these hours between 4 pm and sunset that lap records are broken, and broken yet again; that the highest speeds are registered at Mulsanne; but it is also the time when the dangers of the race are greatest, with the majority of the cars still on the circuit, often moving at widely disparate speeds.

The Porsches had started the race at the head of the field and this was obviously where they intended to stay. Their main competitors were Rondeau and Ford, both launching determined challenges to Porsche's leadership but only succeeding in getting past temporarily whenever the Porsches stopped for fuel. The Porsche turbo engines turned out to be rather thirstier than the Ford-Cosworths, but with the aid of a computer in the pit, and flow meters with digital displays in the cars, the Porsche team had elevated the calculation of fuel consumption to the state of a fine art. The other possible contenders, the Lancia 'Spiders', were dogged by a variety of electrical and mechanical problems – a succession of pit stops soon dropped them to the back of the field. The first retirement came within half an hour when the Grid-Plaza went out with piston failure, while the Dome and one of the Lolas both spent a very long time in the pits soon after the start.

As the afternoon turned into evening, the fastest lap of the race was put in by Jean Rondeau in the car bearing his own name – at 140.527 mph he failed to beat the 1981 lap record which is the record for the current circuit. Meanwhile a number of further retirements had taken place – many of the new Group C cars suffered mechanical breakdowns, while others had calculated their fuel consumption incorrectly or had simply driven with too heavy feet. Several retirements were due to cars running out of fuel on the track.

At 7.30 pm, hopes of an outstanding British performance were partly dashed when the works Nimrod crashed at Mulsanne, after having been driven from twenty-sixth into ninth position. It was believed to have been a slow puncture which developed into a blow-out which caused the accident; the Nimrod began wagging its tail so furiously that Tiff Needell finally lost control and the car went backwards into the Armco, at a speed approaching 200 mph. Tiff was unhurt but the car was extensively damaged. After this, the most spectacular accident of the race, Nimrod's and Britain's hopes rested with the Pace Petroleum car.

With France on continental summer time but Le Mans nearly on the same longitude as London, Le Mans effectively enjoys double summer time and it is light until almost 11 pm, but as darkness finally descended, some cars were in trouble with electrical faults. Ironic that electrical gremlins should still strike after 50 versions of a 24-hour race which was originally arranged ostensibly to promote improvements to electrical systems and lighting. One car which had to retire with electrical faults was the Surer/Ludwig Ford C.100. Then within the hour, the sister car of Winkelhock/Niedzwiedz stopped on the track with engine failure. Before midnight, both Fords had retired, and one major challenge to Porsche supremacy had vanished. Meanwhile the Rondeaus were not faring much better; the three works cars had all retired by half-time, as had one of the privately-entered cars of this make.

After the retirements of the Fords and Rondeaus it must be admitted that some of the interest went out of the race as it seemed there was very little left by the way of competition for the Porsche team which was still intact. Ickx and Bell were leading, followed by Mass and Schuppan, with Martin/Wollek/Martin in the 936 in third place while the Haywood/Holbert/Barth 956 was fifth. In fourth place was the surviving Nimrod which despite its lack of straight line speed had steadily gained place by place on the lap chart due to its impressive regularity and reliability. But the rate of attrition meant that after the first twelve hours there were only 31 cars left in the race. Other retirements by this time included one of the Lancia-Martinis, and both the WM-Peugeots.

The Nimrod held on to its fourth place for some hours early on

Sunday morning but with minor problems developing (brake discs, fuel pressure and finally oil consumption) it dropped back down the scoreboard, while fourth place was taken by a Ferrari Boxer, and several Porsche 935s were coming steadily up from behind – as if ready to pounce should the leaders fail. At one stage the Haywood/Holbert/Barth Porsche dropped as low as ninth place after a door had blown off and a wheel bearing failed, but the car got under way again and had soon re-joined its team mates among the leaders. The Porsche team now showed their mastery of organisation by deliberately keeping speeds as low down as possible, staying ahead of any potential threat by a sufficient margin but not running the cars any faster than they had to. The performance of the team was in a way reminiscent of the Mercedes-Benz and Auto-Union Grand Prix teams of 45 years before, such was the effortless mastery with which Porsche by now held the race in their grasp – though it would be wrong to assume that their control of the situation relied on disciplinary measures in the tradition of Rennleiter Neubauer, instead Porsche's performance must be ascribed to the utter professionalism with which they go racing. But in Derek Bell's quoted remark, 'It's just not very exciting is it?', perhaps one can detect a hint of regret.

Porsche again. The 935 K3T of Verney/Garretson/Ratcliff.

It very nearly did get exciting though when Jacky Ickx had a puncture mid-morning but fortunately it happened at the Virage Ford immediately before the pits so he was able to drive straight home, instead of having to nurse the car round the entire circuit. And in the final two hours of the race, the Porsche works team went into formation establishing a 1–2–3 lead, in numerical order of starting numbers – with car number 4 in fourth place. As a demonstration of their supremacy it was effective, and Le Mans has not seen anything like it since the Ford 1–2–3 victory in 1966 but it was perhaps just a little bit naughty of Porsche. In fact with an hour to go the first six places were occupied by Porsches, and there were reasons for hoping that Stuttgart might equal Modena's all-time record from 1963 when the first six cars home were Ferraris. Alas, this achievement eluded the German make – within the last hour the Martin/Wollek/Martin Porsche 936 C blew its engine.

But the three works-entered 956s crossed the line in 1–2–3 formation – or rather would have done so had not the crowds invaded the track as 4 pm approached on Sunday afternoon, when the marshals and the police finally abandon their twenty-four hour vigilance and permit themselves to be swept aside before the torrent of enthusiastic spectators. This is something which happens at Le Mans every year but in 1982 it was perhaps a bit sooner than in the past and it is doubtful how many cars did in fact cross the actual finishing line! Ickx and Bell repeated their victories of 1981, and 1975, and Ickx's position in the record books became even more impregnable with six wins altogether; while for Porsche, it was their seventh victory. The winning distance was 3,044.140 miles at an average of 126.839 miles – not of course anywhere near the 1971 records but with the exception of 1978 the fastest Le Mans of recent years. Jochen Mass and Vern Schuppan followed in second place, with Haywood, Holbert and Barth in third place. Fitzpatrick and Hobbs in a Porsche 935 were fourth and won the GTX class, while a similar car was fifth; so it was sixth place before another make featured – a Ferrari Boxer.

The Nimrod Aston Martin was seventh despite its troubles in the later stages of the race – to the delight of Victor Gauntlett (who immediately announced his intention to come back to Le Mans in 1983, 'God and cheque book willing') as well as the thousands of British spectators. The Nimrod also gained the award traditionally

The winning Porsche 956T of Ickx/Bell.

presented by *Motor* magazine to the best-placed British car. Cooper/Smith/Bourgognie's Group 5-winning Porsche 935 followed, another Ferrari Boxer was ninth and the highest-placed of the surviving Rondeaus tenth. A Porsche 935 was eleventh, and a Lancia Monte Carlo twelfth, while the single Group 4 car, the Porsche 934 of Cleare, Dron and Jones finished thirteenth and automatically won its class. It was followed by one of the Mazdas, the second surviving Rondeau and in sixteenth place, the GT-class winning Porsche 924 GTR of Busby and Bundy. The two last cars home were a Chevrolet Camaro and a BMW M1 – the other Chevrolet Camaro finished but had been going so slowly, with a race average of little more than 50 mph, that it did not classify.

Apart from filling the first five places, Porsche therefore won every single class or category, equalling their achievement in 1970 and 1971. The Porsche team was the only Group C team to finish intact – only three other Group C cars did finish, the Nimrod and two Rondeaus, a fact not lost on commentators. This was perhaps to be expected, in the first year of a new formula with new and untried designs throughout; yet the Porsche 956 was as new as the rest, and it was remarkable that the vast majority of Ford-Cosworth engined cars should fall by the wayside. It is perhaps in the final analysis difficult to pinpoint any individual reason for Porsche's win in the 1982 race; though one is tempted to mention the fact that the competition was just not good enough, this is unfair to Porsche which would have stood an equally good chance of winning against much stronger opposition. The speed and reliability of the 956, coupled with the efficiency of the team organisation and the race planning, and the rare ability and experience of drivers such as Ickx and Bell – these factors all played their part.

Looking forward to a 1983 Le Mans which will be exclusively for Group C and Group B cars one speculates that this will be a Porsche-versus-the-rest-race, with a number of constructors out to get their own back. One interesting suggestion, prompted by the presence at the 1982 Le Mans race of an official party from Jaguar Cars Limited, was whether this company would contemplate a return to Le Mans – after all if 5.3 litres of Aston Martin V-8 can put up a good show why should not the same size of Jaguar V-12 be able to emulate this performance? A good straight-forward Aston-Jaguar duel has not been seen at Le Mans since 1960; were this to happen again it would undoubtedly more than any other single event at a Le Mans race capture the popular imagination not only in Britain but throughout the world. Meanwhile the outlook for Group C seems bright; even if the fuel consumption restrictions tend to limit speeds compared to the carefree days of the pre-1974 period, the new formula has so far done much to rekindle interest in sports car endurance racing in general, and Le Mans in particular. With a year to sort out the bugs, the 1983 race should see some very competitive entries, from many different makes of many different nationalities. And that is after all what Le Mans is all about.

RESULTS

The following tables are not a complete list of results but list the most important results of each race, as follows: first three cars finishing; all class and category wins; subsidiary awards, such as Biennial Cup and Index wins. The tables are in nine columns as follows:

Column 1:
Overall placing.
Colum 2:
Make and nationality of car; nationalities: B Belgium, CS Czechoslovakia, D Germany, F France, GB Great Britain, I Italy, US U.S.A.
Column 3:
Number of cylinders; where appropriate arrangement of engine if other than in-line as follows: F Flat (horizontally opposed), V V, t/s two-stroke.
Column 4:
Capacity of engine in cc.
Column 5:
Names of drivers; quotation marks indicate pseudonym.
Column 6:
Distance covered, in miles.
Column 7:
Average speed, in miles per hour.
Column 8:
Class-winners only: indicates which capacity class won. Note changes in capacity class structure in 1960. NB: Not listed from 1975 onwards.

Column 9:
Category wins – particularly important from 1975 onwards – and subsidiary awards. Abbreviations used: Bi-cup, Biennial Cup; Tri-cup, Triennial Cup; Ind. Perf, Index of Performance; Index T.E., Index of Thermal Efficiency. Categories: 1959: Sport-prototype and Grand Tourisme; 1960–61: Sports Cars and Grand Tourisme; 1962: Experimental Cars and Grand Tourisme (with subsidiary category for under-2,000 cc GT); 1963–65: as 1962 but Prototypes replace Experimental Cars; 1966: as 1963–65 but with added Sports Car category; 1967: as 1966 but under-2,000 cc GT deleted, and under-1,300 cc Sports Car category added; 1968–71: Sports Car, Sports Prototype and Grand Tourisme – last category is called GT Special 1970–71; 1972–74: Group 5 sports cars, Group 4 GT special, Group 2 special touring; 1975: Group 6 sports-prototypes (with subsidiary two-litre class), and GTX – experimental GT cars – in addition to 1972–74 categories; 1976–81: Group 6, Group 5 and Group 4 as in 1975, GTX now unhomologated production GT cars, new class for GTP – Le Mans prototypes, and categories for I.M.S.A and N.A.S.C.A.R cars. Group 2 category deleted. N.A.S.C.A.R category only in 1976. 1981: Group C cars first admitted.
Note: There have not been entrants, or finishers, in all categories and classes every year.

All results listed in the Appendix have as far as possible been checked against official Automobile Club de l'Ouest figures and have been converted from kilometres to miles using 1.60935 kilometres equals 1 mile.

1	2	3	4	5	6	7	8	9
1st race—1923, 26–27 May. Circuit: 10.726 miles								
33 cars starting, 30 cars finishing. Fastest lap: Clement (Bentley), 66.690 mph								
1	Chenard et Walcker (F)	6 cyl	2,978 cc	A. Lagache/R. Leonard	1,372.937	57.206	3,000 cc	
2	Chenard et Walcker (F)	6 cyl	2,978 cc	R. Bachmann/C. Dauvergne	1,330.033	55.418		
3	Bignan (F)	4 cyl	1,979 cc	de Tornaco/P. Gros	1,287.130	53.629	2,000 cc	
6	Excelsior (B)	6 cyl	5,343 cc	A. Dills/N. Caerels	1,201.320	50.055	8,000 cc	
8	La Lorraine (F)	6 cyl	3,445 cc	G. de Courcelles/A. Rossignol	1,158.416	48.267	5,000 cc	
10	Bugatti (F)	4 cyl	1,495 cc	M. de Pourtales/S. de la Rochefoucauld	1,115.511	46.480	1,500 cc	
12	Salmson (F)	4 cyl	1,086 cc	L. Desvaux/G. Casse	1,051.155	43.798	1,100 cc	
2nd race—1924, 14–15 June. Circuit: 10.726 miles.								
40 cars starting, 14 cars finishing. Fastest lap: Lagache (Chenard et Walcker), 69.076 mph								
1	Bentley (GB)	4 cyl	2,995 cc	J. Duff/F. C. Clement	1,290.794	53.783	3,000 cc	
2	La Lorraine (F)	6 cyl	3,446 cc	H. Stoffel/E. Brisson	1,280.896	53,371	5,000 cc	
3	La Lorraine (F)	6 cyl	3,446 cc	G. de Courcelles/A. Rossignol	1,276.981	53.207		
4	Chenard et Walcker (F)	4 cyl	1,973 cc	Pisard/Chavée	1,191,829	49.659	2,000 cc	
11	Aries (F)	4 cyl	1,085 cc	F. Gabriel/H. Lapierre	979.706	40.821	1,100 cc	

3rd race—1925, 20–21 June. Circuit: 10.726 miles.
49 cars starting, 16 cars finishing. Fastest lap: Lagache (Chenard et Walcker), 70.206 mph

1	La Lorraine (F)	6 cyl	3,473 cc	G. de Courcelles/A. Rossignol	1,388.127	57.838	5,000 cc	
2	Sunbeam (GB)	6 cyl	2,942 cc	J. Chassagne/S. C. H. Davis	1,343.151	55,964	3,000 cc	
3	La Lorraine (F)	6 cyl	3,473 cc	Stalter/E. Brisson	1,335.621	55.650		
7	Rolland-Pilain (F)	4 cyl	1,997 cc	J. de Marguenat/L. Sire	1,255.360	52.306	2,000 cc	
8	Corre La Licorne (F)	4 cyl	1,493 cc	L. Balart/R. Doutrebente	1,185.680	49.403	1,500 cc	
10	Chenard et Walcker (F)	4 cyl	1,095 cc	R. Glaszmann/M. de Zuniga	1,169.572	48.723	1,100 cc	1st Bi-cup
13	Chenard et Walcker (F)	4 cyl	1,095 cc	R. Sénéchal/Loqueheux	1,126.691	46.945		Tri-cup

4th race—1926, 12–13 June. Circuit: 10.726 miles.
41 cars starting, 13 cars finishing. Fastest lap: de Courcelles (La Lorraine), 71.112 mph

1	La Lorraine (F)	6 cyl	3,446 cc	R. Bloch/A. Rossignol	1,585.991	66.083	5,000 cc	
2	La Lorraine (F)	6 cyl	3,446 cc	G. de Courcelles/M. Mongin	1,574.258	65.592		
3	La Lorraine (F)	6 cyl	3,446 cc	Stalter/E. Brisson	1,493.409	62.225		
4	O.M. (I)	6 cyl	1,990 cc	N. Minoia/G. Foresti	1,446.303	59.827	2,000 cc	2nd Bi-cup & Ind. Perf.
9	Salmson (F)	4 cyl	1,094 cc	G. Casse/A. Rousseau	1,189.810	49.575	1,100 cc	
10	Corre La Licorne (F)	4 cyl	1,425 cc	J. Errecalde/A. Galoisy	1,173.491	48.895	1,500 cc	

5th race—1927, 18–19 June. Circuit: 10.726 miles.
22 cars starting, 7 cars finishing. Fastest lap: Clement (Bentley), 73.409 mph

1	Bentley (GB)	4 cyl	2,989 cc	J. D. Benjafield/S. C. H. Davis	1,472.524	61.354	3,000 cc	
2	Salmson (F)	4 cyl	1,094 cc	A. de Victor/J. Hasley	1,255.165	52.280	1,100 cc	
3	Salmson (F)	4 cyl	1,094 cc	G. Casse/A. Rousseau	1,244.088	51.836		3rd Bi-cup & Ind. Perf.
4	S.C.A.P. (F)	4 cyl	1,493 cc	L. Desvaux/F. Vallon	1,190.053	49.585	1,500 cc	

6th race—1928, 16–17 June. Circuit: 10.726 miles.
33 cars starting, 17 cars finishing. Fastest lap: H. R. S. Birkin (Bentley), 79.289 mph

1	Bentley (GB)	4 cyl	4,392 cc	W. Barnato/B. Rubin	1,658.603	69,108	5,000 cc	
2	Stutz (US)	8 cyl	4,888 cc	E. Brisson/R. Bloch	1,650.725	68.780		
3	Chrysler (US)	6 cyl	4,076 cc	H. Stoffel/A. Rossignol	1,549.603	64.560		
6	Alvis (GB)	4 cyl	1,482 cc	C. M. Harvey/H. W. Purdy	1,420.687	59.195	1,500 cc	
7	B.N.C. (F)	4 cyl	1,099 cc	M. Doré/J. Truenet	1,410.548	58.773	1,100 cc	
8	Itala (I)	6 cyl	1,991 cc	R. Benoist/C. Dauvergne	1,403.157	58.465	2,000 cc	
10	Salmson (F)	4 cyl	1,095 cc	G. Casse/A. Rousseau	1,372.258	57.177		4th Bi-cup & Ind. Perf.

7th race—1929, 15–16 June. Circuit: 10.153 miles.
25 cars starting, 10 cars finishing. Fastest lap: H. R. S. Birkin (Bentley), 82.984 mph

1	Bentley (GB)	6 cyl	6,597 cc	W. Barnato/H. R. S. Birkin	1,767.067	73.627	8,000 cc	5th Bi-cup & Ind. Perf.
2	Bentley (GB)	4 cyl	4,398 cc	J. Dunfee/G. Kidston	1,695.951	70.665	5,000 cc	
3	Bentley (GB)	4 cyl	4,398 cc	J. D. Benjafield/A. d'Erlanger	1,614.544	67.273		
8	Lea-Francis (GB)	4 cyl	1,495 cc	K. S. Peacock/S. H. Newsome	1,380.644	57.526	1,500 cc	
9	Tracta (F)	4 cyl	985 cc	L. Balart/L. Debeugny	1,299.678	54.153	1,100 cc	

8th race—1930, 21–22 June. Circuit: 10.153 miles.
17 cars starting, 9 cars finishing. Fastest lap: H. R. S. Birkin (Bentley), 89.696 mph

1	Bentley (GB)	6 cyl	6,597 cc	W. Barnato/G. Kidston	1,821.023	75.876	8,000 cc	6th Bi-cup
2	Bentley (GB)	6 cyl	6,597 cc	F. C. Clement/R. Watney	1,760.017	73.727		
3	Talbot (GB)	6 cyl	2,276 cc	B. Lewis/H. S. Eaton	1,647.856	68.661	3,000 cc	Ind. Perf.
5	Alfa Romeo (I)	6 cyl	1,752 cc	Lord Howe/L. C. Callingham	1,620.319	67.513	2,000 cc	
6	Lea-Francis (GB)	4 cyl	1,496 cc	K. S. Peacock/S. H. Newsome	1,424.107	58.716	1,500 cc	
8	Tracta (F)	4 cyl	986 cc	J. A. Gregoire/F. Vallon	1,306.664	54.444	1,100 cc	

9th race—1931, 13–14 June. Circuit: 10.153 miles.
26 cars starting, 6 cars finishing. Fastest lap: B. Ivanowski (Mercedes-Benz), 86.515 mph

1	Alfa Romeo (I)	8 cyl	2,337 cc	Lord Howe/H. R. S. Birkin	1,875.076	78.128	3,000 cc	7th Bi-cup & Ind. Perf.
2	Mercedes Benz (D)	6 cyl	7,100 cc	B. Ivanowski/H. Stoffel	1,805.163	75.215	8,000 cc	
3	Talbot (GB)	6 cyl	2,970 cc	T. E. Rose-Richards/A. C. Saunders-Davies	1,763.071	73.461		
5	Aston Martin (GB)	4 cyl	1,496 cc	W. Cook/J. Bezzant	1,420.693	59.195	1,500 cc	
6	Caban (F)	4 cyl	1,100 cc	J. E. Vernet/F. Vallon	1,300.019	54.167	1,100 cc	

10th race—1932, 18–19 June. Circuit: 8.383 miles.
26 cars starting, 9 cars finishing. Fastest lap: N. Minoia (Alfa Romeo), 88.506 mph

1	Alfa Romeo (I)	8 cyl	2,337 cc	R. Sommer/L. Chinetti	1,835.547	76.481	3,000 cc	Ind. Perf.
2	Alfa Romeo (I)	8 cyl	2,337 cc	F. Cortese/G. B. Guidotti	1,818.919	75.788		
3	Talbot (GB)	6 cyl	2,970 cc	B. Lewis/T. E. Rose-Richards	1,517.138	63.214		
4	Alfa Romeo (I)	6 cyl	1,746 cc	Mme. Siko/J. Sabipa	1,502.218	62.592	2,000 cc	
5	Aston Martin (GB)	4 cyl	1,495 cc	S. H. Newsome/H. Widengren	1,459.497	60.812	1,500 cc	
7	Aston Martin (GB)	4 cyl	1,495 cc	A. C. Bertelli/L. P. Driscoll	1,409.319	58.094		8th Bi-cup
8	Amilcar (F)	4 cyl	1,089 cc	C. A. Martin/A. Bodoignet	1,269.504	52.896	1,100 cc	

11th race—1933, 17–18 June. Circuit: 8.383 miles.
29 cars starting, 13 cars finishing. Fastest lap: R. Sommer (Alfa Romeo), 90.959 mph

1	Alfa Romeo (I)	8 cyl	2,336 cc	R. Sommer/T. Nuvolari	1,953.607	81.400	3,000 cc	9th Bi-cup
2	Alfa Romeo (I)	8 cyl	2,336 cc	L. Chinetti/P. Varent	1,953.358	81.389		
3	Alfa Romeo (I)	8 cyl	2,336 cc	B. Lewis/T. E. Rose-Richards	1,891.059	78.809		
4	Riley (GB)	4 cyl	1,091 cc	A. W. K. van der Becke/K. S. Peacock	1,604.077	66.836	1,100 cc	Ind. Perf.
5	Aston Martin (GB)	4 cyl	1,495 cc	L. P. Driscoll/S. C. Penn-Hughes	1,583.677	65.986	1,500 cc	
6	MG (GB)	4 cyl	745 cc	J. L. Ford/M. H. Baumer	1,482.208	61.756	750 cc	
8	Alfa Romeo (I)	6 cyl	1,742 cc	A. Rousseau/F. Paco	1,404.726	58.271	2,000 cc	

12th race—1934, 16–17 June. Circuit: 8.383 miles.
44 cars starting, 23 cars finishing. Fastest lap: P. Etancelin (Alfa Romeo), 88.506 mph

1	Alfa Romeo (I)	8 cyl	2,336 cc	L. Chinetti/P. Etancelin	1,793.853	74.744	3,000 cc	
2	Riley (GB)	6 cyl	1,458 cc	J. Sebilleau/G. Delaroche	1,681.078	70.078	1,500 cc	
3	Riley (GB)	6 cyl	1,458 cc	F. W. Dixon/V. Paul	1,670.336	69,597		
4	MG (GB)	6 cyl	1,087 cc	C. E. C. Martin/R. Eccles	1,655.967	68.998	1,100 cc	
5	Riley (GB)	4 cyl	1,087 cc	A. W. K. van der Becke/K. S. Peacock	1,640.845	68.368		10th Bi-cup & Ind. Perf.

13th race—1937, 15–16 June. Circuit: 8.383 miles.
58 cars starting, 28 cars finishing. Fastest lap: Lord Howe (Alfa Romeo), 86.751 mph

1	Lagonda (GB)	6 cyl	4,451 cc	F. S. Hindmarsh/L. Fontès	1,868.330	77.847	5,000 cc	
2	Alfa Romeo (I)	8 cyl	2,331 cc	P. L. Dreyfus('Heldé')/H. Stoffel	1,863.055	77.627	3,000 cc	
3	Aston Martin (GB)	4 cyl	1,494 cc	C. E. C. Martin/C. Brackenbury	1,805.434	75.226	1,500 cc	11th Bi-cup & Ind. Perf.
6	Alfa Romeo (I)	6 cyl	1,774 cc	J. Desvignes/G. Don	1,717.350	71.553	2,000 cc	
9	MG (GB)	6 cyl	1,083 cc	C. Druck/P. Maillard-Brune	1,699.029	70.896	1,100 cc	
27	Austin (GB)	4 cyl	749 cc	J. Barbour/J. Carr	1,189.111	49.546	750 cc	

1936: Race cancelled

14th race—1937, 19–20 June. Circuit: 8.383 miles.
48 cars starting, 17 cars finishing. Fastest lap: J-P Wimille (Bugatti), 96.423 mph

1	Bugatti (F)	8 cyl	3,266 cc	J-P Wimille/R. Benoist	2,043.022	85.126	5,000 cc	Ind. Perf.
2	Delahaye (F)	6 cyl	3,580 cc	J. Paul/M. Mongin	1,979.335	82.472		
3	Delahaye (F)	6 cyl	3,580 cc	R. Dreyfus/H. Stoffel	1,942.044	80.918		
4	Delage (F)	6 cyl	2,984 cc	J. de Valence/L. Gerard	1,806.686	75.278	3,000 cc	

5	Aston Martin (GB)	4 cyl	1,493 cc	J. M. Skeffington/R. C. Murton-Neale	1,720.375	71.682	1,500 cc	
6	Adler (D)	4 cyl	1,679 cc	Graf Orssich/R. Sauerwein	1,719.262	71.636	2,000 cc	
11	Aston Martin (GB)	4 cyl	1,942 cc	M. H. Morris-Goodall/R. P. Hitchens	1,624.186	67.674		12th Bi-cup
12	Simca (F)	4 cyl	996 cc	J. E. Vernet/Mme. Largeot	1,434.682	59.778	1,100 cc	
17	Simca (F)	4 cyl	569 cc	J. Viale/A. Alin	1,222.878	50.953	750 cc	

15th race—1938, 18–19 June. Circuit: 8.383 miles.
42 cars starting, 15 cars finishing. Fastest lap: R. Sommer (Alfa Romeo), 96.177 mph

1	Delahaye (F)	6 cyl	3,558 cc	E. Chaboud/J. Trémoulet	1,976.537	82.356	5,000 cc	
2	Delahaye (F)	6 cyl	3,558 cc	G. Serraud/Y. Giraud-Cabantous	1,959.719	81.655		
3	Talbot-Lago (F)	6 cyl	3,985 cc	J. Prenant/A. Morel	1,839.064	76.627		
5	Peugeot-Darl'mat (F)	4 cyl	1,998 cc	C. de Cortanze/M. Contet	1,800.094	75.004	2,000 cc	
6	Adler (D)	4 cyl	1,679 cc	Graf Orssich/R. Sauerwein	1,774.867	73.952		13th Bi-cup
7	Adler (D)	4 cyl	1,485 cc	O. Löhr/P. von Guilleaume	1,718.108	71.587	1,500 cc	
9	Simca (F)	4 cyl	1,090 cc	A. Debille/P. Lapchin	1,447.514	60.313	1,100 cc	
14	Simca (F)	4 cyl	568 cc	M. Aimé/C. Plantivaux	1,269.307	52.887	750 cc	Ind. Perf.

16th race—1939, 17–18 June. Circuit: 8.383 miles.
42 cars starting, 20 cars finishing. Fastest lap: R. Mazaud (Delahaye), 96.701 mph

1	Butatti (F)	8 cyl	3,251 cc	J-P. Wimille/P. Veyron	2,084.543	86.856	5,000 cc	
2	Delage (F)	6 cyl	2,991 cc	L. Gerard/G. Monneret	2,058.112	85.754	3,000 cc	
3	Lagonda (GB)	V-12	4,479 cc	A. Dobson/C. Brackenbury	2,006.680	83.611		
5	BMW (D)	6 cyl	1,976 cc	von Schaumburg-Lippe/F. Wenscher	1,981.204	82.550	2,000 cc	
10	Simca (F)	4 cyl	1,087 cc	A. Gordini/J. Scaron	1,793.212	74.717	1,100 cc	14th Bi-cup & Ind. Perf.
14	HRG (GB)	4 cyl	1,496 cc	P. C. T. Clark/M. Chambers	1,615.378	67.307	1,500 cc	
19	Simca (F)	4 cyl	566 cc	A. Alin/A. Alin	1,242.410	51.705	750 cc	

1940 to 1948: Race not held

17th race—1949, 25–26 June. Circuit: 8.383 miles.
49 cars starting, 19 cars finishing. Fastest lap: A. Simon (Delahaye), 96.577 mph.

1	Ferrari 166 MM (I)	V-12	1,995 cc	L. Chinetti/Lord Selsdon	1,974.899	82.281	2,000 cc	15th Bi-cup & Ind. perf.
2	Delage D.6 (F)	6 cyl	2,991 cc	H. Louveau/Jover	1,965.129	81.880	3,000 cc	
3	Frazer-Nash (GB)	6 cyl	1,971 cc	N. Culpan/H. J. Aldington	1,884.876	78.536		
5	Delahaye 135 S (F)	6 cyl	3,558 cc	R. Brunet/G. Grignard	1,767.683	73.653	5,000 cc	
8	HRG (GB)	4 cyl	1,496 cc	J. Fairman/E. Thompson	1,700.181	70.841	1,500 cc	
12	Monopole-Simca (F)	4 cyl	1,098 cc	de Montremy/Dussous	1,554.788	64.782	1,100 cc	
15	Aero-Minor (CS)	2 t/s	745 cc	Krattner/F. Sutner	1,486.274	61.928	750 cc	

18th race—1950, 24–25 June. Circuit: 8.383 miles.
60 cars starting, 29 cars finishing. Fastest lap: L. Rosier (Talbot-Lago), 102.830 mph. Note: Two cars attained same Index.

1	Talbot-Lago (F)	6 cyl	4,483 cc	L. Rosier/J-L. Rosier	2,153.121	89.713	5,000 cc	
2	Talbot-Lago (F)	6 cyl	4,483 cc	P. Meyrat/G. Mairesse	2,143.152	89.298		
3	Allard J.2 (GB)	V-8	5,434 cc	S. Allard/T. Cole	2,105.853	87.743	8,000 cc	
5	Aston Martin DB.2 (GB)	6 cyl	2,581 cc	G. Abecassis/L. Macklin	2,094.166	87.256	3,000 cc	Ind. perf.
9	Frazer-Nash (GB)	6 cyl	1,970 cc	T. A. S. O. Mathieson/R. Stoop	1,972.682	82.195	2,000 cc	
16	Jowett Jupiter (GB)	F-4	1,486 cc	T. H. Wisdom/T. Wise	1,819.725	75.821	1,500 cc	
21	Aero-Minor (CS)	2 t/s	744 cc	M. Gatsonides/Hoogeveen	1,547.627	64.484	750 cc	
22	Monopole-Panhard (F)	F-2	611 cc	de Montremy/G. Hémard	1,512.984	63.041		16th Bi-cup & Ind. Perf.
24	Renault 4 CV (F)	4 cyl	760 cc	L. V. Sandt/H. Coatalen	1,438.101	59.921	1,100 cc	

19th race—1951, 23–24 June. Circuit: 8.383 miles.
60 cars starting, 30 cars finishing. Fastest lap: S. Moss (Jaguar XK 120 C), 105.232 mph

1	Jaguar XK 120 C (GB)	6 cyl	3,441 cc	P. Walker/P. Whitehead	2,243.886	93.495	5,000 cc	
2	Talbot-Lago (F)	6 cyl	4,483 cc	P. Meyrat/G. Mairesse	2,166.108	90.253		
3	Aston Martin DB 2 (GB)	6 cyl	2,580 cc	L. Macklin/E. Thompson	2,160.445	90.018	3,000 cc	
12	Lancia Aurelia GT (I)	V-6	1,991 cc	Count G. Lurani/G. Bracco	1,971.221	82.133	2,000 cc	
18	Cunningham C-2 R (US)	V-8	5,426 cc	J. Fitch/P. Walters	1,875.344	78.139	8,000 cc	
20	Porsche 356 (D)	F-4	1,086 cc	J. Veuillet/Mouche	1,765.094	73.545	1,100 cc	
23	Jowett Jupiter (GB)	F-4	1,486 cc	M. Becquart/G. Wilkins	1,707.580	71.148	1,500 cc	
24	Renault 4 CV (F)	4 cyl	747 cc	Landon/Briat	1,658.284	69,095	750 cc	
25	Monopole-Panhard (F)	F-2	614 cc	de Montremy/G. Hémard	1,633.653	68.068		17th Bi-cup & Ind. Perf.

20th race—1952, 14–15 June. Circuit: 8.383 miles.
57 cars starting, 17 cars finishing. Fastest lap: A. Ascari (Ferrari 250 S), 107.596 mph

1	Mercedes-Benz 300SL (D)	6 cyl	2,996 cc	H. Lang/Riess	2,320.071	96.696	3,000 cc	
2	Mercedes-Benz 300SL (D)	6 cyl	2,996 cc	Helfrich/Niedermayer	2,311.657	96.319		
3	Nash-Healey (GB/US)	6 cyl	4,135 cc	L. G. Johnson/T. H. Wisdom	2,195.940	91.497	5,000 cc	
4	Cunningham C-4 R (US)	V-8	5,425 cc	B. Cunningham/Spear	2,112,055	88.002	8,000 cc	
6	Lancia Aurelia GT (I)	V-6	1,991 cc	Valenzano/Ippocambo	2,076.879	86.536	2,000 cc	
11	Porsche 356 (D)	F-4	1,086 cc	J. Veuillet/Mouche	1,836.403	76.516	1,100 cc	
13	Jowett Jupiter (GB)	F-4	1,486 cc	M. Becquart/G. Wilkins	1,751.579	72.976	1,500 cc	
14	Panhard Monopole (F)	F-2	612 cc	G. Hemard/Dussous	1,741.196	72.549	750 cc	18th Bi-cup & Ind. Perf.

21st race—1953, 13–14 June. Circuit: 8.383 miles.
60 cars starting, 26 cars finishing. Fastest lap: A. Ascari (Ferrari 375 MM), 112.866 mph

1	Jaguar C-type (GB)	6 cyl	3,441 cc	A. P. R. Rolt/D. Hamilton	2,540.200	105.841	5,000 cc	
2	Jaguar C-type (GB)	6 cyl	3,441 cc	P. Walker/S. Moss	2,511.074	104.628		
3	Cunningham C-5 R (US)	V-8	5,454 cc	P. Walters/J. Fitch	2,498.112	104.088	8,000 cc	
6	Gordini (F)	6 cyl	2,473 cc	M. Trintignant/H. Schell	2,451.596	102.150	3,000 cc	
13	Frazer-Nash (GB)	6 cyl	1,979 cc	K. Wharton/Mitchell	2,119.449	88.310	2,000 cc	
15	Porsche 356 (D)	F-4	1,488 cc	R. von Frankenberg/P. Frère	2,070.423	86.267	1,500 cc	
17	D.B. Panhard (F)	F-2	745 cc	R. Bonnet/Moynet	1,983.419	82.642	750 cc	
18	Osca (I)	4 cyl	1,093 cc	Damonte/P. L. Dreyfus ('Heldé')	1,943.055	80.960	1,100 cc	
21	Panhard (F)	F-2	611 cc	P. Chancel/R. Chancel	1,869.447	77.893		19th Bi-cup & Ind. Perf.

22nd race—1954, 12–13 June. Circuit: 8.383 miles.
57 cars starting, 18 cars finishing. Fastest lap: P. Marzotto and J. F. Gonzales (Ferrari 375s), both 117.525 mph

1	Ferrari 375 (I)	V-12	4,954 cc	J. F. Gonzales/M. Trintignant	2,523.476	105.145	5,000 cc	
2	Jaguar D-type (GB)	6 cyl	3,442 cc	A. P. R. Rolt/D. Hamilton	2,520.935	105.038		
3	Cunningham C-4 R (US)	V-8	5,482 cc	W. Spear/Johnston	2,367.377	98.640	8,000 cc	
6	Gordini (F)	6 cyl	2,473 cc	Guelfi/Pollet	2,202.514	91.770	3,000 cc	
7	Bristol 450 (GB)	6 cyl	1,979 cc	P. Wilson/J. Mayers	2,178.256	90.760	2,000 cc	
10	D.B. Panhard (F)	F-2	745 cc	R. Bonnet/E. Bayol	2,008.688	83.695	750 cc	20th Bi-cup & Ind. Perf.
12	Porsche 550 (D)	F-4	1,497 cc	J. Claes/Stasse	1,903.958	79.303	1,500 cc	
14	Porsche 356 (D)	F-4	1,089 cc	Z. A. Duntov/G. Olivier	1,803.377	75.140	1,100 cc	

23rd race—1955, 11–12 June. Circuit: 8.383 miles.
60 cars starting, 21 cars finishing. Fastest lap: M. Hawthorn (Jaguar D-type), 122.386 mph

1	Jaguar D-type (GB)	6 cyl	3,442 cc	M. Hawthorn/I. Bueb	2,569.601	107.067	5,000 cc	
2	Aston Martin DB3S (GB)	6 cyl	2,922 cc	P. J. Collins/P. Frère	2,530.852	105.452	3,000 cc	
3	Jaguar D-type	6 cyl	3,442 cc	J. Claes/J. Swaters	2,475.880	103.161		
4	Porsche 550 (D)	F-4	1,498 cc	R. von Frankenberg/H. Polensky	2,379.679	99.153	1,500 cc	21st Bi-cup & Ind. Perf.
7	Birstol 450 C (GB)	6 cyl	1,979 cc	P. Wilson/J. Mayers	2,270.678	94.612	2,000 cc	
13	Porsche 356 (D)	F-4	1,097 cc	Z. A. Duntov/J. Veuillet	2,052.739	85.530	1,100 cc	
16	D.B. Panhard (F)	F-2	745 cc	L. Cornet/R. Mougin	1,974.645	82.276	750 cc	

24th race—1956, 28–29 July. Circuit: 8.364 miles.
49 cars starting, 14 cars finishing. Fastest lap: M. Hawthorn (Jaguar D-type), 115.812 mph

1	Jaguar D-type (GB)	6 cyl	3,442 cc	R. Flockhart/N. Sanderson	2,507.183	104.465	5,000 cc	
2	Aston Martin DB3S (GB)	6 cyl	2,922 cc	S. Moss/P. J. Collins	2,497.057	104,044	3,000 cc	
3	Ferrari 625 LM (I)	4 cyl	2,498 cc	M. Trintignant/O. Gendebien	2,446.713	101.946		
5	Porsche 550 RS (D)	F-4	1,498 cc	Graf W. von Trips/R. von Frankenberg	2,356.389	98.182	1,500 cc	
7	Lotus XI Climax (GB)	4 cyl	1,098 cc	R. Bicknell/P. Jopp	2,111.207	87.966	1,100 cc	
10	D.B. Panhard (F)	F-2	747 cc	G. Laureau/P. Armagnac	1,928.326	80.346	750 cc	22nd Bi-cup & Ind. Perf.

25th race—1957, 22–23 June. Circuit: 8.364 miles.
54 cars starting, 20 cars finishing. Fastest lap: M. Hawthorn (Ferrari 412), 126.147 mph

1	Jaguar D-type (GB)	6 cyl	3,781 cc	R. Flockhart/I. Bueb	2,732.230	113.845	5,000 cc	
2	Jaguar D-type (GB)	6 cyl	3,442 cc	N. Sanderson/J. Lawrence	2,665.388	111.058		
3	Jaguar D-type (GB)	6 cyl	3,442 cc	J. Lucas/Brousselet ('Mary')	2,644.025	110.167		
7	Ferrari 206 (I)	4 cyl	1,984 cc	L. Bianci/G. Harris	2,404.130	100.172	2,000 cc	
8	Porsche 550 RS (D)	F-4	1,498 cc	E. Hugus/G. de Beaufort	2,391.251	99.635	1,500 cc	
9	Lotus XI Climax (GB)	4 cyl	1,098 cc	H. Mackay-Fraser/J. Chamberlain	2,377.982	99.088	1,100 cc	
11	Aston Martin DB3S (GB)	6 cyl	2,922 cc	J. P. Colas/J. Kerguen	2,273.584	94.732	3,000 cc	
14	Lotus XI Climax (GB)	4 cyl	745 cc	C. Allison/J. K. Hall	2,160.605	90.025	750 cc	Ind. Perf.

26th race—1958, 21–22 June. Circuit: 8.364 miles.
55 cars starting, 20 cars finishing. Fastest lap: M. Hawthorn (Ferrari 250 TR), 121.416 mph

1	Ferrari 250 TR (I)	V-12	2,953 cc	O. Gendebien/P. Hill	2,548.813	106.200	3,000 cc	
2	Astron Martin DB3S (GB)	6 cyl	2,993 cc	P. Whitehead/G. Whitehead	2,448.749	102.031		
3	Porsche RS K (D)	F-4	1,587 cc	J. Behra/H. Herrmann	2,429.337	101.222	2,000 cc	
4	Porsche RS K (D)	F-4	1,498 cc	E. Barth/P. Frère	2,420.352	100.873	1,500 cc	
11	Osca (I)	4 cyl	749 cc	A. de Tomaso/C. Davis	2,103.815	87.815	750 cc	Ind. Perf.

27th race—1959, 20–21 June. Circuit: 8.364 miles.
53 cars starting, 13 cars finishing. Fastest lap: J. Behra (Ferrari 250 TR), 124.995 mph

1	Aston Martin DBR 1 (GB)	6 cyl	2,993 cc	R. Salvadori/C. Shelby	2,701.654	112.569	3,000 cc	Sport-proto.
2	Aston Martin DBR 1 (GB)	6 cyl	2,993 cc	M. Trintignant/P. Frère	2,695.229	112.313		
3	Ferrari 250 (I)	V-12	2,953 cc	J. Blaton ('Beurlys')/'Eldé'	2,486.474	103.602		GT
7	A.C. Bristol (GB)	6 cyl	1,971 cc	E. Whiteaway/J. Turner	2,289.647	95.375	2,000 cc	
8	Lotus Elite (GB)	4 cyl	1,216 cc	P. Lumsden/P. Riley	2,259.353	94.140	1,500 cc	
9	D.B. Panhard (F)	F-2	744 cc	L. Cornet/R. Cotton	2,165.752	90.239	750 cc	25th Bi-cup & Ind. Perf.
11	D.B. Panhard (F)	F-2	745 cc	B. Consten/P. Armagnac	2,073.730	86.405		Index T.E.

28th race—1960, 25–26 June. Circuit: 8.364 miles.
55 cars starting, 20 cars finishing. Fastest lap: M. Gregory (Maserati Tipo 61), 123.407 mph

1	Ferrari TR 60 (I)	V-12	2,958 cc	P. Frère/O. Gendebien	2,620.644	109.193	3,000 cc	Sport
2	Ferrari TR 60 (I)	V-12	2,958 cc	R. Rodriguez/A. Pilette	2,587.177	107.798		
3	Aston Martin DBR 1 (GB)	6 cyl	2,992 cc	R. Salvadori/J. Clark	2,558.620	106.609		
4	Ferrari 250 GT (I)	V-12	2,953 cc	F. Tavano/P. Loustel	2,520.231	105.009		GT
8	Chevrolet Corvette (US)	V-8	4,640 cc	J. Fitch/R. M. Grossman	2,350.025	97.917	5,000 cc	
10	Porsche 1600 GS (D)	F-4	1,588 cc	H. Linge/H. Walter	2,249.209	93.716	1,600 cc	
12	MGA Twin-Cam (GB)	4 cyl	1,762 cc	E. Lund/C. Escott	2,188.700	91.195	2,000 cc	
13	Lotus Elite (GB)	4 cyl	1,216 cc	C. Laurent/R. Masson	2,182.879	90.953	1,300 cc	
14	Lotus Elite (GB)	4 cyl	1,216 cc	J. B. Wagstaff/A. E. Marsh	2,146.772	89.448		Index T.E.
15	D.B. Panhard (F)	F-2	702 cc	G. Laureau/P. Armagnac	2,116.042	88.168	850 cc	26th Bi-cup & Ind. Perf.
16	Austin-Healey Sprite (GB)	4 cyl	996 cc	J. F. Dalton/J. K. Colgate	2,055.142	85.630	1,000 cc	

29th race—1961, 10–11 June. Circuit: 8.364 miles.
55 cars starting, 22 cars finishing. Fastest lap: R. Rodriguez (Ferrari TR 61), 125.020 mph

1	Ferrari 250 TR (I)	V-12	2,961 cc	O. Gendebien/P. Hill	2,781.612	115.902	3,000 cc	Sport
2	Ferrari 250 TR (I)	V-12	2,961 cc	W. Mairesse/M. J. Parkes	2,758.086	114.920		
3	Ferrari 250 GT (I)	V-12	2,953 cc	P. Noblet/J. Guichet	2,645.799	110.241		GT
5	Porsche RS (D)	F-4	1,967 cc	M. Gregory/R. Holbert	2,581.456	107.561	2,000 cc	
10	Porsche 695 GS (D)	F-4	1,588 cc	H. Linge/Ben Pon	2,372.811	98.867	1,600 cc	
12	Lotus Elite (GB)	4 cyl	1,216 cc	W. E. Allen/T. Taylor	2,234.916	93.121	1,300 cc	
14	Fiat Abarth (I)	4 cyl	847 cc	D. Hulme/A. Hyslop	2,194.662	91.444	850 cc	
16	Sunbeam Alpine (GB)	4 cyl	1,592 cc	P. Harper/P. Procter	2,182.070	90.919		Index T.E.
18	D.B. Panhard (F)	F-2	702 cc	G. Lauren/R. Bouharde	2,148.182	89.507		Ind. Perf.

30th race—1962, 23–24 June. Circuit: 8.364 miles.
55 cars starting, 18 cars finishing. Fastest lap: P. Hill (Ferrari 330 LM), 126.884 mph

1	Ferrari 330 LM (I)	V-12	3,967 cc	P. Hill/O. Gendebien	2,765.876	115.244	4,000 cc	Experimental
2	Ferrari GTO (I)	V-12	2,953 cc	J. Guichet/P. Noblet	2,724.169	113.507	3,000 cc	GT
3	Ferrari GTO (I)	V-12	2,953 cc	'Eldé'/J. Blaton ('Beurlys')	2,618.375	109.720		
7	Porsche 1600 GS (D)	F-4	1,588 cc	E. Barth/H. Herrmann	2,397.576	99.898	1,600 cc	GT to two-litre
8	Lotus Elite (GB)	4 cyl	1,216 cc	D. W. Hobbs/F. K. Gardner	2,390.451	99.602	1,300 cc	Index T.E.
13	Morgan Plus-Four (GB)	4 cyl	1,991 cc	C. Lawrence/R. Shepherd-Barron	2,255.130	93.963	2,000 cc	
16	Panhard C.D. (F)	F-2	702 cc	A. Guilhaudin/A. Bertaut	2,129.451	88.727	850 cc	Ind. Perf.
17	René Bonnet Djet (F)	4 cyl	996 cc	B. Consten/J. Rosinski	2,126.049	88.585	1,000 cc	

31st race—1963, 15–16 June. Circuit: 8.364 miles.
48+1 cars starting, 12+1 cars finishing. Fastest lap: J. Surtees (Ferrari 250 P), 129.067 mph

1	Ferrari 250 P (I)	V-12	2,953 cc	L. Scarfiotti/L. Bandini	2,834.509	118.104	3,000 cc	Prototype & Ind. Perf.
2	Ferrari GTO (I)	V-12	2,953 cc	J. Blaton ('Beurlys')/G. Langlois	2,700.672	112.528		GT
3	Ferrari 250 P (I)	V-12	2,953 cc	M. J. Parkes/U. Maglioli	2,700.598	112.525		
5	Ferrari 330 LMB (I)	V-12	3,967 cc	J. G. Sears/M. Salmon	2,621.926	109.246	4,000 cc	
7	A.C. Cobra (GB)	V-8	4,728 cc	P. Bolton/N. Sanderson	2,591.833	107.991	5,000 cc	
8	Porsche 718 (D)	F-8	1,962 cc	E. Barth/H. Linge	2,516.703	104.862	2,000 cc	
9	Jaguar E-type (GB)	6 cyl	3,781 cc	Richards/R. M. Grossman	2,372.446	98.851	4,000 cc	
10	Lotus Elite (GB)	4 cyl	1,216 cc	J. B. Wagstaff/Fergusson	2,256.933	94.049	1,300 cc	GT to two-litre
11	Rene Bonnet LM6 (F)	4 cyl	1,108 cc	J. P. Beltoise/C. Bobrowski	2,254.889	93.953	1,150 cc	Index T.E.
—	Rover-B.R.M. (GB)	gas turbine		G. Hill/R. Ginther	2,592.916	107.712		Special A.C.O. award

32nd race—1964, 20–21 June. Circuit: 8.364 miles.
55 cars starting, 25 cars finishing. Fastest lap: P. Hill (Ford GT 40), 131.375 mph

1	Ferrari 275 P (I)	V-12	3,299 cc	J. Guichet/N. Vaccarella	2,917.524	121.563	4,000 cc	Prototype & Ind. Perf.
2	Ferrari 330 P (I)	V-12	3,972 cc	J. Bonnier/G. Hill	2,872.369	119.682		
3	Ferrari 330 P (I)	V-12	3,972 cc	J. Surtees/L. Bandini	2,814.893	117.287		
4	Cobra Ford (GB/US)	V-8	4,727 cc	D. Gurney/B. Bondurant	2,791.243	116.301	5,000 cc	GT
5	Ferrari GTO (I)	V-12	2,953 cc	L. Bianchi/J. Blaton ('Beurlys')	2,778.393	115.766	3,000 cc	
7	Porsche 904 (D)	F-4	1,967 cc	R. Buchet/G. Ligier	2,699.597	112.483	2,000 cc	GT to two-litre
13	Alfa Romeo TZ (I)	4 cyl	1,570 cc	R. Businello/D. Deserti	2,565.152	106.881	1,600 cc	
14	Iso Rivolta (I)	V-8	5,354 cc	E. Berney/P. Noblet	2,560.137	106.672	unlimited	
17	Alpine Renault (F)	4 cyl	1,149 cc	H. Morrogh/R. Delageneste	2,436.379	101.515		Index T.E.
22	Lotus Elite (GB)	4 cyl	1,216 cc	C. Hunt/J. B. Wagstaff	2,222.696	92.612	1,300 cc	

33rd race—1965, 19–20 June. Circuit: 8.364 miles.
51 cars starting, 14 cars finishing. Fastest lap: P. Hill (Ford Mark 2), 138.443 mph

1	Ferrari 275 LM (I)	V-12	3,285 cc	M. Gregory/J. Rindt	2,906.215	121.092	4,000 cc	Prototype
2	Ferrari 275 LM (I)	V-12	3,285 cc	P. Dumay/T. Gosselin	2,859.917	119.163		

3	Ferrari 275 GTB (I)	V-12	3,286 cc	W. Mairesse/J. Blaton ('Beurlys')	2,834.721	118.113		GT
4	Porsche 904 (D)	F-6	1,991 cc	H. Linge/P. Nocker	2,800.825	116.701	2,000 cc	Ind. Perf.
5	Porsche 904 (D)	F-4	1,967 cc	G. Koch/T. Fischaber	2,713.311	113.054		GT to two-lire & Index T.E.
7	Ferrari 365 P.2 (I)	V-12	4,385 cc	P. Rodriguez/N. Vaccarella	2,672.009	111.333	5,000 cc	
9	Iso Grifo (I)	V-8	5,354 cc	R. Fraissinet/J. de Mortemart	2,524.980	105.207	unlimited	
12	Austin-Healey Sprite (GB)	4 cyl	1,293 cc	P. Hawkins/J. Rhodes	2,315.491	96.478	1,300 cc	
13	Triumph Spitfire (GB)	4 cyl	1,147 cc	J. Thuner/S. Lampinen	2,282.770	95.115	1,150 cc	

34th race—1966, 18–19 June. Circuit: 8.364 miles.
55 cars staring, 15 cars finishing. Fastest lap: D. Gurney (Ford Mark 2), 142.979 mph

1	Ford Mark 2 (US)	V-8	6,982 cc	B. McLaren/C. Amon	3,009.350	125.389	unlimited	Prototype
2	Ford Mark 2 (US)	V-8	6,982 cc	K. Miles/D. Hulme	3,009.338	125.389		
3	Ford Mark 2 (US)	V-8	6,982 cc	R. Bucknum/Hutcheson	2,908.987	121.207		
4	Porsche 906 (D)	F-6	1,991 cc	J. Siffert/C. Davis	3,834.770	118.115	2,000 cc	Ind. Perf.
7	Porsche 906 (D)	F-6	1,991 cc	G. Klass/R. Stommelen	2,759.336	114.972		Sports car
8	Ferrari 275 GTB (I)	V-12	3,286 cc	P. Courage/R. Pike	3,617.521	109.063	5,000 cc	GT
9	Alpine Renault A210 (F)	4 cyl	1,292 cc	H. Grandsire/L. Cella	2,600.551	108.356	1,300 cc	
11	Alpine Reanult A210 (F)	4 cyl	1,296 cc	J. Cheinisse/R. Delageneste	2,562.809	106.783		Index T.E.
14	Porsche 911 S (D)	F-6	1,991 cc	J. Dewes 'Franc')/J. Kerguen	2,374.584	98.940		GT to two-litre

35th race—1967, 10–11 June. Circuit: 8,364 miles.
54 cars starting, 16 cars finishing. Fastest lap: D. Hulme and M. Andretti (Ford Mark IVs), both 147.894 mph

1	Ford Mark IV (US)	V-8	6,980 cc	D. Gurney/A. J. Foyt	3,251.567	135.482	unlimited	Prototype & Index T.E.
2	Ferrari P.4 (I)	V-12	3,983 cc	L. Scarfiotti/M. J. Parkes	3,219.063	134.127	5,000 cc	
3	Ferrari P-4 (I)	V-12	3,983 cc	W. Mairesse/J. Blaton ('Beurlys')	3,159.287	131.637		
5	Porsche 907 (D)	F-6	1,991 cc	J. Siffert/H. Herrmann	3,001.558	125.065	2,000 cc	Ind. Perf.
7	Porsche 906 (D)	F-6	1,991 cc	V. Elford/Ben Pon	2,739.899	114.162		Sports car
9	Alpine Renault (F)	4 cyl	1,296 cc	H. Grandsire/J. Rosinski	2,686.797	111.949	1,300 cc	
11	Ferrari 275 GTB (I)	V-12	3,286 cc	R. Steinemann/D. Spoerry	2,660.084	110.836		GT
13	Alpine Renault (F)	4 cyl	1,470 cc	J. Vinatier/M. Bianchi	2,603.092	108.461	1,600 cc	
16	Abarth 1300 GT (I)	4 cyl	1,389 cc	M. Martin/J. Mesange	2,194.386	91.670		Sports car to 1,300 cc

36th race—1968, 28–29 September. Circuit: 8.369 miles.
54 cars starting, 15 cars finishing. Fastest lap: R. Stommelen (Porsche 908), 138.143 mph

1	Ford GT 40 (US)	V-8	4,942 cc	P. Rodriguez/L. Bianchi	2,766.866	115.286	5,000 cc	Sports car
2	Porsche 907 (D)	F-8	2,196 cc	D. Spoerry/R. Steinemann	2,720.805	113.366	2,500 cc	Sport-proto.
3	Porsche 908 (D)	F-8	2,996 cc	R. Stommelen/J. Neerpasch	2,713.038	113.039	3,000 cc	
4	Alfa Romeo Tipo 33 (I)	V-8	1,996 cc	I. Giunti/Nanni Galli	2,688.189	112.007	2,000 cc	
9	Alpine Renault A210 (F)	4 cyl	1,470 cc	A. le Guellec/A. Serpaggi	2,415.818	100.658	1,600 cc	
10	Alpine Reanult A210 (F)	4 cyl	1,296 cc	J-L. Therier/B. Tramont	2,402.452	100.164		Index T.E.
12	Porsche 911 T (D)	F-6	1,991 cc	J-P. Gaban/R. Vanderschriek	2,351.170	97.965		GT
14	Alpine Renault A210 (F)	4 cyl	1,005 cc	J-C. Andruet/J-P. Nicolas	2,273.468	95.051	1,150 cc	Ind. Perf.

37th race—1969, 14–15 June. Circuit: 8.369 miles.
45 cars starting, 14 cars finishing. Fastest lap: V. Elford (Porsche 917 LH), 145.411 mph

1	Ford GT 40 (US)	V-8	4,942 cc	J. Ickx/J. Oliver	3,105.607	129,400	5,000 cc	Sports car & Index T.E.
2	Porsche 908 (D)	F-8	2,996 cc	H. Herrmann/G. Larrousse	3,105.532	129.397	3,000 cc	Sport-proto.
3	Ford GT 40 (US)	V-8	4,942 cc	D. Hobbs/M. Hailwood	3,078.285	128.261		
9	Porsche 910 (D)	F-6	1,991 cc	C. Poirot/P. Maublanc	2,604.416	108.517	2,000 cc	
10	Porsche 911 S (D)	F-6	1,991 cc	J-P. Gaban/Y. Deprez	2,560.392	106.683		GT
12	Alpine Renault A210 (F)	4 cyl	1,005 cc	A. Serpaggi/C. Ethuin	2,443.090	101.795	1,150 cc	Ind. Perf.

38th race—1970, 13–14 June. Circuit: 8.369 miles.
51 cars starting, 7 cars finishing. Fastest lap: V. Elford (Porsche 917), 149.896 mph

1	Porsche 917 K (D)	F-12	4,494 cc	H. Herrmann/D. Attwood	2,863.154	119.298	5,000 cc	Sports car
2	Porsche 917 L (D)	F-12	4,494 cc	G. Larrousse/W. Kauhsen	2,822.231	117.593		Index T.E.
3	Porsche 808 (D)	F-8	2,997 cc	R. Lins/H. Marko	2,797.892	116.578	3,000 cc	Sport-proto. & Ind. Perf.
6	Porsche 914/6 (D)	F-6	1,991 cc	G. Chasseuil/C. Ballot-Lena	2,382.494	99.270	2,000 cc	GT Special
7	Porsche 911 S (D)	F-6	2,253 cc	E. Kremer/Koob	2,355.383	98.141	2,500 cc	

39th race—1971, 12–13 June. Circuit: 8.369 miles.
49 cars starting, 13 cars finishing. Fastest lap: J. Oliver (Porsche 917 LH), 151.854 mph

1	Porsche 917 K (D)	F-12	4,907 cc	H. Marko/G. van Lennep	3,315.203	138.133	5,000 cc	Sports car & Ind. Perf.
2	Porsche 917 K (D)	F-12	4,907 cc	H. Müller/D. Attwood	3,298.448	137.435		
3	Ferrari 512 M (I)	V-12	4,994 cc	S. Posey/T. Adamovicz	3,058.439	127.434		
5	Ferrari 365 GTB 4 (I)	V-12	4,390 cc	R. Grossman/L. Chinetti Jnr.	2,621.405	109.225		Index T.E.
6	Porsche 911 S (D)	F-6	2,381 cc	R. Touroul/'Anselme'	2,554.666	106.444	2,500 cc	GT Special
7	Porsche 907 (D)	F-6	1.981 cc	W. Brun/P. Mattli	2,554.429	106.434	2,000 cc	Sport-proto.

40th race—1972, 10–11 June. Circuit: 8.475 miles.
55 cars starting, 18 cars finishing. Fastest lap: G. van Lennep (Lola T.280), 134.472 mph

1	Matra Simca 670 (F)	V-12	2,993 cc	H. Pescarolo/G. Hill	2,915.059	121.460	3,000 cc	Sport
2	Matra Simca 670 (F)	V-12	2,993 cc	F. Cevert/H. Ganley	2,830.298	117.928		
3	Porsche 908 L (D)	F-8	2,997 cc	R. Joest/M. Weber/M. Casoni	2,751.988	114.665		
5	Ferrari 365 GTB 4 (I)	V-12	4,390 cc	J-C. Andruet/C. Ballot-Lena	2,586.552	107.772	5,000 cc	GT Special & Index T.E.
10	Ford Capri 2600 RS (D)	V-6	2,940 cc	G. Birrell/C. Bourgoignie	2,471.508	102.979		Tour. Spec.
13	Porsche 911 S (D)	F-6	2,466 cc	M. Keyset/J. Barth/S. Grant	2,413.197	100.549	2,500 cc	
14	Lola T 290 (GB)	4 cyl	1,790 cc	R. Ligonnet/B. Smith	2,401.339	100.055	2,000 cc	
15	Chevrolet Corvette (US)	V-8	6,998 cc	D. Heinz/B. Johnson	2,400.910	100.037	unlimited	

41st race—1973, 9–10 June. Circuit: 8.475 miles.
55 cars starting, 21 cars finishing. Fastest lap: F. Cevert (Matra Simca 670B), 138.942 mph

1	Matra Simca 670B (F)	V-12	2,993 cc	H. Pescarolo/G. Larrousse	3,016.095	125.670	3,000 cc	Sport
2	Ferrari 312 P/B (I)	V-12	2,991 cc	A. Merzario/C. Pace	2,965.357	123.556		
3	Matra Simca 670B (F)	V-12	2,993 cc	J-P. Jabouille/J-P. Jaussaud	2,812.417	117.183		
6	Ferrari 365 GTB 4 (I)	V-12	4,390 cc	C. Ballot-Lena/V. Elford	2,685.151	111.880	5,000 cc	GT Special
8	Porsche Carrera RSR (D)	F-6	2,806 cc	Keller/Kremer/Schickentanz	2,678.916	111.621		Index T.E.
11	BMW 3.0 CSL (D)	6 cyl	3,331 cc	T. Hezemans/D. Quester	2,609.381	108.724		Tour. Spec.
12	Chevrolet Corvette (US)	V-8	6,998 cc	H. Greder/M-C. Beaumont	2,571.434	107.142	unlimited	

42nd race—1974, 15–16 June. Circuit: 8.475 miles.
49 cars starting, 20 cars finishing. Fastest lap: J-P Jarier (Matra-Simca 680), 137.008 mph

1	Matra-Simca 670 B (F)	V-12	2,993 cc	H. Pescarolo/G. Larrousse	2,862.380	119.266	3,000 cc	Sport
2	Porsche Carrera (D)	F-6	2,142 cc	G. van Lennep/H. Müller	2,813.220	117.218		
3	Matra-Simca 670 B (F)	V-12	2,993 cc	J-P. Jabouille/F. Migault	2,752.183	114.674		
5	Ferrari 365 GTB 4 (I)	V-12	4,490 cc	C. Grandet/D. 'Bardini'	2,659.773	110.824	5,000 cc	GT Special Index T.E.
15	BMW CSL (D)	6 cyl	3,498 cc	J-C. Aubriet/'Depnic'	2,285.290	95.220		Tour. Spec.
17	Chevron B.23 FVC (GB)	4 cyl	1,790 cc	Y. Fontaine/C. Beckers/M. Laurent	2,248.176	93.674	2,000 cc	
18	Chevrolet Corvette (US)	V-8	6,998 cc	Greder/M-C. 'Beaumont'	2,150.793	89.616	unlimited	

43rd race—1975, 14–15 June. Circuit: 8.475 miles.
55 cars starting, 30 cars finishing. Fastest lap: C. Craft (De Cadenet-Lola T.380), 130.504 mph

1	Gulf-Mirage DFV (GB)	V-8	2,986 cc	J. Ickx/D. Bell	2,855.548	118.981		Sports, over two-litres
2	Ligier JS.2 (F)	V-8	2,983 cc	J-F. Lafosse/G. Chasseuil	2,841.770	118.407		
3	Gulf-Mirage DFV (GB)	V-8	2,986 cc	V. Schuppan/J-P. Jaussaud	2,799.193	116.633		

5	Porsche Carrera (D)	F-6	2,992 cc	J. Fitzpatrick/G. van Lennep	2,676.846	111.535	GT Special
10	Porsche Carrera (D)	F-6	2,992 cc	Maurer/Beez/Straehl	2,508.538	104.522	GT Production
15	Porsche Carrera (D)	F-6	2,142 cc	Beguin/Zbinden/Haldi	2,464.490	102.687	GT Experimental
21	Moynet-Simca (F)	4 cyl	1,994 cc	Hoepfner/Mouton/Dacremont	2,286.263	95.261	Sports, under two-litres
27	BMW 2002 (D)	4 cyl	1,990 cc	Brillat/Gagliardi/Degoumois	2,131.774	88.824	Touring Special

44th race—1976, 12–13 June. Circuit: 8.475 miles.
55 cars starting, 26 cars finishing. Fastest lap: J-P. Jabouille (Alpine-Renault A 442), 136.824 mph

1	Porsche 936 (D)	F-6	2,142 cc	J. Ickx/G. van Lennep	2,963.882	123.495	Group 6 over two-litres
2	Mirage-DFV GR.8 (GB)	V-8	2,986 cc	J-L. Lafosse/F. Migault	2,871.218	119.634	
3	Lola-DFV T.380 (GB)	V-8	2,996 cc	C. Craft/A. de Cadenet	2,860.715	119.196	
4	Porsche 935 (D)	F-6	2,808 cc	R. Stommelen/M. Schurti	2,809.390	117.058	Group 5
8	Inaltera-DFV (F)	V-8	2,993 cc	H. Pescarolo/J-P. Beltoise	2,587.559	107.815	GT Prototype
12	Porsche Carrera (D)	F-6	2,992 cc	'Segolen'/Ouviere/Gadal	2,477.977	103.249	Group 4
14	Porsche Carrera (D)	F-6	2,992 cc	Laffeach/Rullon Miller/Vaugh	2,402.533	100.106	IMSA
15	Lola-Cosworth T292 (GB)	4 cyl	1,998 cc	F. Trisconi/G. Morand/A. Chevalley	2,370.524	98.772	Group 6 under two-litres
24	BMW CSL (D)	6 cyl	3,003 cc	J-L. Ravenel/J-M. Detrin/J. Ravenel	2,003.017	83.459	Group 2

45th race—1977, 11–12 June. Circuit: 8.475 miles.
55 cars starting, 20 cars finishing. Fastest lap: J. Ickx (Porsche 936), 140.736 mph

1	Porsche 936 (D)	F-6	2,142 cc	J. Ickx/H. Haywood/J. Barth	2,902.805	120.950	Group 6 over two-litres
2	Mirage-Renault (GB/F)	V-6	1,999 cc	V. Schuppan/J-P. Jarier	2,808.457	117.019	
3	Porsche 935 (D)	F-6	2,856 cc	C. Ballot-Lena/P. Gregg	2,676.565	111.524	Group 5
4	Inaltera-DFV (F)	V-8	2,993 cc	J. Ragnotti/J. Rondeau	2,675.248	111.469	GT Prototype
6	Chevron-ROC (GB)	4 cyl	1,996 cc	M. Pignard/J. Henry/A. Dufrene	2,575.002	107.292	Group 6 under two-litres & Index T.E.
7	Porsche 934 (D)	F-6	2,991 cc	B. Wollek/P. Gudjian/'Steve'	2,526.529	105.272	Group 4
8	BMW CSL (D)	6 cyl	3,152 cc	J. Xhenceval/P. Dieudonne/S. Dini	2,473.415	103.059	IMSA

46th race—1978, 10–11 June. Circuit: 8.475 miles.
55 cars starting, 17 cars finishing. Fastest lap: J-P. Jabouille (Renault-Alpine A 443), 142.445 mph

1	Renault-Alpine A442 (F)	V-6	1,997 cc	D. Pironi/J-P. Jaussaud	3,134.514	130.605	Group 6, over two-litres
2	Porsche 936/78 (D)	F-6	2,140 cc	B. Wollek/J. Barth/J. Ickx	3,087.035	128.626	Index T.E.
3	Porsche 936/77 (D)	F-6	2,140 cc	H. Haywood/P. Gregg/R. Joest	3,070.016	127.917	
5	Porsche 935/77A (D)	F-6	3,000 cc	B. Redman/D. Barbour/J. Paul	2,862.907	119.288	I.M.S.A.
6	Porsche 935/77A (D)	F-6	3,000 cc	J. Busby/C. Cord/R. Knoop	2,853.929	118.914	Group 5
9	Rondeau-DFV M 378 (F)	V-8	2,989 cc	B. Darniche/J. Rondeau/J. Haran	2,497.294	104.054	GT Prototype
11	Chevron-Chrysler B36 (GB)	4 cyl	1,996 cc	M. Pignard/L. Rossiaud/L. Ferrier	2,409.799	100.408	Group 6, under two-litres
12	Porsche Carrera (D)	F-6	2,994 cc	A-C. Verney/X. Lapeyre/F. Servanin	2,372.337	98.847	Group 4

47th race—1979, 9–10 June. Circuit: 8.467 miles.
55 cars starting, 22 cars finishing. Fastest lap: J. Ickx (Porsche 936), 141.053 mph

1	Porsche 935 (D)	F-6	2,993 cc	Ludwig/Whittington/Whittington	2,593.556	108.065	Group 5
2	Porsche 935 (D)	F-6	2,993 cc	D. Barbour/P. Newman/R. Stommelen	2,540.041	105.835	I.M.S.A.
3	Porsche 935 (D)	F-6	2,993 cc	L. Ferrier/F. Servanin/F. Trisconi	2,478.177	103.257	
4	Porsche 934 (D)	F-6	2,991 cc	A. Pallavicini/H. Müller/M. Vanoli	2,468.541	102.856	Group 4
5	Rondeau M 379 (F)	V-8	3,000 cc	B. Darniche/J. Ragnotti	2,433.837	101.410	Group 6, over two-litres
14	W.M. P 79 (F)	V-6	2,661 cc	J-D. Raulet/M. Mamers	2,263.994	94.333	GT Prototype
17	Chevron-Ford B 36 (GB)	4 cyl	1,998 cc	A. Charnell/R. Smith/R. Jones	2,189.790	91.241	Group 6, under two-litres

48th race—1980, 14–15 June. Circuit: 8.467 miles.
55 cars starting, 25 cars finishing. Fastest lap: J. Ickx (Porsche 908/80), 138.176 mph

1	Rondeau M 379 B (F)	V-8	2,993 cc	J. Rondeau/J-P. Jaussaud	2,863.280	119.303	Group 6, over two-litres & Index T.E.

2	Porsche 908/80 (D)	F-6	2,140 cc	J. Ickx/R. Joest	2,847.924	118.663	
3	Rondeau M 379 B (F)	V-8	2,998 cc	G. Spice/J-M. Martin/P. Martin	2,789.873	116.244	GT Prototype
5	Porsche 935 K.3 (D)	F-6	3,164 cc	J. Fitzpatrick/B. Redman/R. Barbour	2,688.700	112.029	I.M.S.A
8	Porsche 935 (D)	F-6	2,991 cc	Schornstein/Grohs/von Tschirnhaus	2,652.220	110.509	Group 5
16	Porsche 911 SC (D)	F-6	2,994 cc	T. Perrier/R. Carmillet	2,374.629	98.942	Group 4
17	Chevron-ROC B 36 (GB)	4 cyl	1,994 cc	P. Hesnault/B. Sotty/Laurent	2,342.897	92.620	Group 6, under two-litres

49th race—1981, 13–14 June. Circuit: 8.467 miles.
55 cars starting, 18 cars finishing. Fastest lap. J. Mass (Porsche 936/81), 142.437 mph

1	Porsche 936/81 (D)	F-6	2,649 cc	J. Ickx/D. Bell/J. Barth	2,998.321	124.930	Group 6, over two-litres
2	Rondeau M 379 CL (F)	V-8	2,998 cc	J. Haran/J-L. Schlesser/P. Streiff	2,882.731	120.114	GT Prototype
3	Rondeau M 379 CL (F)	V-8	2,998 cc	G. Spice/F. Migault	2,840.405	118.350	
4	Porsche 935 K 3 (D)	F-6	3,122 cc	J. Cooper/C. Bourgoignie/D. Wood	2,800.833	116.701	Group 5
5	Ferrari BB-512 (I)	F-12	4,942 cc	J-C. Andruet/C. Ballot-Lena	2,777.167	115.715	I.M.S.A GTX
11	Porsche 924 Carrera (D)	4 cyl	1,983 cc	Schurti/A. Rouse	2,673.724	111.355	I.M.S.A. GTO
17	Porsche 934 (D)	F-6	2,943 cc	V. Bertapelle/T. Perrier/B. Salam	2,322.328	96.763	Group 4
18	Lola-BMW T.298 (GB)	4 cyl	1,998 cc	J-P. Grand/Y. Courage	2,308.226	96.175	Group 6, under two-litres & Index T.E.

50th race—1982, 19–20 June. Circuit: 8.467 miles.
55 cars starting, 18 cars finishing. Fastest lap: J. Rondeau (Rondeau M.382), 140.527 mph

1	Porsche 956 (D)	F-6	2,649 cc	J. Ickx/D. Bell	3,044.140	126.839	Group C
2	Porsche 956 (D)	F-6	2,649 cc	J. Mass/V. Schuppan	3,018.696	125.779	
3	Porsche 956 (D)	F-6	2,649 cc	H. Haywood/A. Holbert/J. Barth	2,883.216	120.134	
4	Porsche 935 (D)	F-6	2,676 cc	J. Fitzpatrick/D. Hobbs	2,788.810	116.200	I.M.S.A. GTX
8	Porsche 935 K.3 (D)	F-6	3,121 cc	J. Couper/P. Smith/C. Bourgoignie	2,676.430	111.518	Group 5
13	Porsche 934 (D)	F-6	2,994 cc	R. Cleare/T. Dron/R. Jones	2,466.970	102.790	Group 4
16	Porsche 924 GTR (D)	4 cyl	2,008 cc	J. Busby/H. Bundy	2,307.880	96.162	I.M.S.A. GT

INDEX

Numbers in italics refer to illustrations
General

Abecassis, 80
A.C.O., *see* Automobile Club de l'Ouest
Adamovicz, 164
Ahrens, 161–62
Allard, Sidney, 90, 93
Allison, 105
Amon, Chris, 136, 147, 164–65
Andretti, Mario, 153, 190
Andretti, Michael, 190
Ascari, 84, 86–7
Attwood, 162–64
Auriet, 167
Austin, Herbert, 10
Automobile Club de France, 11
Automobile Club de la Sarthe, 11
Automobile Club de l'Ouest, 11–12, 14–15, 18, 23, 28, 34, 52, 64, 72, 74, 95–6, 98, 126, 161, 167, 169, 172, 184, 186
Auto-Union. 194
Baillie, 110
Balestre, Jean-Marie, 25
Bandini, L, 115, 126–27, 130
Barbour, Dick, 182–84
'Bardini', 167
Barnato, W, 15, 38–9, 43, 45, 66
Barth, J, 169–72, 181–83, 191, 193–94
Beasley, 181
Beaumont, 168
Beckers, 169
Behra, J, 98, 100, 105–106
Bell, D, 163, 167–68, 170, 172, 181, 183, 186, 191–95
Beltoise, J-P, 164–67, 169
Benjafield, Dr. J D, 32, 35–6, 38, 60
Benoist, 64, *65*, 66
Bertaut, *116*
Bentley, W O, 28, 34, 38, 70, 72, 78
Bertelli, 60
Beurlys, 153
Bianchi, 153, 156, 159
Biondetti, 66, 82
Bira, B, 70
Birkin, 'Tim', 38–9, 43, 45, 50, 52, 54, 59
Bloch, 30, 35, 38
Boillot, 34
Bol d'Or 24-hour race, 15
Bollée company, 10
Bollée, A, 10
Bollée, Leon, 10–11
Bondurant, Bob, 130
Bonnet, R, *114*, 135
Bonnier, Joachim, 165
Bouharde, *114*
Bourgognie, 195
Bouriat, 43, 54
Boutsen, 187
Brabham, J, 100
Bracey, I, 181, 185
Brackenbury, C, 62, 70
Brisson, 38
Broadley, Eric, 151, 191
Brooklands track, 14–15, 45
Brook, 98, 101, 103
Brousselet, 'Mary', 103
Bucknum, 147
Bueb, I, 92, 95–6, 98–101
Bugatti, Ettore, 64
Bugatti, Jean, 47, 50, 72
Bundy, 195
Busby, 182, 195

Callingham, 36, 45
Camoradi team, 109
Caracciola, 45
Casoni, 165
Casse, 36, 38
Castelloti, 93
Cevert, 165–66
Chaboud, 66, 84
Chapman, C, 21, 93, 95
Chassagne, 32, 34, 36, 38
Chasseuil, 168
Chinetti, L, 22, 54, 59–62, 66, 72, 78, 80, 83–4, 168
Chiron, L, 50, 54, 59
Clark, Jim, 110, 114
Cleare, 195
Clemens, 14
Clement, F, 15, 28, 30, 32, 34, 36, 38, 45
Clifford, 60
Cloître, 59
Cole, Tom, 86
Collier brothers, 80, 82
Collières, Dr, 14
Collins, P, 84, 95–6, 98, 101
Connaught, 93
Consten, 106
Cooper, 195
Coquille, Emile, 18
Cord, 182
Cornet, 105
Cortese, 54–5, 59
Cotton, 105
Courage, Piers, 163
Courcelles, 35
Craft, Chris, 164–65, 168–70, 172, 181–82, 185
C.S.I., 98–9, 109, 140, 153, 164, 168
Culpan, Norbert, 78
Cunningham, B, 80, 84, 92–3, 96, 109, 114–15, 125–26
Cunningham-Reid, 98
Czaikowski, 54

da Silva Ramos, 105
Davis, Colin, 103, 147
Davis, 'Sammy', 10, 32, 34–6, 59–60, 74
Daytona 24-hour race, 15, 25, 169
de Adamich, 162, 164
de Broc, Marquis, 10
de Cadenet, A, 163, 165, 170, 172, 181–83
Delettrez brothers, 78
de Montrémy, 83
Depailler, 159, 166, 172, 181
'Depnic', 167
de Portago, Marquis de, 96
Derby, 60, 62
d'Erlanger, Baron, 36, 38
de Sauge, 62
Desprez, Mme, 59
de Tomaso, Allessandro, 103, 164
Dobson, A, 70
Dolhem, 169
Donahue, 153, 163
Downe, Viscount, 191
Dreyfus, P-L, *53*, 54, 62
Dron, 195
Duff, J, 28, 30, 32, 34
Duller, 32, 34, 36
Dumont, 50
Durand, G, 18, 74

Dussous, 84
Duvergne, 34

Ecurie Ecosse, 48, 96, 98–100, 109, 116
Ecurie Francorchamps, 96
Edge, S F, 14
Edwards, G, 181, 183, 187, 192
Elford, V, 161–63, 166
Embiricos, 78
Enever, Syd, 82
England, Gordon, 32
Ericksson, 105
Escott, 110
Essex Motorsport, 183
Etancelin, P, 60–61, *60*, 66
Evans, B, 183, 185, 191
Eyston, George, 14, 43, 62

Fairfield, Pat, 65
Fairman, J, 82, 96, 105, 110
Fangio, J-M, 92–3, 95
Faroux, C, 18, 74
Faure, Nick, 181, 185
Fitch, 82–3, 90
Fitzpatrick, 194
Flockhart, R, 93, 96, 98, 114
Fontes, 62, *63*
Foresti, 35
Forestier, 65, 72
Fox, 61
Foyt, A. J, 153, *153*
French Grand Prix, 11, 14, *14*, 18, 24, 64
Frere, P, 95–6, 105, 110
Friderich, E, 11–12, 54

Gallop, 34
Ganley, 165
Garretson, 15
Gastaud, 62
Gauntlett, V, 192, 194
Gavin, S, 159
Gendebien, 0, 96, 98, 103, 105, 110, 114–15, *114*, 125, 172
Gérard, 72
Gillett, T, 14
Ginther, R, 114, 116, 126, 130, 144
Giraud-Cabantous, 68
Gonzalez, J-F, 89–90, 110
Good, Alan, 72
Goodall, 66
Gordini, A, 62, 64, 66, 72, 74, 93
Grandet, 167
Grant, 144, 147
Green, Willie, 181
Gregg, 181–82
Grégoire, 36
Gregory, M, 110, 130, 136
Grob, 181
Grohs, H, 192
Guichet, 125, 130, 136,
Guidotti, 54–5, 64
Guilbert, Andre, 34
Guilhaudin, *116*
Günter, 62
Gurney, D, 105, 110, 130, 144, 147, 153, *153*

Hadley, Bert, 80, 85
Hahne, 15
Hailwood, Mike, 161–62, 166–67
Hall, E R, 22, 82
Haller, Andre, 170
Hamilton, D, 85–6, 89–90, 92, 95, 100–101, 103
Hamilton, R, 171–72, 183, 191
Hanon, Bernard, 183
Hansgen, W, 110
Hawthorn, M, 86, 92–3, 95–6, 98, 101, 106, 125
Hay, 78
Haywood, 170–72, 181–82, 186, 191, 193–94
Hedges, Andrew, 130
Heinz, Bino, 127
Helfrich, 84
Hémard, 83–4
Héméry, Victor, 11
Hermann, H, 153, 161–63
Héry, Louis, 96
Heyer, 183–84
Hill, Graham, 114, 116, 126, 165
Hill, Phil, 92–3, 96, 98, 101, 103, 105, 114–15, *114*, 125, 130, 135–36, 153
Hindmarsh, 62, *63*
Hitchens, 66
Hobbs, 153, 161–64, 183, 194
Holbert, 191, 193–34
Hopkirk, Paddy, 126, 130
Howe, Lord, 43, 45, 50, 52, 54, 60, 62
Hugus, 105
Hulme, Denis, 144, 147, 153
Hutcheson, A, 126, 147

Ickx, Jacky, *6–7*, 15, 22, 25, 147, 153, 159, 161–62, 166, 168–72, 181–83, 185–86, 191–95
Indianapolis, 14, 18, 129
Iwanowski, 50

Jabouille, J-P, 165–67, 169–72, 181–82
Jacobs, Dick, 95
Jaray, 65
Jarier, 167, 172, 181
Jaussaud, 166, 168–69, 171–72, 181–83, *181*, 185, 191
Joest, R, 165, 168–70, 182, 185–86
Joest Racing, 190
Johnson, L, 80, 82, 84–5
Johnston, 90
Jones, 195
Jousset, 34
Jover, 78
Juncandella, 163

Kauhsen, 161, 163
Kidston, 45
Kippeurt, 65
Klenk, 84
Kling, 84, 90, 93
Knoop, 182

Labric, D, 59, 62, 64, 66
Lafitte, 172
Lafosse, J-L, 168, 170, 187
Lagache, 28, 30, 34
Lago, A, 62
Laly, 36
Lang, 84
Larivière, 82
Larrousse, G, 161, 163, 116–117
Laureau, *114*
Lawrence, Chris, 116
Lawson, H. J, 10
Lees, G, 191
Le Mans, *1*, *8–9*, *24*, *28*
Leonard, 28
Levegh, P, 22, 82–4, 86, 90, 93–4
Lewis, B, 59–60, 62
Ligier, G, 162
Links, 161
Lins, 163
Lombardi, Lelia, 168
Loos, 170
Louveau, 78
Lucas, 80, 83
Ludwig, K, 183–84, 190, 193
Lumsden, 125
Lund, Ted, 110

McLaren, B, 130, 136, 147, 153
Macklin, 80, 84, 93–4, 184
Maggs, 114
Maglioli, U, 89–90, 93, 126
Mairesse, 80, 82–3, 114–15, *114*, 126, 153
Mallock, Ray, 191
Manzon, 89–90
Maranello, 105
March, Earl of, 15
March engineering company, 183, 185, 191
Marchand, 82, 84
Maréchal, P, 78
Marinoni, *49*, 53
Marko, H, 163–64
Martin, 62, 185, 191, 193–94
Martini Racing Team, 163, 167, 170–72, 181, 185
Marzotto brothers, 86, 89–90, 93
Mass, J, 181, 186, 191, 193–94
Masson, 98
Mazard, 72, 74, 78
Mereuse, Mme, 43, 50
Merz, 14
Merzario, 166
Mestivier, Marius, 34
Meyrat, 80, 82–3
Migault, F, 167–68, 170, 183, 191
Mignot, 183
Miles, 136, 144, 147
Mille Miglia, 47, 59, 74, 82, 85
Moir, K, 32
Moll, 59
Monneret, 72
Monte Carlo Rally, 18, 192
Montier, C, 28
Montlhéry motor race track, 14–15, 34
Monza Grand Prix, 25
Morris, W, 11, 66
Moss, Stirling, 82–3, 85–6, 89, 92, 95–6, 100–101, 105, 114, 181
Muir, 153
Müller, 163–64, 167
Murphy, Jimmie, 14
Musso, 98
Navone, 82
Needell, Tiff, 191, 193
Neerpasch, 159
Newman, Paul, 183–84
Nichol, 61
Nicholas, Prince of Roumania, 59, 62
Niedermayer, 84
Niedziwedz, 190, 193
Noblet, 125
Nürburgring, 25, 130, 191
Nuvolari, Tazio, *18*, *57*, 59–60, *59*, 66

Oliver, J, 161, 163–64
Orssich-Sauerwein, Graf, 68

Pabst, 114–15
Pace, 166
Paco, 59
Paget, Hon. Dorothy, 45
Panhard, Paul, *114*
Parkes, 114–15, *114*, 126, 136, 144, 153
Parnell, Reg, 90, 105
Peacock, 60–61
Pescarolo, H, 159, 165–72, 181, 185, 191
Philippe, 43
Philips, G, 78, 80, 82, 181
Philips, S, 191
Pilette, 110
Piper, Ken, 162
Pironi, 172, 181–82, *181*
Poirier, 36
Polensky, 95
Poore, 85
Poulain, 183
Pozzi, 84, 86

Ragnotti, 122, 185, 191
Rahal, 15
Ramponi, 15
Ravel, 34
Redman, 15, 161, 182–83
Redman, B, 161–62, 166
Reutemann, 166
Riess, 84
Rigal, 34
Rindt, Jochen, 136
Rodriguez, Pedro, 99–100, 114–16, 125, 144, 156, 159, 163–64
Rodriguez, Ricardo, 99, 110, 114–16, 125
Rolls, C S, 10
Rolt, Tony, 85–6, 88–90, 92, 95
Rondeau, J-P, 25, 169, 172, 181, 185, 191, 193
Rose-Richards, 59–60
Rosier, L, *79*, 80, *81*, 82, 89–90
Rossignol, 35
Rost, M, 50
Rouse, A, 191
Rousseau, 36, 38, 59
Rubin, B, 38, 43
Rudge-Whitworth Cup, 18–19, 34

Salmon, M, 191
Samuelson, Sir Francis, 32
Salvadori, Roy, 90, 105, *106*, 110, 114, 125
Sanderson, 96
Sargent, 125
Saunders-Davis, 60
Scarfiotti, L, 126–27, 136, 144, 153
Scaron, 66, 68, 72
Schell, 86, *90*, 95
Schenken, 166
Schetty, P, 163
Schumann, *53*, 54
Schuppan, V, 167–68, 170, 172, 183, 186, 191, 193–94
Schurti, 170, 183–84
Segrave, 32
Selsdon, Lord, 70, 78, 80
Serrauld, 68
Shelby, C, 105, *106–107*, 130
Siffert, Jo, 147, 153, 161–63
Siko, Mme, 43, 50, *53*, *58*
Silverstone, 15, 25, 191
Simon, 78, 90, 93, 96, 98
Sommer, R, *18*, 22, 54–6, *55*, *57*, 59–60, 62, 64–6, 68, 70, 72, 80
Spa, 15, 25
Spear, 84, 89–90
Spence, Mike, 153
Spice, G, 183, 185, 190
Stalter, 30
Staniland, C S, 15
Stewart, Mrs. G, 60
Stewart, 86
Stoffel, 50, 62
Stuck, Hans, 185
Stommelen, R, 159, 161, 170, 183–84
Surer, 190, 193
Surtees, J, 126–27, 130, 136, 153
Szisz, F, 11

Tabourin, 36
Tambay, 169, 171
Tarante, Mme, 59
Targa Florio, 18, 85
Thatcher, Mark, 185
Thistlethwayte, 34
Thompson, 85, 114–15, 184
Towns, Bill, 129
Tremoulet, 66, 72
Trevoux, 53, 59
Trimmer, 183
Trintignant, M, 86, 89–90, *90*, 95–6, 98, 101, 103, 105, 110

Vaccarella, 130, 163, 165
van Lennep, G, 163–65, 167, 169–70
Varent, 59–60
Varzi, A, 50
Veyron, 62, 64, 66, 68, *73*
Villoresi, 85–6
van der Becke, 60–61
van Frankenberg, 95
von Trips, W, 114

Wagner, 34
Waleran, Lord, 70
Walker, P, 82–3, 86, 89
Walters, 82–3
Watney, 45
Watson, Ian, 166
Wéber, 165
Werner, 45
Whitehead, G, 100–101
Whitehead, P, 82–3, 86, 100–101
Whittington brothers, 183–84
Willys-Knight, 34
Wilson, Desire, 184
Wimille, 64–6, *65*, 68, 72, *73*, 74
Winkelhock, 183, 191, 193
Wisdom, 'Bill', 62, 66, 78
Wisdom, Tommy, 62, 66, 84
Wollek, 166, 181–83, 191, 193–94
Woolfe, J, 161
Wyer, J, 151, 154, 159, 161, 166–69

CARS
Abarth, 114–15, *115*, 125–26, 153
A.C.: Ace, 105, 109, 114, 116; Cobra, 126–27, 129–30, *129*, 133, *136*; Cobra Daytona, 130; Six, 14, 32, 98–100, 103
ACR, 185–86
Aero-Minor, 78, 80, 82
Adler, 21, 64, 66, 68–9, *68–9*, 72
Alfa Romeo: 15, 16–18, 24, *44*, 45, 52–6, *57–8*, 59–60, *59–60*, 62, 64–6, 70, 72, 85–6, 125–26, 130, 159, 161, 165–66, 168, 192; **8C-2300**, 47, *48–9*; **Disco Volante**, 85; **Giulietta**, 100, 109; **SZ GT**, 109; **Tipo 33**, 154, *154*, 159, 162–65; **TZ**, 130; **TZII**, 133
Allard, 80, 82–5
Alpine Renault: 25, *125*, 126–27, 130, *129–30*, 135, *142*, 144, 147, *148–49*, 151, 153, 161, 168, 182, *182*; **936**, 170–72; **A110**, 154; **A210**, *157*; **A220**, 156, *156*, 159; **A310**, 170; **A443**, 172, *172*, 181–82
Alta, 52
Alvis, 38, 40, 78
Amilcar, 28, 34, 166
Aries, 30, 32, 34–6, 38
Arnott, 98
Arrol-Aster, 48
Asa, 144
Aston Martin: 24, 38, 48, 50, 52, 56, *56*, 59–62, *61*, 64, 66, 70, *75*, 78, 83–4, 88–90, *88*, 95, *99*, 100–101, 103, 106, *105–106*, 110, 125, 130, 169–70, 172, 183–84, 192, 195; **212**, 116, 125; 215, 126; **DB**, 85, 88, 92, 96, 98, 101, 103, 114, 116, 126, *126*, 184; **DBR**, 97–8, 100, 104–105, 109, 114; **Ulster**, 15
Atlanta, 66
Austin, 64; Seven, 32, 59–62, 64
Austin Healey: 85, 93–4, 109, 114, 116, 126; Sprite, 109–10, 114, 130, 135–36, 144, 153, 156, 159
Autodelta, 154, 159

Ballot-Lena, 172
Beelzebub, 10
Bentley: 11, 15, 20, 22, 24, 28, *29*, 30, 32, 34, 36, *37*, 38–9, *40*, 43, 45, *45*, 47–8, 50, *52*, 59, 61, 78, 80, 82–3, 184, 192; Mulsanne, 38, 192; Speed Six, 39–40, *40–41*, 43, *43*, 45, 52–4, 192; TT, 80, 82
Bignan, 15, 28, 30
Bizzarini, 142, 144

BMW: 15, 64, 74, 165; **320**, 170; **328**, 65, 70, *70*, 72, 78; **2002**, 168–69; **CS**, 164; **CSL**, 166–68, 170, 172; M.1, 183–86, 190–91, 195
BNC, 62
Bollée Voiturette, 10
Bonnet, 125–27, 130
Borgward, 85
Bristol, 85, 90, 93, *92–3*, 95; **450**, 85, 89
Bugatti: 24, 28, *29*, 48, 50, 59–62, 64–6, 72, *73*, 74, *74*; **Type 13**, 12, 43, 45; **Type 50**, 47, 50, *50–51*; **Type 55**, 52, 54, *54–5*; **Type 57G 'Tank'**, 64; **Type 57S 'Tank'**, 66; **Type 57 'Tank'**, 68

Caban, 50, 56
Cadillac, 80, 82
Callista, 82
CD: Panhard, *116*, 125, 130; DKW, 126; Peugeot, 144, 147, 153
Chapparal, 140, 148, 153–54
Cheetah, 169–70, 181, 183
Chenard et Walcker, *27*, 28, 30, *31*, 32, 34, 36, 64, 192
Chevrolet: Camaro, 186, 191, 195; Corvette, 109–10, 116, 151, 154, 161–64, 166, 167; Monza, 181
Chevron, 156, 159, 161–62, 164, 166–67, 169–70, 172, 181–83, 185
Chrysler: 32, *32–3*, 39–40, 43, *46–7*, 48, 82; **Model 72**, 38
Citroen: 52; SM, 165
Cooper: 93, 96, 98; 'Monaco', 104, 114
Corre La Licorne, 30, *35*
Costin-Nathan, 153
Cougar, 191
Coventry-Motette, 10
Crosley, 82
Cunningham: 82–4, 90, 95; **C4R**, 88; **C5R**, 85; **C6**, 92

Datsun, 260Z, 170
DB (Deutsch et Bonnet), 78–9, 82, 89, 98, 109
DB-Panhard, 87, 90, 93, 95–6, 100, *103–104*, 105–106, 109–10, 114–15
De Cadenet, 167–70, 172, 183–86, 191
Deep Sanderson, 126, 130, 156
Delage, 12, 28, 64, 66, 69, *69*, 72, 74, *74–5*, 78–9, 82
Delahaye: *20*, 24, 62, 64, *64*, *67–8*, 68–9, 72, 74, 78–9, 82; **Type 135**, 64, 66; **Type 145**, 66
Delettrez, 78–9, 82
de Tomaso, Pantera V8, 164, 167–68
Deutsch, 125, 135, 144
Diatto, *30*, 32
Dino, 133, 135, 142, 156
DKW, 98
Dome: Amada, 191, 193; Zero, 183, 185–86
Duckham-Ford, 164–65
Duesenberg, 14, 59, 62
Du Pont, 40, 43
Dyna Panhard, 82
d'Yrsan, 40

Elva-BMW, 133
Excelsior, 28

Ferrari: 15, 24, 78, 80, *80*, 82–90, 93, 95–6, 98–9, *99*, 101, *102*, 103, 105–106, *108*, 110, 112, *112–14*, 114–16, 125, 127, *128*, 129, *137*, 140, *141*, *150*, 153–54, 161, 163, 168, 192; **121LM**, 92, 131; **250GT**, 104–105, 109–10, *111*, 112, 114–15, 126; **250GTO**, *22*, 125, 127; **250P**, 126, *127*; **250TR**, 99, *100–101*; **275GTB**, 131, 133, 136, 140, 147–48, 153–54, 159; **275LM**, *134–35*, 136, 154, *158*, 159; **275P**, 130; 290, 98; 312, 98, 165–67; **312P**, 159, 161; **330GT**, 115, *126*; **330LM**, 115, 125; **330PZ**, 130, *135*, 136, 140; **365**, 164–65; **365P2**, 140, 148; **365 Daytona**, 163–64, 166–68; **375 'Plus'**, 88; **412**, 98; **512LM**, 163; **512M**, 164; **512S**, 161–63; **625**, 96; **Boxer**, 170, 172, 181, 183, 185–86, 191, 194–95; **Dino**, 104, 164, 167; **Testa Rossa**, 98, 104–105, 109–10, 112, 114–16
Ferry-Renault, 79
Fiat: 11, 80, 85; Abarth, 109–10, 161; Ballilla Sport, 62
Ford: 15, 25, 130–31, 136, *141*, 147, 156, 181–82, 190, 193; **C.100**, 186, 191–93; **Capri RS V6**, 165–67; **GT 40**, 21, 129–30, *131*, 133, 140, 148, 159, *160*, 161, 169, 192; **M10**, 183; **Mk II**, 133, 135, 140, *140*, 144, *142–45*, *151*; **Mk IV**, 147–48, *152*, 153; **Ten**, 64, 66
Frazer-Nash, 61, 64–5, 78, 80, 82, 84–5, 87, 89, 93, 95, 97–8, 105

Gordini: *72*, 79, 83–90, *89*, 92, 95–8
Grac-Gotti, 20, 167
Grid-Plaza, 191–93
Gulf, 25, 151, 153–54, 159, 161, 163, 165–69, 186
Healey, 78, 80, 156, 159, 161–62
Howmet, 156, 159
HRG, 64, 66, 68, 70, 78

Ibec, 185–96
Inaltera, 169–72, 181
Invicta, 40, 43
Iso: Grifo, *131*, 133; Rivolta, 129–30
Itala, 38

Jaguar: 24, 82, 85–7, 90, 93, 95–6, 98–101, 103–104, 112, 126, 130, 184, 192; **C-type**, *4–5*, 82–6, 88–90; **D-type**, 21, 88–9, 92, 95–6, *97*, 98–100, 104–105, 109–10, 181; **E-type**, 109, 116, 125–27; **E2A**, 110; **XK120**, 80; **XK120C**, 82; **XK140**, 95; **V-12**, 195
Janspeed, 185
JCB, 181
Jowett: 83–5; Jupiter, 80, 82, 84; R.1 type, 82

Kieft, 89, 93
Kremer, 170, 183, 186, 190–92

Lago-Talbot, 69
Lagonda: 24, 38, 40, 62, *62–3*, 72, 74, 78, *88*, 89, 95, 106, 185, 192; Rapide, 61, 64; Rapier, 60; V12, 70, *71*, 88, 92
Lancia: 25, 84–6, 191–93; Aurelia GT, 82–3; Beta, 184; Beta Montecarlo, 186–87, 191, 195; D.20, 85; 'Spider', 193; Stratos, 170, 184
Lea-Francis, 40, 43, 45
Lenham, 169
Ligier, 162–68
L'Obeissante, 10
Lola: 25, 109–10, 126, 129, 151, 153, 163, 165, 167–70, 181–86, 192–93; **294**, 181; **296**, 181; **297**, 181; Chevrolet, *154–55*, 159, 161–62; Ford, 166; **T280**, 164–65; **T292**, 167; **T600**, 187; **T610**, 191
Lorraine, *13*, 28, 30, 32, 34–5, 47, 50, 59–62
Lotus: 23, 21, 95–6, 98–100, 104, 114, 125–7, 130; IX Climax, 93; XV Climax, 100; Elan, 130; Elite, 105, 109–10, 114–15; Europa, 47, 151

MAP, 80
March, 25, 168
Marcos, 144, 147
Maserati: 84, 92–3, 95, 97–8, 100, *110*, 112, 115, 125–26, 129–31, *132*, 133, 136, 181; A6G, 89, 92; Spyder, 98; Tipo 61, 109–10, 114; Tipo 63, *111*, 114; Tipo 151, 115, 126
Matra-Simca: 25, 135, 142, 147, *146–47*, 161–67; **630**, 156, 159; **660**, 164; **660C**, 165; **670**, 162, 164–68; **680**, 162–64, 166–68; BRM, 151, 153, 159
Mazda, *254*, 191, 195; RX-3, 167; RX-7, 15, 183, 185–86
Mercedes-Benz, 21, 24, 45, *46–7*, 50, 52, 54, 64, *85*, 90, *91*, 93–6; SSK, 48; 300SL, 83–4, *83*, 96; SLR, 90
MG: 50, 52, 61, 64, 66, 68, 70, 80, 95, 131; Ex.182, 93; Magnette, 60–61; PB-type, 66; TC, 78; TD, 82; Midget, 15, 59–60; C-type, 48; J4, 60; M-type, 45; PA-type, 62; MGA, 82, 93, 105, 109–10, 114; MGB, 126, 130, 133, 136
Mini-Marcos, *141*, 153
Minoia, *16–17*, 35, 53
Mirage: 171–72, 181, 183–84, 190–92; Ford-DV, 169–70, *171*
Monopole, 78–9, 82, 89; Panhard, 80, 83–4
Montier-Special, 28
Moretti, 96
Morgan: 21–2, 125; **66**, 68, 70; Plus 4, 84, 116
Morris: Léon Bollée, 11; Martin, 181; Mini, 10
Moynet: 156; Simca, 168

Napier, 14
Nardi, 21, 89, 93, 95
N.A.R.T. (North American Racing Team) 275LM, 136, 164, 167–68, 170
Nash-Healey, 82–5
Nimrod, 25, 191, 193–95
Nomad, 161

O.M., *31*, 32, 34–5
Osca, 84–5, 87, 89, 93, 95–6, 98, 101, *101*, 103, 105, 109, 114
Osella, 170, 181, 185

Panhard: 79, 82–3, 85, *85–7*, *90*, 95–6; CD, *116*, 125; Monopole, 93, 98, 100
Porsche: *2–3*, 15, 25, 82–5, 87, 89–90, *90*, 93, 95–6, 98–101, 103, 105, 109–10, *109*, 114–15, 125–27, 130, 133, 163, 183–84, 190, 192–94; **Carrera**, 165, 167–68, 181–82, 184, 186,; **Carrera 911**, 166–70; **Mitter/Davis 904**, *21*; **550**, *94*; **807**, 163; **903**, 163; **904**, 130, *133*, 136; **906**, 140, *145*, 147–48, 153–54; **907**, 148, 153–56, 159, 161, 164; **908**, 154, 156, 159, *159*, 161–65, 168–69, 186; **908/936**, 185; **910**, 148, 156, 159, 161, 164, 166–67; **911**, 140, 147–48, 154, 159, 161, 163–64, 185; **914**, 161, 163; **917**, 159, 161–63, *162*, 186; **924**, 185–86, 191; **930**, 190; **934**, 169–70, 172, 181, 183–87, 191, 195; **935**, 169–73, 181–87, 191, 194–95, *194*; **936 Spyder**, 169–70, 172, 181–83, 186, *187*, 191–92, 194; **944**, 186–87; **956**, *25*, 191–93, 195
Pegasos, 85
Peugeot: 34, 64, 66, 68, 169; Constantin, 84–5, *86–7*, 89, 93, 169; Lion, 12; Quadrillette, 14

Rally, 60
RB, 96
Renault: 11, 78–9, 82–3, 85, *86–7*, 172; **l'Etoile Filante**, 99
Riley: 60–62, 64–6, 70, 78, 80; Model 9, 59–60
Rolls-Royce: 45, 70; Phantom, 39
Rondeau, 25, 182–87, 191–93, 195
Rover-BRM, 25, 125–26, 129, 131, 133, 136

SAAB, 105–6, 183
Salmson, 28, 34, 36, *37*, 38–9, 60, 93, 97
S.A.R.A., 28, 34, 36, 39, 59
Sauber, 170, 181, 191–92
Serenissima, 114, 142
Shelby, 151
Sigma: Mazsa, 167; Toyota, 168
Simca: 24, 66, 68, *68–9*, 78–9, 82, 186; Cinq, 65–6, 68, *72*, 74; Fiat, 64–6; Gordini, 78, 82
Singer: 61–2, 64, 66, 70; Nine, 59–60, 66, 68, 78
Sizaire, Berwick, 32
Skoda, 80
Spuker, 14
Stanguellini, 93, 96, 98, 100, 105, 109
Stutz, 38, *39*, 40, 43, 45, 47, *45–7*, 52–3, 82
SU, 34
Sunbeam: 30, *31*, 32, 34; Alpine, 114–15, 126; Tiger, 129
Sygma, 166

Talbot, *20*, 25, 32, 45, *45*, 48, 50, 52, 54–6, 62, 64–6, *67*, 68–9, 72, 74, 78–80, *79*, *81*, 82–6, 88–9, 97–8, 192
Th. Schneider, 36
Toj, 183, 185
Tojeiro: Climax, 100, 116; Jaguar, 104
Tom Walkinshaw Racing, 186, 191
Tracta, 36, 38–40, 43, 45, 60
Triumph: 110; Peerless, 100, *100*, 103; Spitfire, 130, 135–36; TR2, 89–90, 93, 95, *95*, TR7, 185; TRS, 109, 114–15; TRS Sabrina, 105
T.V.R., 125

UMG 400, 82
U.R.D., 190

Voisin, 28
VP-Renault, 93, 96, 98, 100

Willys-Overland, 34; Six, 34
WM-Peugeot, 25, 69–70, 181, 183, 185–87, 190–93
Wolseley, 10

Zakspeed, 190

ACKNOWLEDGEMENTS

Every author who writes on the history of the Le Mans 24-hour race must acknowledge a debt to Roger Labric. Himself a driver in every race from 1931 to 1937, Labric spent the war years in accumulating data for his monumental tome which was published in 1949 as the Automobile Club de l'Ouest's official history of the 16 pre-war races, under the title *Les 24 Heures du Mans*. It is perhaps strange that this book was never translated into English and published in Britain or the U.S.A., and regrettably it was limited to 1,000 copies – both factors have contributed to denying Labric's work the wider currency it deserves. The book was superbly printed and delightfully illustrated by Geo. Ham, the outstanding French motoring artist – although the modern researcher regrets that Labric's book contains no photographs. I have been in doubt about facts and figures pertaining to the pre-1940 races, I have considered Labric's book to be the final word.

Since 1949 there has been a Le Mans book at regular intervals, each bringing the story up to date. First came another French author, Georges Fraichard, whose *La Ronde Impitoyable* (*The Merciless Circuit*) was published in Paris in 1953, and subsequently translated by Louis Klemantaski who added extra chapters on the 1953 and 1954 races. It went through two editions under the rather less dramatic title *The Le Mans Story*, published by The Bodley Head. Fraichard's work was written in a delightful anecdotal style, reflecting his long personal experience of the Le Mans races as a journalist and writer. In 1963, Temple Press published *The Le Mans 24-Hour Race* by David Hodges, a straightforward well!researched story of the 31 races from 1923 to 1963, ending on a high note with the Rover-B.R.M. gas turbine car. With meticulously detailed appendices listing every car and driver taking part, together with individual results, Hodges' book is still the most complete guide published in English to the pre-war races.

Then in 1973, the Automobile Club de l'Ouest celebrated the fiftieth anniversary of the first race by publishing the second volume of the official history of the Le Mans race. Confusingly enough this book also appeared under the title *The Le Mans 24-Hour Race* in its English version. The author and editor was Christian Moity, and the English translation was by D. B. Tubbs. The book was a collaborative effort between the A.C.O. and *Automobile Year* and was published by Edita, Lausanne, and by the American Chilton Book Company. Moity chose to rely mainly on a collection of some 300 photographs, accompanied by long captions and additional notes, together with tables covering the 25 races from 1949 to 1973 and the usual comprehensive appendices. One could not wish for a better guide to the races of this crucial period in the history of Le Mans.

These books have all been consulted in the course of preparing this book. So, inevitably, have those two invaluable guides edited by G. N. Georgano – *The Complete Encyclopedia of Motorcars* and *The Encyclopedia of Motor Sport* – together with the books of the late W. O. Bentley; *French Vintage Cars* by John Bolster; *German High-Performance Cars* by Sloniger and von Fersen; *Lost Causes of Motoring, Europe, Vols 1 and 2* by Lord Montagu of Beaulieu; and many one-make histories too numerous to mention though perhaps *Jaguar – A Biography* by Montagu deserves to be singled out as a classic model for many other books that have appeared in the 20 years following its publication.

Contemporary magazine race reports have naturally been invaluable and I found the following particularly useful: *Autocar, Automobile Year, Autosport, Classic and Sportscar* (formerly *Old Motor*), *Motor, Motor Sport*, and *Thoroughbred and Classic Car*. I would therefore like to record my thanks to the editors of these magazines.

It remains for me to thank Peter Brockes, the reference librarian of the National Motor Museum who was as always patient and helpful; all members of the gallant but ill-fated Canon-Porsche team in the 1982 race but particularly Richard Lloyd and Peter Stevens – not only because they made it possible for me to gain much more insight into to-day's Le Mans races but also for their hospitality; Mike McCarthy who answered silly questions on Porsche at a crucial stage; my colleagues at BL Heritage Limited who were as always wonderfully understanding in coping with my bouts of creativity while the research and writing was going on; Derek Avery of Winchmore Publishing Services Ltd who was as patient as I could wish for when it came to extending deadlines; Dave Jack, mechanic of the Nimrod team, who was an entertaining travelling companion to and back from Le Mans 1982; and finally, Jacky Ickx for writing the foreword.

Anders Ditlev Clausager
Birmingham, July 1982

The publishers would like to thank Sports Agency Magazines in Paris for their superb and speedy effort in carrying out the picture research without whose assistance this publication would not have been possible. Our gratitude is also due to Colin Maher for his special photography in Le Mans and Jaguar Cars for their last lap rescue.

The streamlined Porsche 956 of Mass and Schuppan finished second in the 50th Le Mans race held in 1982. 1st and 3rd places were filled by similar Porsche cars with the Ickx/Bell partnership repeating their 1981 victory.